Vocabulario Vaquero/Cowboy Talk

Vocabulario Vaquero/Cowboy Talk

A Dictionary of Spanish Terms from the American West

By Robert N. Smead

Foreword by Richard W. Slatta
Illustrations by Ronald Kil

UNIVERSITY OF OKLAHOMA PRESS : NORMAN

Publication of this book is made possible in part by a grant from the Charles Redd Center for Western Studies, Brigham Young University.

Library of Congress Cataloging-in-Publication Data

Smead, Robert N. (Robert Norman), 1954–
    Vocabulario vaquero = cowboy talk : a dictionary of Spanish terms from the American west / by Robert N. Smead ; illustrations by Ronald Kil ; foreword by Richard Slatta.
        p. cm.
    Includes bibliographical references.
    ISBN 0-8061-3594-8 (alk. paper)
    1. Cowboys—Language—Dictionaries. 2. English language—West (U.S.)—Foreign words and phrases—Spanish—Dictionaries. 3. English language—Dialects—West (U.S.)—Dictionaries. 4. Spanish language—Influence on English—Dictionaries. 5. Americanisms—West (U.S.)—Dictionaries. I. Title.

PE3727.C6S64 2004
427'.978—dc22

2003061298

1 2 3 4 5 6 7 8 9 10

*To buckaroos, ranchers, and vaqueros everywhere—and to my wife,
Gloria, and my children, Jessica, Justin, Richard, and Jonathan*

Contents

Foreword

by Richard W. Slatta

Language ranks among the most visible, extensive, and useful cultural evidence that human societies create. Indeed, according to the *Encyclopedia Britanica*, language is "manifestly a part, probably the most important part" of culture.[1] The rich bounty of Spanish-origin words gathered into this volume provides an enlightening view into the origins and cultural workings of the western cattle industry. The absorption of such a large number of ranch-related words from Spanish into English offers striking evidence of the importance of that heritage to the history of the American West. Anyone curious about ranch life, cowboys, "westernisms," history, culture (material and otherwise), or the fun of exploring word origins and their meanings is in for a real treat with *Vocabulario Vaquero*.

By exploring the etymology of many western terms intensively and extensively, Robert Smead thus makes a substantial contribution to western and Borderlands studies with his minute examination of the western vocabulary. Students of the American West, the Borderlands, Latino studies, and language will find much to learn and enjoy from his work. Historical and anthropological linguists will find a bounty of material, nicely gathered and ready for further study. Smead's linguistic research also puts the final nail in the coffin of the British "Carolina cowpens theory" of the origin of the western range livestock industry.

Linguists have long appreciated the importance of Spanish-origin words in the western vocabulary. But how have the Spanish origins of so many things western remained neglected by so many others for so

---

1. "Language," "Linguistics," *Encyclopædia Britannica Online*.

long? In popular history and culture, the Spanish legacy has been largely uncommented upon or suppressed, and there are many reasons why.[2] For one, racial discrimination has colored our vision of the American West. As in other regions of the country, Native American, African, and Hispanic influences have been ignored. In traditional narratives, history begins when white men show up. Descendants of those white men either ignored or actively erased traces of prior influences in constructing their heroic myth of white expansionism and progress.[3] Early Anglo ranchers in Texas dismissed Hispanic ranchers and ranching with facile racial stereotypes. Recollections of these Anglo pioneers exhibit a blend of what one historian described a "fallacy and fact [that became] intertwined into a self-serving paean of Anglo superiority."[4] Turning a blind eye to preexisting Spanish and Mexican ranching and culture also made it easier to appropriate land, animals, and water rights.

Another reason the Spanish/vaquero roots of the western range cattle industry have gone relatively unnoticed is a lack of historical sources. Frontier regions, including those devoted to ranching, generate fewer permanent records than do urban centers, where political and economic power concentrates. Newspapers of the past and present devote disproportionate space and attention to city matters, thus limiting the extent of the paper trail for cattle frontiers. Such a working-class social group as cowboys does not generate as much documentation as do the wealthy, powerful, and landed. Thus we have a more limited store of primary sources produced by ranch hands. This problem is compounded among the generally illiterate Latin American ranch hands, including Spanish colonials and later Mexican vaqueros. They did not write diaries, memoirs, or letters home. Fortunately, many Anglo cowboys on the western ranges did leave firsthand accounts of their lives, documents that well illustrate the importance of Spanish roots and antecedents.[5]

2. For a quick history of the Mexican vaquero and his significance, see Richard W. Slatta, *The Cowboy Encyclopedia* (Santa Barbara and New York: ABC-CLIO, 1990; W. W. Norton, 1994), pp. 380–86.

3. Ibid. pp. 103–4.

4. Jack Jackson, *Los Mesteños: Spanish Ranching in Texas, 1721–1821* (College Station: Texas A&M University Press, 1986), p. 593.

5. On the usefulness of memoirs by real, working cowboys, see Richard W. Slatta, "In Their Own Words: Cowboy Memoirs," *Cowboys & Indians* 2: 1 (Spring 1994):

Not all scholars have ignored the Spanish/vaquero origins of the western range cattle industry. During the 1920s and 1930s, Philip Ashton Rollins and Paul L. Wellman clearly delineated the Anglo cowboy's debt to his vaquero predecessors.[6] More recent scholarship, generally termed the "new western history," has likewise revealed a diverse and multiethnic West. Historians have pointed up the activities of a wide range of immigrant and other ethnic groups as well as women.

Texas scholars, in particular, built a solid case for the origins of the western livestock industry in the brush country (*brasada*) of their state. Historian Walter Prescott Webb and folklorists J. Frank Dobie and Joe Graham established an unmistakable lineage from the Mexican vaquero to the Anglo cowboy.[7] Later, Sandra L. Myres explored more fully the Spanish roots of Texas ranching, thus highlighting important Hispanic elements.[8] Despite the hard work of these scholars, the larger public narrative of Texas and western history often omitted Spanish origins in favor of the story of white, Anglo-Saxon (mostly male) triumphalism. As Myres complained in 1969, "In comparison to the hundreds of studies of Anglo-American ranching, little has been written on Spanish-American ranching practices."[9]

Conversely, cultural geographer Terry G. Jordan reacted a few years later to what he viewed as an overemphasis on the Hispanic influences on western cattle ranching. In *Trails to Texas: Southern Roots of Western Cattle Ranching* (1981), Jordan resurrected an argument first made decades earlier by Frederick Jackson Turner, who theorized that "the experiences of the Carolina cowpens guided the

45–50; Richard W. Slatta and Jeanne Ronda, "Cowboying at the Chapman-Barnard Ranch," *Persimmon Hill* 21: 3 (Spring 1993): 36–41.

6. Philip Ashton Rollins, *The Cowboy: An Unconventional History of Civilization on the Old-Time Cattle Range* (rev. ed. 1922; reprint, with Foreword by Richard W. Slatta, Norman: University of Oklahoma Press, 1997, 2001), pp. 1–4; Paul I. Wellman, *The Trampling Herd: The Story of the Cattle Range in America* (1939; reprint, Lincoln: University of Nebraska Press, 1967, 1988), pp. 26–32.

7. Lawrence Clayton, Jim Hoy, and Jerald Underwood, *Vaqueros, Cowboys, and Buckaroos* (Austin: University of Texas Press, 2001), pp. 68–69.

8. Sanda L. Myres, "The Spanish Cattle Kingdom in the Province of Texas," *Texana* 4: 3 (Fall 1966): 233–46; *The Ranch in Spanish Texas, 1691–1800* (El Paso: Texas Western Press, 1969); "The Ranching Frontier: Spanish Institutional Backgrounds of the Plains Cattle Industry," in Myres, et al. *Essays on the American West* (Austin: University of Texas Press, 1969), pp. 19–39.

9. Myres, "The Ranching Frontier," p. 37.

ranchers of Texas."[10] This theory, like many aspects of Turner's work, led subsequent generations of historians up a blind draw. Nonetheless, Jordan provided a few needed correctives. He pointed out that brand designs used by western Anglo ranchers differed considerably from the larger, more ornate styles Hispanics favored. In discussing the Spanish *Mesta*, an organization representing powerful, pastoral interests in Spain, however, Jordan erroneously referred to it as the Meseta (plateau, flat-top mountain).[11] As often happens in scholarship, Jordan overreached his evidence.[12] In a desire to replace Hispanic origins with Anglo influences from the American South, he erred on several points. Most telling is the sin of omission: The citations to *Trails to Texas* include only two Spanish-language articles.[13]

Criticism of Jordan's overrevisionism appeared quickly. Historian Jack Jackson greatly expanded on the earlier work by Sandra L. Myres with his richly documented, seven-hundred-page study, *Los Mesteños: Spanish Ranching in Texas, 1721–1821* (1986). Jackson observed that Jordan's "list of practices that supposedly distinguished the Anglo herding tradition from the Hispanic shows at least two-thirds common to both." Aside from such details as the use of dogs and whips, scattering salt on the range or setting fire to it, the two traditions, he concluded, "were closely akin. The grand scale of ranching in Texas made them more so, not less, and the Spanish system prevailed, for it was already adapted to the land and its unpredictable vicissitudes."[14]

In 1993, Jordan amended many of his earlier notions in an impressively researched book, *North American Cattle-Ranching Frontiers.*

10. Frederick Jackson Turner, *The Frontier in American History* (New York: Holt, Rinehart and Winston, 1920, 1947, 1962), p. 16.

11. Terry G. Jordan, *Trails to Texas: Southern Roots of Western Cattle Ranching* (Lincoln: University of Nebraska Press, 1981), pp. 8, 120, 147. Jordan now uses the name Jordan-Bychkov.

12. For a more extended critique of historical overrevisionism, see Richard W. Slatta, *Comparing Cowboys and Frontiers: New Perspectives on the History of the Americas* (Norman: University of Oklahoma Press, 1997, 2001), pp. 183, 188–210.

13. The only recent author to propagate the Jordan thesis and ignore Spanish sources is novelist Laurie Winn Carlson. See her thinly documented book, *Cattle: An Informal Social History* (Chicago: Ivan R. Dee, 2001) and summary article, "Cattle: A Bevy of Bovine Story Ideas," *Roundup Magazine*, 11: 2 (December 2001): 6–8.

14. Jackson, *Los Mesteños*, p. 594.

His new analysis showed that Hispanic influence reached the American West along many trails: by way of Texas northward but also from California, Arizona, New Mexico, Louisiana, and Florida.[15] He also acknowledged that open-range ranching in Latin America preceded any ranching activities in what is now the United States by more than a century.[16] Thus chronology supports linguistic and other evidence.

Hispanic culture and practices even crossed the Pacific Ocean in the 1830s, when three vaqueros from California, likely mestizos or Native Americans, taught Hawaiians how to handle cattle. The Hawaiian term for cowboy, *paniolo*, is likely an adaptation of *español* (Spaniard or of Spanish language). In 1832, at King Kamehameha III's request, the vaqueros landed in the Kona district on the western shore of the island of Hawaii. They taught native Hawaiians how to handle wild cattle. Hawaii's cowboys rode horseback and chased wild cattle decades before the arrival of the first Anglo ranchers and cowboys in most of the mainland American West.[17] Scholars with the Kona Historical Society and the Paniolo Preservation Society are researching and recovering the history of ranching on the island of Hawaii.[18]

In his minutely researched regional study, *Tejano Legacy: Ranchers and Settlers in South Texas, 1734–1900,* Armando C. Alonzo clearly demonstrated the important Spanish origins of the economy and society of the lower Rio Grande valley. His exemplary work of local history makes excellent use of country tax and probate records that "demonstrate a strong, early presence of Tejano ranchers." Citing the research of John E. Rouse, Alonzo also disputes, as have many others, Jordan's assertion that "the origin of the cattle industry in Texas is of South Carolinian background."[19] Likewise, Gerald E.

15. Terry G. Jordan, *The Overemphasis of Texas as a Source of Western Cattle Ranching,* Charles L. Wood Agricultural History Lecture Series (Lubbock: Texas Tech University, International Center for Arid and Semiarid Land Studies, 1992); Jordan, *North American Cattle-Ranching Frontiers,* pp. 153, 256.

16. Jordan, *Trails to Texas,* p. 5.

17. L. A. Henke, *A Survey of Livestock in Hawaii* (Honolulu: University of Hawaii Research Publication No. 5, August 1929), p. 21.

18. For information on Hawaiian ranching, see http://www.cowboyprof.com. Select the link to "Explore ranch and paniolo life in Hawaii."

19. Armando C. Alonzo, *Tejano Legacy: Ranchers and Settlers in South Texas, 1734–1900.* (Albuquerque: University of New Mexico Press, 1998), pp. 9, 193, 206; John E. Rouse, *The Criollo: Spanish Cattle in the Americas* (Norman: University of Oklahoma Press, 1977), pp. 86–88, 191–96.

Poyo and Gilberto M. Hinojosa offer an unambiguous explanation of the "Tejano origins in eighteenth-century San Antonio." The regional identity of greater San Antonio "involved the adaptation of a Mexican ranching culture at the Texas frontier."[20]

Smead's wonderful compendium of Spanish-origin linguistic evidence and oral tradition bolsters the historical arguments drawn from the built environment and material culture. If cattle frontiers have been somewhat light on paper sources, they make up for it with leather. Material culture—saddles, tack, boots, hats, and other clothing, weapons, and equipment—often survive long after their owners are deceased and paper has disintegrated. Saddle-maker and historian George Necer has documented variations in saddles throughout the world. His work traces the spread of saddlemaking and saddle types from Spain through Latin America and into the American West.[21] Fortunately, many countries have museums and private collections where items of material culture have been preserved. This wealth of leather material culture offers overwhelming tangible evidence of Hispanic influences.[22]

Smead's work shows that many essential items of tack originated in the Spanish culture. The *bozal*, usually rendered *bosal*, for example, is the nose band of a headstall or hackamore (the latter from the Spanish term *jáquima*). Western cowboys still show the Spanish origins of their ubiquitous leather leggings or chaps, by pronouncing the words "shaps." That pronunciation stems from the original Spanish *chaparreras*, also pronounced with the "sh." The ever-present *lariat* comes from *la reata*; *McCarty* (a fine horsehair rope) from *mecate*. *Theodore* (a small-diameter rope used on a horse as a chin-strap or throat latch) is an adaptation of *fiador*.

Jerald Underwood does a masterful job of describing vaquero saddles, tack, and technique in *Vaqueros, Cowboys, and Buckaroos*. Historian Lawrence Clayton shows the profound influence of vaquero tradi-

20. Gerald E. Poyo and Gilberto M. Hinojosa, eds. *Tejano Origins in Eighteenth-Century San Antonio* (Austin: University of Texas Press for the University of Texas Institute of Texan Cultures at San Antonio, 1991).

21. George Necer, "Saddles of the World" (unpub. MS, 1982, copyright January 11, 1991, TXu 89.427).

22. See the 130 illustrations and the excellent explanatory text in Clayton, *Vaqueros, Cowboys, and Buckaroos*.

tions on the Anglo cowboy when he quotes south Texas cowboy Frank Graham describing the vaquero as a "master teacher." "He was here before Anglos came," Graham explained, "and he gave his terminology to us." He showed Anglos "how to work cattle in this wild, open country. And the vaquero knew the brush; the English did not."[23] Historian Jim Hoy traces the Hispanic roots all the way north to the buckaroos of Nevada's Great Basin, southern Idaho, and eastern Oregon.[24] Spanish terms, equipment, and practices reached throughout the West and even crossed the border into Canada.

Texas still exhibits many elements of its strong Hispanic past and present, wonderfully illustrated by Helen Simmons and Cathryn A. Hoyt in *Hispanic Texas: A Historical Guide*. Spanish music and dance, established during the eighteenth century, persist. Andrew F. Muir visited San Antonio in 1837 and commented on the residents' love of *fandangos*, lively dances. "There are seldom less than three or four during the night in different portions of the city."[25] Missions and churches, Spanish Revival architecture, place names, statues, paintings, festivals, and many other cultural elements of Texas reflect powerful, extensive Hispanic roots.[26] Kathleen Mullen Sands examines the history and persistence of Mexican rodeo in her study *Charrería Mexicana*.[27]

Ned Martin, Jody Martin, and James Gorton have produced two lavishly illustrated and highly informational books that document the origins and transmission of important elements of horse gear from Spanish/Moorish roots to Mexico and northward into the United States. They indicate exactly how the exigencies of Spanish and Mexican riding shaped the equipment that *vaqueros* and *charros* used. "The sliding stops and spectacular spins of the California *vaquero's* horse," wrote James Gorton, "required a greater degree of control than the more conventional performance of the Texas Quarter Horse,

23. Clayton, *Vaqueros, Cowboys, and Buckaroos*, p. 71.
24. Clayton, *Vaqueros, Cowboys, and Buckaroos,* passim.
25. Quoted in Manuel Peña, *Música Tejana* (College Station: Texas A&M University Press, 1999), p. 27; on music see pp. 37–49.
26. See the many essays and illustrations in Helen Simmons and Cathryn A. Hoyt, *Hispanic Texas: A Historical Guide* (Austin: University of Texas Press, 1992).
27. Kathleen Mullen Sands, *Charrería Mexicana* (Tucson: University of Arizona Press, 1993).

and the *vaquero* found the spade bit best accomplished the control required."[28] Gorton also noted that "Spurs in the West came north with the Mexican *vaqueros* and developed differently in Texas and in California. . . . The most significant transition of design occurred after 1870 when hand-wrought workmanship reached a high degree of development. The best craftsmen were still those from Mexico who came to California and continued to reproduce favorite old Spanish design elements."[29]

Ralph Emerson has demonstrated that both Spanish and British influences shaped the development of horse equipment in North America. However, he unequivocally states that "the first bits and spurs in the New World originated in Spain," introduced by Columbus. Anglo-American influences on Texas gear do not become significant until some 350 years later, during the 1840s and 1850s.[30] Texans used mostly Mexican spurs during much of the nineteenth century. Not until about 1872 did Joseph Carl Petmecky of Austin, Texas, begin crafting stronger, lighter-weight one-piece spurs of tempered spring steel that supplanted the older, heavier, more elaborate Mexican varieties.[31]

All this "horse furniture" had the same purpose: to control horses. Horse breeds of the New World demonstrate the primacy and ubiquity of Hispanic influences. Many authorities have traced the Spanish introduction and subsequent spread of horses throughout the Americas. Most recently, Deb Bennett, in *Conquerors: The Roots of New World Horsemanship*, states the case simply. "The Spanish jennet— that intelligent, noble, handsome, brave, and worthy animal—is the one equine which contributed to the ancestry of all horse breeds originating in the Americas."[32] Bennett adds strong evidence of the pri-

28. James Gorton, "Bit Styles, Components and Use," in Ned Martin and Jody Martin, eds., *Bit and Spur Makers in the Vaquero Tradition: a Historical Perspective* (Nicasio, Calif.: Hawk Hill Press, 1997), p. 20.

29. Gorton, "The Spur: History, Parts and Uses," in Martin and Martin, *Bit and Spur Makers in the Vaquero Tradition*," pp. 47–48.

30. Ralph Emerson, "Origins of Horse Equipment in North America," and "Nineteenth Century Texas Settlement and Cattle Ranching," in Ned Martin, Jody Martin, and Kurt House, *Bit and Spur Makers in the Texas Tradition: A Historical Perspective* (Nicasio, Calif.: Hawk Hill Press, 2000), pp. 12, 25.

31. Martin, Martin, and House, *Bit and Spur Makers in the Texas Tradition*, pp. 45, 193.

32. Deb Bennett, *Conquerors: The Origins of New World Horsemanship* (Solvang, Calif.: Amigo Publications, 1998), p. iii.

macy and power of Hispanic influences gathered by prior researchers, including Frederic Remington, Robert M. Denhardt, Glenn R. Vernam, and David Dary.[33]

In sum, Robert Smead has completed the case for the significance and primacy of Spanish origins of the western range cattle industry, with his extensive, elegant, entertaining body of linguistic evidence. Wherever we look—language, including slang and jargon, gear, clothing, horses, the built environment—we see that Spaniards and/or Mexicans laid the foundations, and that later-arriving Anglos built upon those origins. As Jack Jackson has written, "Anglo contributions to the industry generally came in the post–Civil War period and consisted of things like the introduction of northern breeding stock (shorthorns), barbed wire fences, windmills, and market-oriented developments such as packeries, railroad shipment, and stockyard operations."[34] That is, Anglo contributions came later.

To understand cowboys and ranch life in the American West, we cannot begin at the very late period of Anglo arrival during the nineteenth century. We must go back many centuries to Columbus and his importation of Spanish cattle, horses, and horsemanship into the New World. We must trace the dissemination of the vaquero culture as it moved into northern New Spain, what is now California and the American Southwest. Finally, we must recognize that just because a latter-day Anglo-American demographic wave washed over the West, it did not drown all preexisting cultures. Buckaroos of the Northwest, vaqueros of the Southwest, and *paniolo* in Hawaii offer living testimony that Spanish roots run deep and still constitute living cultures.

Enjoy this fascinating ride, guided by Robert Smead, through the rich Spanish-origin language of the American West. *Vocabulario Vaquero* explores the Spanish origins of many ranching terms, as well

33. Frederic Remington, *Pony Tracks* (Norman: University of Oklahoma Press, 1961), pp. 70–82; Remington, *The Collected Writings of Frederic Remington,* ed. Peggy Samuels and Harold Samuels (n.p.: Castle, 1986), pp. 120–39; Robert M. Denhardt, *The Horse of the Americas* (Norman: University of Oklahoma Press, 1947, 1975); Glenn R. Vernam, *Man on Horseback: The Story of the Mounted Man from the Scythians to the American Cowboy* (Lincoln: University of Nebraska Press, 1964, 1972); David Dary, *Cowboy Culture: A Saga of Five Centuries* (Lawrence: University Press of Kansas, 1981, 1989).

34. Jack Jackson, "Hispanic Ranching Heritage," in Simons and Hoyt, *Hispanic Texas,* p. 56.

as the concepts, equipment, and practices associated with those words. Everyone from linguistic specialists to "word buffs" to western historians and history fans will learn from and appreciate Smead's labors. You'll encounter many delightful surprises (the term *vigilante* is of Spanish origin), punctured misconceptions (the origin of the ten-gallon hat), and just plain fun.

Acknowledgments

This dictionary was inspired, in part, by Mackey Hedges' *Last Buckaroo*. His short glossary at the end of the novel drew my attention to the fact that cowboy vocabulary contains a significant number of Hispanicisms, far more than is usually acknowledged. I wish to thank several of my students who also researched the subject matter: Mark Richardson, who has cowboyed in North and South America, and Bo and Taylor MacDonald, who have a great deal of ranching and beef experience. They all shared their insight and expertise with me. I also owe a profound debt of gratitude to my research assistants: Heather Robles, who completed the bulk of the research and without whom this dictionary would not have been completed, Cecilia Tocaimaza, whose careful editing and close reading helped correct errors and oversights, and Allen Rasmussen, whose help in the final editing process has proven invaluable. I also thank Jeff Turley, of our department, for his suggestions and help with the Latin etymologies. Likewise, a special thanks to Don Norton and his staff for help in editing the initial manuscript. Thanks also to the Department of Spanish and Portuguese, the College of Humanities, and the Charles Redd Center for Western Studies at Brigham Young University for their generous financial support. I also owe a debt of gratitude to Charles Rankin and the OU Press editorial staff for their active promotion of this project; to Richard Slatta for his careful appraisal of the historical aspects and for his helpful suggestions; and to Ronald Kil for his fine illustrations. Last, but not least, I wish to thank my family for all their unfailing support.

Introduction

J. Halvor Clegg and I have written elsewhere, "The lexicon of all languages is the sum of their cultural and linguistic history."* In this particular case, the major cultural and linguistic elements that were brought together in the Old West include distinct dialects of American English, a number of American Indian languages, and at least three or four varieties of Spanish. With regard to the Spanish varieties, these can be identified as the Peninsular Spanish of the early colonizers and Californios; Southwestern Spanish, including the variety spoken in northern New Mexico and southern Colorado; and educated as well as uneducated varieties of Mexican Spanish. Each of these linguistic varieties responds to and encompasses cultural distinctions and orientations.

Most contemporary dictionaries of the American West, such as those utilized in the preparation of this work, catalog terms from English, Spanish, and indigenous sources. This dictionary is unique, however, because it focuses solely on the words and expressions used in ranching and cowboying that trace back to Spanish. Furthermore, claims that a particular term owes its existence to Spanish-English contact in the western United States have been carefully scrutinized. Both the origins (etymology) and usage in English as well as Spanish have been carefully documented for each term or expression. In sum, this work represents a scholarly linguistic treatment of its subject matter—a treatment that is often found lacking in other sources.

*Unpublished course materials for "Border Spanish" (Spanish 423, Brigham Young University, 2000).

Methodology

The Hispanicisms collected here derive from several sources. Some are referenced in scholarly works of a wide scope, including the *Oxford English Dictionary*, *Dictionary of American Regional English* (Vols. I–III), and Félix Rodríguez González's anthology titled *Spanish Loanwords in the English Language: A Tendency towards Hegemony Reversal*. Others were collected by my students, some of whom have worked as cowboys or ranchers in the western United States. The bulk of the terms referenced, however, derive from popular lexicons of the (Old) West. These include Adams's *Western Words: A Dictionary of the Old West*, Blevins's *Dictionary of the American West*, Clark's *Western Lore and Language*, Hendrickson's *Happy Trails: A Dictionary of Western Expressions*, Smith's *Southwestern Vocabulary: The Words They Used*, and Watts's *Dictionary of the Old West*. Other scholarly sources that proved invaluable are Bentley's *Dictionary of Spanish Terms in English, with Special Reference to the American Southwest*, Carisle's "Southwestern Dictionary," and Hoy's *Spanish Terms of the Sonoran Desert Borderlands: A Basic Glossary*.

Each term (extracted from the sources summarized above) was referenced to several Spanish sources. The etymologies derive in the main from Corominas's dictionaries: *Breve diccionario etimológico de la lengua castellana* and *Diccionario crítico etimológico castellano e hispánico*, the latter written with José A. Pascual, comprising five volumes. Scholarly works of a wide scope that were consulted include the Royal Academy's *Diccionario de la lengua española* and Simon and Schuster's *International Dictionary, Spanish/English and English/Spanish*. Other key sources include Santamaría's *Diccionario de mejicanismos*, Sobarzo's *Vocabulario sonorense*, and Islas's *Vocabulario campesino nacional* for Mexican Spanish; Cabrera's *Diccionario de aztequismos* for Nahautlisms or Aztequisms; Cobos's *Dictionary of New Mexico and Southern Colorado Spanish*, and Galván's *Dictionary of Chicano Spanish/El diccionario del español chicano* for Southwestern Spanish. Please see the bibliography for other pertinent details on the English and Spanish sources.

Lexical Borrowing: Some Linguistic Notions

In order to comprehend the complicated process known as lexical borrowing, one must first understand what is transferred from one language to another when borrowing occurs. According to Ferdinand de Saussure, generally recognized as the father of modern linguistics, a word or expression constitutes a *linguistic sign*. A linguistic sign, in turn, is composed of two elements: a *signifier* (*form* or *signal*) that evokes the *signified* (*meaning* or *message*). Thus, the sign *clock*, for example, consists of a form which serves to transmit the meaning associated with that particular term in English.

$$\text{Sign} = \text{Signified} + \text{Signifier}$$

$$Clock = \quad \bigcirc \quad + \text{ /klák/}$$

It is generally accepted that a linguistic sign can refer to any particular object, concept, or other phenomenon in the real world. The term most utilized to describe this today is *referent*. The exact nature of the relationship between the referent and the linguistic sign is unknown, but need not concern us here. To recapitulate, a word or expression (known as a linguistic sign) has both a form (signifier or signal) as well as meaning (signified or message). These components and their relationship to one another are key to an understanding of linguistic borrowing.

The term *borrowing* generally refers to the process of adopting and integrating non-native words or expressions into one's native language. Note that the term is not precise (one doesn't plan to return the borrowed word, for instance). It might be preferable to speak of linguistic copying or even cloning, but the term *borrowing* is quite entrenched and has not yet yielded to other possibilities.

Borrowing begins with a *model*, that is, the term or expression (linguistic sign) in the *donor* or *source* language (Spanish, in this case). The *model* is copied in an inexact form, and is known as a *replica*. The language that adopts, adapts, and accommodates the replica is referred to as the *host* language (in this case, English). For example, the Spanish model *mecate* 'horsehair or *maguey* rope' was borrowed into English as *macardy*, *macarte*, *McCarthy*, *McCarty*, *mecarte*. These forms represent the replicas coined by English speakers. Note that in two cases, the speakers misindentified the Spanish term with a supposed English-language surname, perhaps incorrectly assuming that a cowboy or saddlemaker lent his last name to that particular type of rope. The intrusive {r} probably results from a spelling pronunciation where the Spanish {t} was tapped or flapped. A similar process occurred with *chaps*; the Spanish model *chaparreras* 'leather leggings' was shortened and the Northern Mexican pronunciation of the letter {ch} was retained (as /ʃ/ "sh").

A Simplified Example of Borrowing into English

Source Language Model ➡ Host Language Replica

mecate (Spanish—Nahuatl) ➡ macardy (English)

chaparreras (Spanish—pre-Roman) ➡ chaps (English)

As this graphic illustrates, Spanish is the immediate source for these terms (as well as all others included in the dictionary, except in cases where we conclude the term in question is not a Hispanicism). In many cases, however, Spanish itself borrowed the term from some other source. In this case, *mecate* derives from Nahuatl, the language of the Aztecs, but was borrowed into Spanish first before the original cowboys learned it from the Mexican vaqueros. *Chaparreras* probably derives from a pre-Roman term, perhaps Basque in its origin, which was first borrowed into Spanish before both the referent and word *chaps* appeared in cowboy dress and speech. Such cases of multiple borrowings are common. From our point of view, all such terms are Hispanicisms since Spanish speakers have granted them a sort of naturalized citizenship in their language (and most lay persons are unaware of their foreign origins). In any event, Spanish acts as the vehicle for their adoption into English.

Both of these examples illustrate the borrowing of the entire linguistic sign—the signifier as well as the signified of the Spanish model have been copied (not without some adaptation of the form and/or meaning). This type of borrowing, termed a *loan* or *loanword*, is most typical of language contact situations. However, it is not the only manifestation of this process. The other type of lexical borrowing that we will consider is termed *calquing*. If a term or terms are calqued, the host language borrows only the signified and superimposes the foreign meaning (Spanish, in this case) on a native signifier (English). A *multiword calque* is one modeled on a foreign phrase or expression. It may take the form of an apparent "literal" or word-for-word translation. The following chart provides an example of a paired loanword and calqueword as well as a paired loanword and phrasal calque.

A Typology of Lexical Borrowing

Loanword	Calqueword	Multiword Calque
manzana	apple	
hombre bueno		good man

In the western United States, the loanword *manzana* and the calqueword *apple* have acquired the specialized meaning of 'saddlehorn,' since one style of Mexican saddles features a horn shaped like an apple cut in half. Note that the loanword imports both the form and meaning from Spanish into English. The calqueword imports only the meaning, superimposing it on an English-language translation equivalent for the Spanish word. A similiar process occurs with *hombre bueno* and *good man*, meaning 'arbitrator.' The compound loanword transfers both meaning and form from Spanish into English, while the multiword calque translates the Spanish compound into English, retaining the original meaning. Thus, a *good man* in this sense, is not only one who is morally upright, but one who fulfills a specific legal function in settling disputes.

Contents of the Dictionary

This dictionary contains 416 headwords (primary terms or expressions) and 347 derived or related terms (indented under the headwords). Thus, the lexical entries total 763 terms or expressions. Of the 416 headwords, 226 (54 percent) derive from Latin. This is to be expected, since Spanish descends directly from Latin and inherited most of its vocabulary from that source. American Indian borrowings, which originated during the Spanish conquest of the Americas, compose 48 (12 percent of the total). The bulk of these, 26 (6 percent), derive from Nahuatl, the language of the Aztecs. Arabic accounts for 25 (6 percent) of the terms referenced. Arabisms entered into Spanish during the Moorish occupation of the Iberian Peninsula from A.D. 711 to 1492. An additional 18 (4 percent) derive from other Romance languages, notably French (10) and Italian (6). Eighteen (4 percent) of the headwords can be traced no further than Spanish itself. Some of the oldest terms in the Spanish language, those that predate the Roman conquest of 218 B.C., are also represented in the dictionary— they total 13 (3 percent). Terms of Germanic origin, introduced into Spanish following the fall of the Roman Empire and the subsequent invasion of barbarian tribes at the beginning of the fifth century A.D., add up to 12 (3 percent). Another 9 (2 percent) can be classified as toponyms or place names (not included elsewhere). Finally, a total of 30 (7 percent) of the headwords cannot be definitively classified: they are of uncertain, disputed, or unknown origin. (The remaining 17, or 4 percent, are of miscellaneous origin.)

Semantic Fields

As an indication of the lexical need that triggers borrowing, we provide a brief summary of the types of terms which entered Cowboy English via Spanish. We have limited our analysis to the top four categories of borrowings: (1) those that derive directly from Latin, (2) those that derive from an American Indian language other than Nahuatl, (3) Aztequisms, and (4) Arabisms.

The Latin-Spanish borrowings fall into several semantic fields. Thirty-six terms (16 percent) can be classified as cultural artifacts, institutions, and practices—they make specific reference to Spanish or Mexican cultural realities, including foods and types of clothing. Some examples include: *ajicola, colear, compadre/comadre, fandango,* and *hacienda.* Another twenty-five (11 percent) make reference to tack, and thirteen terms deal with the saddle itself. These include: *cinch, corus, fiador, fuste,* and *romal.* A total of twenty-four (11 percent) of the terms refer to the horse. They include colors such as *bayo* and *pinto* and descriptors like *caponera*, *mustang*, and *yegua*, as well as other related terms. Twenty-three terms (10 percent) refer to professions related to cowboying or ranching. These include: *agregado*, *buckaroo*, *desperado*, *remudadero*, and *wrangler*. Nineteen borrowings (8 percent) deal with cattle. *Cimarron, ladino, querencia, toro*, and *vaca* are a few pertinent examples. An additional nineteen terms (8 percent) provide synonyms (often jocular or pejorative in tone) for common English words. *Dinero, hoosegow, mosey, pungle*, and *savvy* are illustrative of this register change.

Other semantic fields represented in this dictionary by only a few of the Latin-Spanish borrowings include: sixteen terms (7 percent) classified as geographical descriptors (*canyon, mesa, monte, salina, sierra*); thirteen terms (6 percent) naming indigenous flora and fauna, excluding cattle and horses (*abrojo, burro, grama grass, lobo*, and *palo verde*); eleven (or 5 percent of the total Latin-Spanish borrowings) are roping terms (*dally, honda, lasso, reata*, and *tarrabee*); another eleven (5 percent) are toponyms or place names (*Colorado, El Paso [del Norte], Montana, Nevada*, and *[Rio] Grande*); an additional eleven terms (5 percent) are exclamations or taboo words (*andale, cabron, diablo, pendejo*, and *pronto*); eight terms (4 percent) reference that all-important commodity, water (*agua [dulce], bebedero, hueco tanks, ojo [caliente]*, and *tinaja*); seven terms (3 percent) are gentilics, referencing groups of people (*Chato, Cristianos, hombre, manso*, and *Piñoneros*); five terms (2 percent) are used as vocatives or forms of address (*corazon, cuñado, doña, dulce*, and *mugre*).

The lexical contribution from Nahuatl via Spanish can be divided into three semantic fields. The first of these—cultural artifacts, institutions, and practices—is composed of twelve terms (46 percent). It includes terms like *chongo, jacal, metate, teguas*, and *temescal*. The category of flora and fauna is represented by nine entries (35 percent). *Mesquite, nopal, tule, zacate*, and *zopilote* are a few examples. A third and final category, fermented beverages, includes the five remaining borrowings (19 percent): *colonche, mescal, pulque, tequila, tiswin*.

The other twenty-two American Indian borrowings fall principally into three semantic fields: cultural artifacts, institutions, and practices; gentilics; and flora and fauna. Culturally related items come to ten (45 percent) and are represented by terms like *cacique, chaquira*, *guancoche, huarache,* and *jerky.* Gentilics, referencing groups of people, total six (27 percent). Such terms include *Apache, Comanche, Moqueño, Savanero,* and *Tejano.* The third semantic field, flora and fauna, includes a total of five terms (23 percent), namely, *Cibola, guaco, maguey, pitahaya,* and *saguaro.* The remaining term, *Texas,* is, of course, a toponym or place name.

The Arabic-Spanish borrowings can be classified into five semantic fields. The largest category, made up of twelve terms, concerns horsemanship, as exemplified by *Alice Ann, a(r)cion, bayo azafranado, hackamore,* and *jinete.* Flora is represented by four terms. *Alfalfa, alfilaria, bellota,* and *loco*(weed) are common southwestern plants whose names derive ultimately from Arabic. Three semantic fields, those of architecture; cultural artifacts, institutions, and practices; and water are represented by three terms each. Elements of Arabesque architecture common in the southwestern United States provide the terms *adobe, almagre,* and *azotea. Alcalde, alguacil,* and *arroba* derive from Arabic institutions and practices. *Alberca, jarro,* and *noria,* referring to water deposits or vessels, relate to the constant need for potable water in arid regions.

Spanish Phonetic Symbols

Vowels

Phonetic Symbol	Approximate Value	Articulatory Description
a	{a} in f<u>a</u>ther, {o} in h<u>o</u>t	low central
e	{e} in w<u>e</u>t, st<u>e</u>p	mid front
j	{y} in <u>y</u>es, <u>y</u>ard	front semiconsonant
i	{ee} in m<u>ee</u>k, {ea} in w<u>ea</u>k	high front
i̯	{y} in maguey̯	front semivowel
o	{o} in g<u>o</u>, {ow} in b<u>ow</u>	mid back
w	{w} in <u>w</u>alk, <u>w</u>illow	back semiconsonant
u	{oo} in b<u>oo</u>t	high back
u̯	{w} in hoosego<u>w</u>	back semiconsonant

Consonants

Phonetic Symbol	Approximate Value	Articulatory Description
b	{b} in <u>b</u>rother, <u>b</u>oy	voiced bilabial occlusive
β	As in blowing out a candle plus voicing	voiced bilabial fricative
tʃ	{ch} in <u>ch</u>arity	unvoiced palatal affricate
d	{d} in <u>d</u>octor	voiced dental occlusive
δ	{th} in <u>th</u>en	voiced interdental fricative
f	{f} in <u>f</u>irst	unvoiced labiodental fricative
g	{g} <u>g</u>ood	voiced velar occlusive
γ	As in gargling	voiced velar fricative
ǰ	tenser than English {y}	voiced palatal fricative
k	{k} in <u>k</u>ite	unvoiced velar occlusive
l	{l} in <u>l</u>aw	voiced alveolar lateral
l̪	see below*	voiced dentalized lateral
m	{m} in <u>m</u>other	voiced bilabial nasal
n	{n} in <u>n</u>one	voiced alveolar nasal
n̦	{n} in i<u>n</u>sure	voiced palatalized nasal
ŋ	{n} in so<u>ng</u>	voiced velarized nasal
n̦	see below*	voiced dentalized nasal
ɲ	{ny} in ca<u>ny</u>on	voiced palatal nasal
p	{p} in <u>p</u>art	unvoiced bilabial occlusive
r	intervocalic {t} or {d} in bu<u>tt</u>er, la<u>dd</u>er	voiced alveolar flap

r̄	"rolled r"	voiced alveolar trill
s	{s} in <u>s</u>ong	unvoiced alveolar fricative
ṣ	{z} in <u>z</u>oo	voiced alveolar fricative
t	{t} in <u>t</u>ime	unvoiced dental occlusive
x	{h} in <u>h</u>ome	unvoiced velar fricative

Other phonetic symbols

á, é, í, ó, ú	stressed vowel, acoustically prominent
ã, ẽ, ĩ, õ, ũ	nasalized vowels, e.g. m<u>o</u>m, m<u>e</u>n, m<u>i</u>nk, m<u>oa</u>n, m<u>oo</u>n
v͜v	(last and first vowels of separate words fall in the same syllable)

*English has no dental or dentalized consonants. The dentalized nasal and lateral are formed with the tip of the tongue placed where the gum ridge and the inside face of the upper incisors meet. This occurs in Spanish in anticipation of a following dental consonant /t, d/.

Etymological Symbols

ā, ē, ī, ō, ū	denotes long vowel in Latin
* (starred form)	hypothetical/reconstructed form

Key to Sources Frequently Cited

For stylistic purposes some sources are cited twice
For complete reference see bibliography

Adams	*Western Words: A Dictionary of the Old West*
Bentley	*A Dictionary of Spanish Terms in English, with Special Reference to the American Southwest*
Blevins	*Dictionary of the American West*
Cabrera	*Diccionario de aztequismos*
Carlisle	"A Southwestern Dictionary"
Clark	*Western Lore and Language: A Dictionary for Enthusiasts of the American West*
Cobos	*A Dictionary of New Mexico and Southern Colorado Spanish*
Corominas	*Breve diccionario etimológico de la lengua castellana* or *Diccionario crítico etimológico castellano e hispánico*
DARE	*Dictionary of American Regional English*
DM	*Diccionario de mejicanismos*
DRAE	*Diccionario de la Real Academia Española*
Hendrickson	*Happy Trails: A Dictionary of Western Expressions*
Hoy	*Spanish Terms of the Sonoran Dessert Borderlands: A Basic Glossary*
Islas	*Vocabulario campesino nacional*
OED	*Oxford English Dictionary*
Royal Academy	*Diccionario de la Real Academia Española*
Santamaría	*Diccionario de mejicanismos*
Sobarzo	*Vocabulario sonorense*
Smith	*A Southwestern Vocabulary: The Words They Used*
VCN	*Vocabulario campesino nacional*

VS   *Vocabulario sonorense*
Watts   *A Dictionary of the Old West*

Key to Dictionary Entries

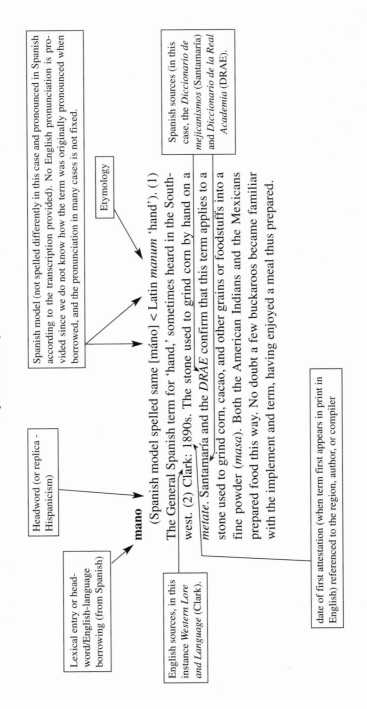

Headword (or replica - Hispanicism)

Lexical entry or head-word/English-language borrowing (from Spanish)

Etymology

Spanish model (not spelled differently in this case and pronounced in Spanish according to the transcription provided). No English pronunciation is provided since we do not know how the term was originally pronounced when borrowed, and the pronunciation in many cases is not fixed.

Spanish sources (in this case, the *Diccionario de mejicanismos* (Santamaría) and *Diccionario de la Real Academia* (DRAE).

mano

(Spanish model spelled same [máno] < Latin *manum* 'hand'). (1) The General Spanish term for 'hand,' sometimes heard in the South-west. (2) Clark: 1890s. The stone used to grind corn by hand on a *metate*. Santamaría and the *DRAE* confirm that this term applies to a stone used to grind corn, cacao, and other grains or foodstuffs into a fine powder (*masa*). Both the American Indians and the Mexicans prepared food this way. No doubt a few buckaroos became familiar with the implement and term, having enjoyed a meal thus prepared.

English sources, in this instance *Western Lore and Language* (Clark).

date of first attestation (when term first appears in print in English) referenced to the region, author, or compiler

Vocabulario Vaquero/Cowboy Talk

abrojo:

(Spanish model spelled same [aβróxo] < Latin *aperi oculum* 'open your eye!'). Texas: 1931. According to the *DARE*, this term can refer to any of a variety of chaparral shrubs, including *Condalia globosa.* Often refers to the "lotebush" and "squawbush." The *DRAE* defines *abrojo* as a plant of the zygophyllaceous family, with long creeping stems, composite leaves, almost spherical fruit, and many sharp, sturdy spines. It is harmful to crops. Santamaría glosses this term as a common name for any of a number of plants, belonging to several different families, that all have stems or fruit bristling with many sharp, sticky, or barbed spines. In Mexico, *abrojo* is applied to such diverse plants as: *Triumpheta semitriloba, Microrhamnus ericoides, C. spatulata*, and *C. obtusifolia.* The cowboy wore chaps and relied on his boots and *tapaderos* to protect his feet and legs from the sharp spines of these plants. *Ladino* cattle often hid in thickets of *abrojo* or *chaparral*, making his job difficult, indeed.

acion:

(Sp. model spelled same [asjón]< Arabic *as-siyūr*, plural of *sair* 'leather strap or belt'). Adams: 1944. Extreme SW, border country, and California, according to Watts. Both Adams and Watts reference this term as "a stirrup leather." The *DRAE* provides a similar gloss: a leather strap that hangs from the stirrup. Spanish horsemanship was strongly influenced by the Moors who conquered and controlled most of Spain for nearly eight centuries (A.D. 711–1492). *Ación* is one of a significant number of terms that was borrowed from Arabic into Spanish and subsequently made its way into English via the Spanish/Mexican vaqueros.

adios:

(*adiós* [aðjós] < Spanish *a Dios* 'to God' < Latin *deus* 'God'). SW: 1844. General Spanish term for good-bye or farewell. Watts notes its relationship to another common leavetaking, *vaya con Dios*, 'go with God.' Hendrickson remarks that Texans also have used it as a verb meaning 'get going, vamoose,' as in "you better adios before the law comes." According to Bentley, Kit Carson is said to have uttered "Doctor, compadre, adios" in 1856 as his last words.

adobe:

(Sp. model spelled same [aðóβe] < Arabic *aṭ-ṭub* 'the brick'). *DARE*: 1759. (1) Sundried brick made of clay, straw, and water. (2) A structure, usually a house, made from the same material. (3) Clay suitable for fashioning such bricks. The first definition is attested to in the *DRAE*; Santamaría confirms the usage of the second in the Southwest, providing the example "She lived in her old *adobe*," also noting that the lot or grounds on which such a structure was to be built could be referred to as "an *adobe* sole." (*Sole*, according to the *OED*, is an obsolete term meaning "the foundation of a building; the site of a city, etc.") Spanish architecture was also greatly influenced by the Moors who introduced styles and materials now intimately associated with the Southwest. (4) As an adjective, several English sources note that the term denotes Mexican origin and usually connotes inferiority. For instance, the Mexican dollar or silver peso was called a "dobie dollar," or "dobie," for short. Cowboys were familiar with adobe as building material on the ranches and haciendas where they worked. Cowboy English is the source of the expression *dobe wall* listed below, according to Bentley, Adams, and Watts. (5) Hendrickson's contention that *adobe* is the model for *doughboy* (military personnel) is not supported by any of the sources consulted. See the *OED* for possible etymologies. *Doughboy* is attested, however, by the *OED* as slang for (1). *Common compounds:* adobe brick, adobe block, adobe house. *Alternate forms:* adabe, adaube, adaubi, adobey, adobi, adobie, adoby, 'dobe, 'dobie, dob, doba, dobbey, dobby, dobie, doby, dogie, doughboy.

adobe dollar:

SW: 1909. A Mexican peso. Cowboys and rustlers, who often worked on both sides of the border, were undoubtedly familiar with Mexican currency. *Alternate form:* 'dobe dollar.

adobera:

(Sp. model spelled same [aδoβéra] < *adobe* [see above] plus -*era* 'place where the lexical root is made or an object used for making the same'). The most common meaning of this term (also referenced by Hoy) is "a wooden mold used for making adobe bricks." The *DRAE*, as well as the Mexican sources consulted, also states that it may refer to the place where adobes are made.

adobero:

(Sp. model spelled same [aδoβéro] < *adobe* [see above] and the agentive suffix -*ero* 'occupation, profession, job'). Hoy's definition is correct: "a maker of adobes." Hendrickson also notes that the phrase "adobe-maker" was used pejoratively to refer to Mexicans.

'dobe wall:

(adobe wall): According to Watts (who, in turn, refers to Adams), this expression meant to put a man up against a wall and shoot him, and probably originated in the 1870s when Texan cattle rustlers (or retrievers) were caught and executed in Mexico and the Southwest.

agregado:

(Sp. model spelled same [aɣreɣáδo] < Latin *aggregāre* 'to add to, join' and the nominalizing suffix -*do*). New Mexico: 1871. Watts glosses the term as "a farmhand or a man allowed to work for himself on part of the landowner's soil." The *DRAE* provides a similar definition for Latin American Spanish, stating that it refers to someone who occupies another's property and may or may not pay rent or perform odd jobs for the privilege. A cowboy who settled down and married could become an *agregado* on his (former) **patron**'s property.

agua:

(Sp. model spelled same [áɣwa] < Latin *aquam* 'water'). As Blevins notes, this term may refer to water or rain. The plural *aguas* is the usual form for rain. No doubt the cowboy working in the borderlands among Mexicans used this term in searching for a source of drinking water for himself for the cattle under his care. Several common compounds exist, including:

agua caliente or **aguas calientes:**

(Sp. model spelled same [áɣwa] [see above] and [kaljéŋte] < Latin *calentis*; the plural agglutinated Aguascalientes is the name of a state in northern Mexico. As Carlisle observes, this compound means "literally 'hot water(s),' now a place name used to refer to many settlements in the West near Hot Springs [*sic*]."

agua dulce:

(Sp. model spelled same [áɣwa] [see above] and [ðúlse] < Latin *dulcis* 'sweet'). As Blevins states, this term means literally 'sweet water,' which in Spanish can refer to water fit for human consumption or to water low in concentration of mineral salts, according to the *DRAE*.

aguaje:

(Sp. model spelled same [aɣwáxe] < Latin *aquam* 'water' and the Spanish suffix -*aje* 'abundance of'). SW: Texas, Arizona, New Mexico, and California, according to the *DM*. According to Hoy, "any place for obtaining water." The *DRAE* notes an older, maritime usage meaning a provision of water or a place for obtaining potable water. All Spanish sources also note its usage as a watering hole, spring, or drinking trough for wild or domesticated animals, particularly cattle. The borderlands cowboy was undoubtedly familiar with this term since potable water in the desert regions of the Southwest was a primary concern for both humans and animals.

aguardiente:

(Sp. model spelled same [aɣwarðjéŋte] compound, agglutinated Spanish form < Latin *aqua* 'water' and *arder* < Latin *ārdēre* 'to burn, be on fire' plus the Spanish suffix -*iente* equivalent to the English -*ing*, in this case, literally burning water; hence, fire, or fiery, water). *DARE*: 1818. According to the *OED*, it originally referred to "a coarse kind of brandy made in Spain and Portugal" and was extended to native whiskey in the Southwest. Watts notes the continued evolution of the term: it also came to refer to spirits distilled from Mexican red wine or rum. As the Spanish sources note, it can refer to any distilled drink where the resultant alcohol is diluted with water. Hence it is a generic term translatable as booze (Blevins), strong (alcoholic) drink, or liquor (Hendrickson). It is likely that this generic meaning was the one used by cowboys and American Indians alike. *Alternate forms:* agua ardiente, aguadiente, aguadinte, aguardent, aquadiente, aquadinte, aquardiente, aquedent, aquediente, argadent, awerdente, awerdenty.

ajicola:

(*ajícola* [axíkola] < compound form agglutinated from Spanish *ajo* 'garlic' < Latin *ālium*, Spanish *y* 'and'; *cola* 'glue' < Latin *collam*). Smith states that the term refers to "a sort of mucilage or glue made in the Southwest by cowhands from leather-cuttings mixed with garlic and boiled into a paste." The *DRAE* provides a similar definition, although neither source indicates how it was used by buckaroos.

alazan: *See* **Alice Ann.**

albardon:

(*albardón* [alβarðón]; *albarda* < Arabic *al-barḍa'a*, 'the saddle,' plus the Spanish augmentative suffix *-on*). Both Smith and Blevins define this term as a packsaddle similar to the aparejo. The *DRAE* concurs for the root form *albarda*, but both *albardón* and *albarda* are glossed in the *DM* as types of riding saddles. According to the Royal Academy, the *albardón* is a riding saddle fashioned higher and hollower than the *albarda*. Santamaría, however, defines the term as an English riding saddle that is flat and lacks a bolster or cantle. Garulo's analysis of these terms can be construed to indicate that in Andalusia they were used indiscriminately to refer to packsaddles as well as riding saddles. Thus, it is possible that cowboys, muledrivers, and others intended the usage referred to in the English sources.

alberca:

(Sp. model spelled same [alβérka] < Arabic *al-birka* 'the pool or pond'). West Texas: 1892. According to Clark, "a water hole or watering place." The *DRAE* indicates that this term can refer to small accumulations of water, such as a pond or a pool, or a larger source, such as a dam or reservoir. In dry, dusty west Texas (as well as in other desert regions), an *alberca* was a welcome sight to thirsty cowmen and cattle.

alcalde:

(Sp. model spelled same [alkáḷde] < Arabic *al-quāḍī* 'the judge'). *DARE*: 1821 (Texas). Hoy notes that in colonial times this term referred to a town leader who wore several hats. He could act as judge in both civil and some minor criminal matters. He was also the presiding authority in the *alcaldía*, holding a higher position than the *regidores*, city legislators who collected tribute along with the alcalde. In Texas, during the 1830s, the term broadened significantly in meaning. Watts indicates that what it signified was roughly equivalent to a combination of mayor, chief of police and judge in the Southwest, particularly among the Mexican **poblados**. Clark adds that the term was also used to refer to a "somewhat important or self-important local person." Bentley notes that the term is sometimes confused with Spanish *alcaide*, meaning "the officer charged with the defense of a fort or castle." According to the *DRAE*, the term can refer to the president of a town council (or mayor) or to a municipal judge. *Alternate forms:* alcade, alcaide. Although Hollywood has greatly exaggerated the type and frequency of criminal activities that cowboys engaged in, no doubt a few renegades appeared before an alcalde to answer to the demands of justice.

alfalfa:
 (Sp. model spelled same [alfálfa] < Arabic *al-fasfaṣa*). *OED:* 1880s. A plant of the genus *Medicago sativa*. When in bloom it bears cloverlike purple flowers. The plant is widely used as animal fodder and as a cover crop. Spanish sources concur. It made its way to the Southwest from Mexico, having been originally introduced by the Spanish. *Also known as* lucern(e). It is still in common use among cowmen and ranchers today.

 alfalfa cube:
  "Cake of pressed alfalfa used to feed cows during the winter," states Blevins.

 alfalfa desperado:
  The hay hand on a ranch. *See also* desperado.

alfarga, alfarge, alfarky: *See* **alforja(s).**

alfilaria:
 (*alfilería* [alfilería] < *alfilerillo* < *alfiler* < Arabic *al-ḫilĕl* 'pin,' plus the diminutive suffix *-illo*; hence, 'small pin'). *OED:* 1868. A common forage in the Southwest, *also known as* pin grass (*Erodium cicutarium*). According to Cobos, *alfilería* (also *alfilerillo*) is used in New

Mexican and Southern Colorado Spanish to denote a plant of the Cranesbill family called pinclover. He indicates that the term derives from *alfilerillo*, which the *DRAE* defines as an herbaceous plant used as forage in Argentina and Chile. It is likely that the Argentine and Chilean varieties are unrelated to the southwestern *alfilaria* or *alfileria*, but share the common characteristic of a pinlike shape. No doubt the cowboy distinguished among the various types of forage that cattle would eat, since there was always the danger that they might ingest locoweed or some other poisonous plant. *Alternate forms:* alfilena, alfileria, alfilerilla, filaree, fileree.

alfilena, alfilerilla: *See* **alfilaria.**

alforche, alforki: *See* **alforja(s).**

alforja(s):
    (Sp. model spelled same [alfórxa] < Arabic *al-jurŷa* 'the saddlebags'). Bentley: 1847. A pair of bags or boxes made of rawhide, canvas, or wood suspended from a packsaddle; saddlebags. Spanish sources also register this meaning, among others. Another Arabic term introduced into Spanish in the Iberian Peninsula and brought to the New World by Spanish horsemen. Mexican vaqueros subsequently introduced *alforja(s)* to the ranchers, riders, and ropers in the Southwest. The range of spellings and pronunciations attests to the widespread usage of the term. *Alternate forms:* alfarga, alfarge, alfarky, alforche, alforga, alforge, alforka, alforki, alforje, alforkus.

algarroba: *See* mesquite—honey mesquite.

alguacil:
    (Sp. model spelled same [alɣwasíl] < Arabic *al-wazīr* 'the minister'). Southwest, especially Arizona and New Mexico: 1888. According to the *DARE*, "a constable or justice of the peace." The *DRAE* references one of several meanings similar to this one. According to Santamaría, the term is used in the Mexican state of Tabasco to refer to a law enforcement officer of the lowest order. It is an unpaid public office that all citizens are required to perform in turn. Just as they faced an **alcalde**, no doubt a few cowboys were arrested and jailed by the *alguacil*, the Spanish/Mexican equivalent of the sheriff or marshal. *Alternate form:* alguazil.

Alice Ann:

(*alazán* [alasán] < Arabic *al-azár* 'reddish'). Cowboy pronunciation of the Spanish color *alazán*—sorrel, or reddish. This may reflect a spelling pronunciation or a misconstrual of the model. Some poor cowman may have read the term with English phonology or mistakenly assumed that it originally referred to a redheaded female named Alice Ann. The *DRAE* describes the color as reddish or the color of cinnamon. Santamaría describes *alazán* with reference to horses' coloring. He notes that the term combines with other adjectives to describe a variety of colors. *Alazán claro* (light sorrel), *alazán jilote* (corn-colored sorrel), and *alazán mulato* (mulatto sorrel) are some examples.

almagre:

(Sp. model spelled same [almáγre] < Spanish *almagra* 'rust' < Arabic *al-magra* 'the red earth'). Carlisle: 1893. An early Spanish meaning for this Arabic term was iron oxide (rust) or oxidation. It also came to signify iron oxide as a pigment in clay. In the Southwest the term is closer to the original Arabic, referring to red earth or Indian red (where iron oxide may or may not be the principal pigment), used to paint adobe walls and houses. Cowboys familiar with construction methods and techniques that the Spaniards in the Old World learned from the Moors would have known this term also.

alze:

(*alce* [álse] < imperative form of the Spanish verb *alzar* [alsár] 'to lift up' < Vulgar Latin *altiāre* 'to raise, lift up'). In the game of monte, to expose the first card in a deck. According to the *DRAE*, the term means to cut the deck. Monte was a common diversion in the Old Southwest. Buckaroos, cattle rustlers, and hustlers played such card games in **cantina**s and in bunkhouses.

amansador:

(Sp. model spelled same [amãnsaðór] < Vulgar Latin *mãnsum* 'tame, gentle' plus Spanish agentive suffix -*dor* 'one who tames or domesticates'). SW and California: 1950. In the Southwest, a horsebreaker, especially one who employs the "hackamore," or rope halter and lead rope. Spanish sources concur. Santamaría notes that this meaning of the term is particular to the Americas. Its use illustrates a process known as foregrounding. The Spanish word *amansador* refers principally to someone who breaks horses following methods and techniques introduced by the Spanish **caballeros** and Mexican **vaqueros**. As such, the Spanish term foregrounds or highlights the Hispanic way of taming horses. *Alternate form*: mansador.

andale:

(*ándale* [áŋdale]; from Spanish verb *andar* < Romance variant of Latin *ambulāre* 'walk around' plus Spanish dative pronoun *le* 'a command to walk, go on'). Bentley: 1932. An exclamation meaning "hurry up" or "get going." This term is common in the Southwest and was used often when driving cattle. *See also* **avance**. Bentley adds that "a mother sending her child or servant on an errand might be expected to conclude her instructions with 'Now, *andale*' or 'Now, *andale pronto* (quick).'" Spanish sources concur. *Alternate form:* odale (probably from *órale*, another similar Mexican expression).

anquera:

(Sp. model spelled same [aŋkéra] < Italian or Old Provençal *anca* 'croup or hindquarters' plus Spanish suffix -*era*, 'place where something is used'; hence, 'an item that is used on the horse's hindquarters'). Mexico and California: 1881. A wide, often highly decorated piece of leather at the base of a western saddle lacking a rear jockey. Watts indicates that the *anquera* was used when another rider was placed to the rear of the first. Its practical function was to safeguard the second rider from contact with a sweaty horse. Other sources (including Blevins and Rossi, as cited in Watts) claim that the *anquera* had principally a decorative function. This term is not found in the *DRAE*, but the *DM* defines it as a type of leather cover attached to the cantle behind the saddle. Decorated with a string of small iron bells, it covers the horse's hindquarters and extends to the hocks. It is used in the breaking of a horse and as protection during bullfights or when the animal is thrown on the ground. According to Santamaría, the term is rarely used in Spanish today. The *anquera* is considered a characteristic feature of nineteenth-century Mexican saddles.

Apache:

(Sp. model spelled same [apátʃe] from the Zuni *ápachu* 'enemy' via Mexican Spanish). Clark: 1740s. The Zuni term for 'enemy' originally

Apache

referred to the Navajo. After it was incorporated into Spanish, its reference broadened to include a number of southwestern or Mexican Indian tribes who spoke varieties of the Athapaskan language. The Apaches are especially famous for their bellicose behavior and are inextricably linked in the popular mind with the cowboy. Spanish sources concur with the principal meanings cited here.

Apache plume:
New Mexico: 1889. A shrub of the Southwest (*Fallucia paradoxa*), which sports a "reddish seed cluster, resembling an Indian headdress," according to Watts. *Also known as* poñil.

Apache state:
Clark: 1930s. One of several nicknames for the state of Arizona, according to Watts.

aparejo:
(Sp. model spelled same [aparéxo] < Spanish verb *aparejar* 'to prepare' < Spanish prefix *a-* plus *parejo* < Latin *pariculum*, dimunitive of *parem* 'equal'). SW: 1844. A type of packsaddle consisting of a large stuffed leather or canvas pad attached to a wide cinch and an exceptionally wide breeching that fits under the animal's tail. It is especially designed for awkward heavy loads and may be used on horses, mules, and other animals. Spanish sources define it both as a packsaddle or riding gear. Bentley notes this item became so common that the U.S. Army has its own official version of the **aparejo**. Such packsaddles were common on long trail drives. *Alternate forms:* aparayho, arapaho.

aparejo grass:
Western Texas: 1894. A variety of grass in the Southwest, either *Sporobolus depauperatus* or *Muhlenbergia utilis* according to Clark, used to stuff aparejos, or packsaddles.

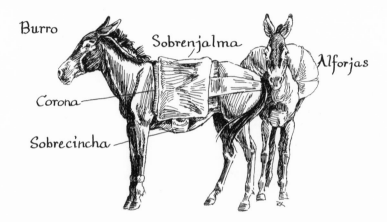

apple:
(Probable calque/loan translation from Spanish *manzana* 'apple'). Northwestern Texas: 1933. A type of saddlehorn (more fully described below). Santamaría provides the same definition for **manzana**.

apple-horn:
Adams: 1880s. A saddle that features a horn similar in shape to half an apple. *Also*: applehorn.

choke or grab the apple:
Southwest Texas: 1937. An attempt to remain in the saddle. Said of an unexperienced or unskilled rider who grabs hold of the saddlehorn. *Alternate expressions:* grab the nubbin/the post.

aquadinte, aquedent: *See* **aguardiente.**

Arapaho:

(1) Glossed by Hendrickson as "a name of uncertain origin for an Indian of a Western plains tribe of the Algonquian family. The name may derive from a Pawnee word for trader or from a Spanish word meaning 'the ragged ones.'" Hendrickson's definition is not supported by Spanish sources and it is unlikely that *harapo* [arápo], meaning rag or scrap of clothing, is the source of this southwestern term. Watts derives it from *aparejo* (see above); however, his claim is also unsubstantiated in the Spanish sources consulted. (2) *See* **aparejo.**

arciones:

(Sp. model spelled same [arsjónes] < Arabic *as-siyūr*, plural of *sair*, leather strap). Watts's definition of "stirrup-leathers" agrees with that of Santamaría, who notes the presence of an intrusive /r/ and assignment of the masculine to a term originally accorded feminine gender. He also indicates that it may refer to the saddlehorn (sometimes called the apple or *manzana*). The *DRAE* observes that this form arose through a blend of *ación* and *arzón*, the latter derived from the Latin *arcionis* 'forepart or bow of the saddletree.' *See* **acion.**

arena:

(Sp. model spelled same [aréna] < Latin *harēnam* 'sand'). Sand. Spanish sources concur. Its use in the Southwest as in *rodeo arena* may not be a Hispanicism since both the *OED* and the *DRAE* define it similarly ("sand-strewn place of combat") and attribute its origin to Latin.

areñeros:

(Sp. model spelled same [areɲéros] < Spanish *arena* '*sand*' [see above] plus Spanish suffix *-ero*, here the meaning is probably 'place abounding in sand' or 'sandy place'). The Sand Papago Indians who lived in the sands of the *Pinacate/Gran Desierto* region. Spanish sources do not reference this term, but the morphological derivation is legitimate. *Alternate form:* areñeñeros.

argolla del entreatador:

(Sp. model spelled same [argójaðeleŋtreataðór] < Arabic *al-gulla* 'the collar or handcuffs' (meaning 'iron ring' in Spanish) and *del* 'of the' and *entreatador* 'one that ties among two or more straps' < *entre* 'among or between' and *atador* (*atar* < Latin *aptāre* 'to adjust or adapt' and agentive suffix *-dor*; hence, the term refers to an iron ring used to tie between several straps). According to Watts, this term was used in the Southwest and California to refer to "the ring of the rigging straps, part of the saddle equipment." The *DRAE* defines *argolla* as a ring, generally made of iron, used with a rope to tie or catch something. *Entreatador* does not appear in any Spanish source but is a legitimate creation. This term was used among Mexican **vaquero**s and may have found its way into some varieties of cowboy English; no doubt it was a mouthful for the buckaroo who spoke little or no Spanish.

armas:

(Sp. model spelled same [ármas] < Latin *arma*, '(pieces of) armor, shield'). Clark: 1930s. Large leather flaps attached to the saddle to protect the rider's legs against brush and thorns. Watts indicates that they were a precursor to more modern chaps. The *DM* defines *armas de agua/de pelo* as two large pieces of goat hide, with the hair left on, that were attached to a saddle or to the belt of a rider to cover his legs and feet and protect them from water. Santamaría also notes that *armas* were sometimes used as mats for sleeping. Some were richly decorated. He also mentions that they have been substituted more recently by chaps or *chaparreras*, which do not protect the feet and cannot be used for sleeping. A similar definition can be found in the *VCN*, where *armas de agua* or *armas de pelo* are leather flaps that protect a rider's legs and the saddle from rain. *Armas de pecho* are defined as similar devices used mainly by vaqueros in Jalisco, Mexico, to defend themselves against rain and rugged terrain.

armitas:

(Sp. model spelled same [armítas] < Spanish *armas* [see above] plus diminutive suffix *-ita* 'small shields, armor'). West: 1942. This term may refer to a short leather apron worn by cowboys to protect their legs from rubbing and chaffing (sometimes caused by the **reata**) or to a short variety of **chaps**, *also known as* **chinks**, that extended only to the knees.

arriero:

(Sp. model spelled same [ařjéro] < Spanish *arre*, an exclamation used to urge animals on and *-ero* 'profession or occupation'). *DARE*: 1824. A muleteer; an owner of packmules, or one who directs a mule train transporting cargo. Spanish sources concur. This Hispanicism frequently singled out a muleteer of Mexican origin.

arroba:

(Sp. model spelled same [ařóβa] < Arabic *ar-rub* 'the fourth part of a quintal'). *DARE*: 1824. In terms of weight or quantity, a measurement equal to about twenty-five pounds or thirty-two pints. Spanish sources concur. Often used to measure longhorn cattle, cowhide, or tallow. According to Watts, Bentley, and the *DARE*, the term was used by Hispanics and Anglos. Bentley notes that an American in a border community could have asked for "an *arroba* of flour."

arroyo:

(Sp. model spelled same [ařójo] < Latin *arrugia* 'mining trench or riverbed'). Northwestern Texas: 1806. A deep-cut channel made by a creek or rivulet. It may be filled with water or be dry. Dry arroyos are referred to as *arroyos secos* in Arizona. According to Hendrickson, the term may refer to a "brook, creek, channel, gully, dry wash, stream bed, or valley." Bentley notes that the terms *cañon* and *arroyo* may substitute for each other, in a non- technical sense. Spanish sources concur with all the meanings listed except 'valley' and 'canyon,' which are clearly extensions of the original meanings. This term, along with others such as **canyon** and **mesa**, is used frequently in literature and films depicting the cowboy in the Southwest. *Alternate forms:* aroya, arroya, royo. *Also called* a wash, often pronounced with an intrusive /r/.

atajo:

(*hatajo* [atáxo] < verb *atajar* < prefix *a-* plus verb *tajar* < Latin *taliāre* 'to cut,' meaning group that has been separated or set apart from a larger group). New Mexico: 1844. A string of packmules or pack horses. Bentley indicates "a typical *atajo* may have consisted of from fifteen to forty animals equipped with *aparejos* and cared for by drivers or *atajaderos*." Santamaría concurs. The *DRAE* and the *VCN* give "a group of livestock" as an alternate definition. These pack animals were a necessity on the long cattle drives and some borderland cowboys certainly knew the Spanish term. *Alternate forms:* atago, hatajo.

avance:

(Sp. model spelled same [aβánse]< Spanish verb *avanzar* < Latin *abantiāre* 'to advance, press forward'). Carlisle: 1850. Glossed by

Carlisle as a command form meaning 'get along,' used in cattle drives, for example. Spanish sources concur. *See also* **andale**.

awerdente, awerdenty: *See* **aguardiente.**

ayate:

(Sp. model spelled same [aǰáte]< Nahuatl *ayatl* 'thin cloth made of maguey fiber'). Glossed by Carlisle as a square or rectangular piece of plaid cloth used to carry diverse items by southwestern Indians. It was fashioned into a sling and served to transport pottery, foodstuffs, and other things. The term is referenced in the *DRAE, DM,* and *VCN.* All three Spanish sources say that the term refers to a woven fabric made of **maguey** fiber used as a sort of bag to carry fruit and other items. The *DRAE* indicates that the fabric could have been made of palm fibers, henequen, or cotton. Buckaroos who resided in Indian territory likely would have seen this artifact and known its name.

azote:

(Sp. model spelled same [asóte] < Arabic *as-sūṭ* 'whip'). Texas: 1892. According to Clark, this term may refer to "a switch, whip, a slender tree branch that may be used as a whip." The *DRAE* concurs. Borderland cowhands probably used this Hispanicism along with or in place of the English term whip.

azotea:

(Sp. model spelled same [asotéa] < Arabic *as-suṭaiha* 'small, flat roof or terrace'). Texas: 1844. A southwestern architectural feature that has its roots in the Moorish practice of using the flat roof or upper terrace as a porch or patio. The *DRAE* concurs. Bentley notes that the term is widely used in the Southwest. No doubt some cowboy studied the landscape or watched the sun go down from the *azotea* of the **casa grande** on a southwestern ranch.

baccaro, bacquero: *See* **buckaroo (1).**

baile:

(Sp. model spelled same [báįle] < Spanish verb *bailar* 'to dance' < Latin *ballāre* 'to dance'). (1) New Mexico and Arizona: 1844. A dance or ball, especially one in which the participants or the dances are Mexican. (2) New Mexico: 1880. Also referenced by Clark and the *DARE* as a dance hall. The *DRAE* concurs with both definitions. No doubt a buckaroo or two could be found at such gatherings.

bajada:

(Sp. model spelled same [baxáða] < Spanish verb *bajar* 'to go down' < Latin *bassiāre* 'to go down' plus Spanish derivational suffix *-da*). *OED*, SW: 1866. This term is referenced by Hendrickson, Hoy, Clark, Watts, the *DARE*, and the *OED*. It is generally defined as an incline sloping downward formed by the merging of several alluvial fans (composed of rock debris, such as gravel, sand, and silt). The term may also refer to a steeply descending trail. The *DRAE* also references *bajada* as a trail that leads downward. Santamaría adds that in Mexico the term also refers not only to a trail, but to any downward slope. The trail boss and drivers encountered many *bajadas* and *subidas* (trail leading up) in the uneven, rocky, and sometimes treacherous western terrain.

balling up:

Adams: 1944. Defined by Watts as the "bunching up" of cattle. This could occur at narrow passages in the terrain, at the entrance to a corral or pen, and when attempting to drive the cattle across a river or other body of water. It was often necessary to break a large herd into smaller groups to avoid this overcrowding. This term may be a calque derived from the Spanish term *bola* [bóla] 'ball' meaning a large, disorderly crowd. According to the *DM*, the term *bola* refers to "a noisy get-together of disorderly people; a fight or tumult," and the phrase *hacerse bola* means "to lose order or formation, said of a troop or a gathering."

ballo: *See* **bayo** (1).

banda:

(Sp. model spelled same [báŋda], of disputed origin; the *DRAE* indicates that it comes from Germanic *band* 'sash, band'; according to Corominas it is from Old French *bende, bande* 'sash, band, or bandage'). Carlisle: 1925. Referenced by Carlisle as "a bright-colored triangular or square shaped piece of material folded to make a strip about 3 or 4 inches wide and worn around the forehead; used extensively by the male Indians of the Southwest." Similiar to a *bandana*, a term of Hindustani-Portuguese origin, according to the OED.

bandido:

(Sp. model spelled same [baŋdíðo], past participle of *bandir*, of disputed origin; the *DRAE* claims that *bandir* comes from Gothic *bandwjan*, meaning to outlaw or banish; Corominas indicates it is from Frankish *bannjan*, which was confused with Gothic *bandwjan* 'to make a sign'). *DARE*: 1898. A bandit, bandito, or desperado. This item also foregrounds the origin of the referent; the Spanish term usually denotes a bandit of Mexican origin. The *DRAE* concurs with the principal meaning of bandit. Such figures are stock characters in the literature and film depicting the Old West.

baquero: *See* **buckaroo** (1), **vaquero**.

barboquejo:

(Sp. model spelled same [barβokéxo] probably from a derivative of the Latin *barbam* 'chin' > **barbuco*, according to Corominas and the Spanish diminutive or pejorative suffix *-ejo*). Carlisle: 1929. (1) A chin strap on a cowboy's hat. This definition is confirmed by Spanish sources. (2) According to Adams and Blevins, the term was also used to refer to "a halter that fit under the jaw of a horse." (3)

According to Smith, the term could also refer to "a bandage placed under the chin of a corpse as it awaited burial." The latter two definitions here are not confirmed by Spanish sources, but may be extensions. *Alternate form:* barbiquejo.

basto:
(Sp. model spelled same [básto] < Vulgar Latin *bastum* 'packsaddle'). Mexico and California: 1881. According to the *DARE*, "the skirt of a saddle; also, the leather lining of a saddle." The *DRAE* notes the American usage of this term and defines it as the cushions that make up the saddle pads. Santamaría mentions that the term is usually plural, *bastos*, and that it refers to two pieces of leather that rest on the frame of a saddle and protect the backside of the horse. They can be made several ways and are generally lined with coarse woolen cloth or unshorn sheepskin. Cobos defines *basto* as a "saddle skirt made of sole leather lined with undressed lambskin." *Alternate forms:* bastas, bastos. Also sometimes referred to as **sudadero**.

bayeta:
(Sp. model spelled same [baǰéta], probably from Old French *baiette*, diminutive of *bai* 'gray; brown'). *DARE*: 1852. Watts indicates that *bayeta* refers to a woolen yarn as well as fabric composed of the same produced by the Pueblo Indians. The *DRAE* describes *bayeta* as a loosely woven wool cloth or a sort of flannel used to mop floors and other surfaces. Cobos defines it as "woolen homespun." No doubt a few cowpokes were familiar with this fabric. *Alternate forms:* bayjeta, vayeta.

bayeta blankets:
Blankets made by the Navajo out of *bayeta* cloth. These were popular among settlers and traders in regions of the Southwest, according to Clark. Some cowboys probably incorporated these blankets in their **cama**s or bedrolls.

bayo:
(Sp. model spelled same [βáǰo] < Latin *badium* 'bay-colored'). (1) California: 1855. Glossed by Clark as "a small reddish or bay-colored bean, especially used in Northern California as a baking bean." The *VCN* mentions a bean of the same name that is yellowish white in color. *Alternate form:* bayo bean. (2) Southern California: 1857. A

horse of a dun or light bay color, generally with black points (such as ears, muzzle, and lower legs). The *DRAE* indicates that this term refers to a horse of a yellowish-white color. The *VCN* says the horse is of a bright yellow straw color with mane, tail, muzzle, and feet of either white, dark, black, or saffron. Cobos references *bayo* as dun-colored. *Alternate form:* ballo. (3) Clark: 1850s. According to Clark, "a bay or dun horse with a dark stripe running down its back."

bayo azafranado:

(Sp. model spelled same [báǰo̯asafranáðo]; Spanish *bayo* [see above] plus *azafranado* past participle of *azafranar* 'to color with saffron' < *azafrán* < Arabic *az-za'farān* 'saffron'; hence, 'saffron-colored bay'). A saffron-colored horse, somewhere between dun and sorrel. The *VCN* concurs.

bayo blanco:

(Sp. model spelled same [báǰoβláŋko]; Spanish *bayo* [see above] plus *blanco* < Germanic *blanc(k)* 'white or brilliant'; pale bay). A horse of a pale dun color. This color is not referenced in Spanish sources.

bayo cebruno:

(*bayo cervuno* [báǰoserβúno]; Spanish *bayo* [see above] plus *cervuno* < *ciervo* 'deer' < Latin *cervus* 'deer'; deer-colored bay). A horse of a smoky-dun color. The *DRAE* does not reference this combination, but it does mention the use of *cervuno* ('deer-colored') to describe horses. The *VCN* describes the *bayo cervuno* as a dark variety of *bayo* whose color is similar to that of a deer, generally with a dark mane, muzzle and feet.

bayo coyote:

(Sp. model spelled same [báǰokoǰóte]; Spanish *bayo* [see above] plus *coyote* < Nahuatl *coyotl* 'coyote'; coyote-colored bay). A dun horse with a black dorsal stripe. Southwestern sources list this term as a synonym of *bayo lobo*, but Santamaría indicates that the terms are not synonymous in Mexico. According to the *DM*, *bayo coyote* is used more often for mules than for horses. It is a lighter color than *bayo lobo* and a horse so designated often has white spots on its head, flank, and belly. The *bayo lobo* horse, on the other hand, has dun and black hairs that blend to produce a darker shade of dun. *Alternate form:* **bayo lobo**. *Also known as* coyote dun, lobo dun.

bayo lobo:

(Sp. model spelled same [báǰolóβo]; Spanish *bayo* [see above] plus *lobo* < Latin *lupum* 'wolf'; wolf-colored bay). *See also* **bayo coyote** above.

bayo naranjado:

(*bayo anaranjado* [báǰo̯anaraŋxáðo]; Spanish *bayo* [see above] plus *anaranjado*, Spanish prefix *a-* plus *naranja* < Arabic *nāranŷā* 'orange' plus derivational suffix -*do*; orange bay). A dun horse of an orange hue. Santamaría describes a *bayo anaranjado* as a dun-colored horse with a white mane and tail.

bayo tigre:

(Sp. model spelled same [báǰotíɣre]; Spanish *bayo* plus *tigre* < Latin *tigrem* 'tiger'; tiger bay). According to Hendrickson, "a dun horse with stripes around the legs and along the shoulders," similar to the zebra dun. Spanish sources do not make mention of this color. *Also known as* **gateado**.

bebedero:

(Sp. model spelled same [beβeðéro] < *beber* < Latin *bibere* 'to drink' plus Spanish derivational suffix -*dero*; drinking place). Hoy gives a general and a specific meaning for this term. Broadly, it refers to an artificial receptacle for watering animals. On the Sonoran Desert, it refers to "a concrete water trough, generally connected to a corral and windmill." The *DRAE* defines this term as a drinking place for birds. Santamaría indicates that in Mexico the term refers to a watering hole for all kinds of animals. The southwestern or borderlands cowhand was pleased to find a *bebedero,* whether manmade or natural, for his thirsty *dogies.*

beefalo:

(Combination of English *beef* and *buffalo* < Spanish *búfalo* [búfalo] < Late Latin *bufalus* < Classical Latin *būbulus* 'cattle; beef'). Kansas: 1889. The offspring of a male buffalo and a domesticated cow. Blevins, citing Webster, says that the animal is "five-eighths beef and three-eighths bison." Ranchers have tried to breed cattle and buffalo to produce an animal that yields more meat, but consumers have balked at the combination. *See also* **cattalo.**

bellota:

(Sp. model spelled same [bejóta] < Arabic *ballūṭa* 'oak; acorn'). An oak found in the Southwest (*Quercus arizonica*). Can also refer to a type of bread made from ground acorns, reportedly eaten by some of the indigenous peoples. None of the Spanish sources consulted referenced this term as the name of a tree, although the term in General Spanish means acorn. It is possible that cowboys and ranchers were familiar with this term, particularly if they resided in Indian territory.

blanco:

(Sp. model spelled same [bláŋko] < Germanic *blanc(k)* 'white or brilliant'). Glossed by Hendrickson as a term used by Indians to refer to white men. The *DRAE* confirms the use of *blanco* to refer to European or Caucasian people. Many buckaroos were blancos, but there was a significant number of blacks, mestizos, and Indians who rode the range.

bosal:

(*bozal* [bosál]< *bozo* < Latin *bucceus* 'from the mouth,' and *-al* 'pertaining to'). New Mexico: 1844. A rope; a leather, or rawhide halter; or a metal ring that fits around the nose of a horse and is used as part of a **hackamore** in place of a bit. It can also refer to the rope used for such a halter. A *bosal* is often used when breaking a horse or riding an unruly horse. The *DRAE* gives several definitions for *bozal*, but notes that in the Americas it refers to a rope that, when tied to the neck of an animal, functions as a halter. In Spain, the more common term is *bozo*. Santamaría expands on the definition found in the *DRAE* and indicates that a *bozal* is made by loosely looping a rope around an animal's neck and securing it with a knot, then tying the rest of the rope around the horse's nose, using the end as a single rein. *Alternate forms:* bonsal, bosaal, bozal.

bosal brand:

Adams: 1961. According to Adams, a brand in the form of "a stripe burned around an animal's nose." No Spanish source refers to *bosal* with this meaning.

bota:

(Sp. model spelled same [bóta] < French *botte* 'boot'). New Mexico: 1834. A leather riding boot or dress boot, especially one that is "intricately decorated with carved leather, often with silver ornaments" or **conchas**, according to Clark. The *DRAE* references this term as a leather boot, but not as one that is exceptionally ornamental. The southwestern usage probably derives from the dress boot used by Mexican **vaqueros** and **charros**.

brasada:

(*brazada* [brasáða], apparently a combination of *brazo* 'arm' < Latin *brachium* 'arm' and -*ada*, a Spanish derivational suffix; in this case, it may mean accumulation of arms or tree branches, or it may refer to a measure of the amount of firewood or brush that can be carried in both arms). Texas: 1929. A region characterized by dense undergrowth, known as brush country. West Texas features such vegetation; the cattle that graze in such areas are remarkably well-adapted to the rugged terrain. Southwestern sources give a variety of possible etymologies for this word, since no Spanish dictionary contains a similar definition. The *VCN* and *VS* reference *brazada* as a unit of measurement roughly equivalent to that which can be carried in one's open arms. The *DRAE* includes both *brazada* and *brazado* as a measurement for the amount of firewood, sticks, grass, or straw that can be carried in a person's open arms. Blevins's theory that it derives from Spanish *bruzada* 'brush' (for scrubbing and cleaning), is doubtful. It is more likely, as Bentley and Adams suggest, that the term somehow derives from the Spanish *brazo*, meaning arm or tree branch. *Alternate form:* brazada.

brasada measure:

A measurement; according to Watts, "the stretch of a man's arm along a *reata* held taut in both hands." The Spanish measurement was the distance between the two thumbs when the arms were held in a horizontal position out from the body.

brasaderos:

(*brazadero* [brasaðéro] < *brazada* [*see* above] and Spanish suffix -*ero*, indicating profession or office). Carlisle: 1929. Cowboys who work in the brush country. Also refers to cattle in that region.

brasero:

(Sp. model spelled same [braséro] < *brasa* 'red hot coal' of Latin or pre-Roman origin, and -*ero*, a Spanish nominal suffix; hence, a place to put hot coal or firewood). Southern Texas: 1892. A type of brick oven used by Pueblo Indians and Mexicans, according to Watts. Also a container for holding hot charcoal, used for cooking or for heating. Carlisle comments that the term sometimes refers to a pile of hot coals. These definitions vary somewhat from those found in Spanish sources. The *DRAE* indicates that a *brasero* is a deep, circular metal dish with a rim in which one builds a fire for heating. It generally rests on a stand made of wood or metal. Santamaría notes that in Mexico it is a cooking range or stove. He also mentions a portable *brasero* and a smaller dish, or *braserito*, which was made of porcelain, clay, or silver and was an essential household item for smokers before the invention of the match. *Alternate form:* brassero.

brasil:

(Sp. model spelled same [brasíl], probably from *brasa* [see above], because of the plant's red color). Western Texas: 1891. Clark glosses this term as "a common *chaparral* plant" that grows in western Texas. It is used for limited grazing. He gives the genus and species as *Condalia obovata*. According to the *DARE*, "bluewood," "logwood," "capulin," and "purple haw" are other names for this plant. Santamaría references the diminutive *brasilillo*, for several varieties of rhamnaceous plants common to northwestern Mexico. It is unlikely that the *brasil* plant described in the *DRAE* is related to the southwestern *brasil*; according to that source, it can be either a papilionaceous tree that grows in tropical regions or a red pigment used as a cosmetic by women. *Alternate form:* brazil.

bravo:

(Sp. model spelled same [bráβo] < Latin *prāvus* 'evil, uncouth'). (1) Bentley: 1836. Brave; wild or fierce, referring to animals or people. (2) A shortened form of the Río Bravo (del Norte); the Mexican name for the Rio Grande. (3) According to Bentley, a shout of encouragement at "some public performance or competition." It may also mean excellent or well done, notes the *DRAE*. (4) Bentley: 1929. Also "a bandit or villain." The *DRAE* indicates that this term may mean brave or ferocious. Perhaps that definition arises from the fierce, tempermental character attributed to many outlaws. The *DM* further notes that *bravo* may mean wild, angry, irascible, or irritable and can be applied to animals as well as humans. Some cowpunchers, ranchers, and not a few of the animals they rode or herded were considered bravo—no doubt a number of cowboys understood and employed this term.

bravura:

(Sp. model spelled same [braβúra] < *bravo* [see above] and the nominalizing suffix *-ura*). Carlisle: 1922. Ferocity or courage. Also refers to a show of manliness or bravado. The *DRAE* concurs.

bronco:

(Sp. model spelled same [bróŋko], of uncertain origin; may be from Latin *broncus*, via *broccus* 'having long, uneven teeth' as the *DRAE* concludes; or from an early Spanish term meaning originally 'piece of a cut branch' or 'knot in wood' < Vulgar Latin **bruncus*, a cross between *broccus* 'pointed object' and *truncus* 'trunk' as Corominas hypothesizes). Clark: 1850s. Hendrickson, Clark, and Blevins all reference this term. (1) Originally applied to a wild or unbroken horse. It could be used as an alternate term for *mustang*. It was later applied more loosely to any unmanageable or vicious horse. More recently, the term refers to any horse used by a cowboy. (2) The term could also be an adjective describing an unruly horse or a wild, rebellious person. The *DRAE* references the adjective *bronco*, meaning crude, rough, or unrefined, and also mentions a noun form used in Mexico meaning an untamed horse. Santamaría concurs, describing a bronco as a horse that has not yet been broken and therefore fights the reins and rider. *Alternate forms:* bronc, bronch, broncho. Cowboys came to prefer the anglicized form *bronc*.

bronca:

Arizona: 1931. Referenced by Carlisle as the feminine form of *bronco*. She does not indicate whether it referred to horses or women. Spanish sources define it as a fight, uproar, or dispute.

bronc belt:

Adams includes this term, meaning "a broad leather belt sometimes worn by bronc fighters to support their back and stomach muscles."

Bronc & Bronc Buster

Bronco & Amansador

bronc fighter:

May be used as a synonym for *bronco buster*, but Blevins cites Adams as saying that it might also refer to a rider who spoils a horse instead of breaking it. *See also* **bronco buster** below.

bronc fits:

DARE: 1963. Refers to outbreaks of a horse when the animal becomes unmanageable and kicks and bucks uncontrollably.

bronco buster:

West: 1888. A cowboy who breaks wild horses. According to Adams, he is no ordinary run-of-the-mill horsebreaker, but a highly skilled rider who takes great pride and satisfaction in doing his job well. *Also known as:* bronc breaker, bronc buster, bronc fighter, bronc peeler, bronc rider, bronc scratcher, bronc snapper, bronc squeezer, bronc stomper, bronc twister, bullbat, buster, contract buster, flesh rider, gentler, hazer, horsebreaker, **jinete**, **(a)mansador**, peeler, rough-string rider.

bronco busting:

Southwest: 1891. According to Hendrickson, "breaking wild horses for the saddle."

bronco grass:

California: 1967–68. Hendrickson references this term, noting that it is a bromegrass of the Southwest (*Bromus secalinus*). *Also known as* devil's darning needle (because it has inch-long needles that catch on clothing). Probably not preferred forage for cattle.

bronc saddle:

According to Blevins, "a saddle designed for breaking horses." It has a wide, undercut fork, a deep-dished cantle, and bulges in the back. *Also known as* a bronc tree.

bronc spur:

Defined by Blevins as "a spur whose shank turns in toward the horse, to make scratching the bronc easier."

bronc stall:

Blevins notes that this term refers to a horse stall that is built just large enough so that a horse can stand in it but so narrow that the horse cannot kick or bite (similar to a rodeo chute). Adams indicates that such stalls are common on ranches where horses are broken for the harness, but cowboys prefer to break their horses in a wide-open corral.

bronc stomper:
As Adams observes, either a synonym for *bronco* buster or a man who is skilled in riding and able to ride a vicious horse. *See also* **bronco buster** above.

last year's bronc:
According to Adams, "a horse in his second season of work."

oily bronc:
Adams says this refers simply to "a bad horse." It may refer to the fact that such a horse is hard to stay mounted on, hence "oily" or "slippery."

raw bronc:
Glossed by Watts as "an inexperienced or unbroken horse."

start a bronc:
To begin to break a horse, to ride it for the first time.

brujo:
(Sp. model spelled same [brúxo], of uncertain origin, probably pre-Roman). Southwest: 1940. All of the English language sources reference this term. In their dealings with indigenous peoples, cowboys most likely ran across this Spanish term for wizard, medicine man, shaman, or one who practices black magic (as well as the derivatives below). The *DRAE* concurs.

bruja:
(Sp. model spelled same [brúxa], of uncertain origin). New Mexico: 1912. A witch, hag, or an owl. The *DRAE* concurs. Mexican folklore claims that a *bruja* may assume the form of an owl.

brujería:
(Sp. model spelled same [bruxería] < *brujo*, of uncertain origin, and Spanish suffix *-ería* that denotes collectivity or plurality). Carlisle: 1931. According to Carlisle, "witchcraft or sorcery." The *DRAE* concurs.

buchario: *See* **buckaroo (1).**

buckaroo:

(*vaquero* [bakéro] < Spanish *vaca* 'cow' < Latin *vaccam* 'cow'and Spanish suffix *-ero* 'profession or office.' Mason's speculation that a Nigerian form *mbakara* > *bakara* 'white man' is the model can easily be dismissed on linguistic grounds. See Cassidy and Hill for further details). (1) Texas: 1827. A working cowboy; later it came to mean any ranch hand. Watts suggests that the term was popularized in pulp literature because it conjures an image of a man on a bucking horse; indeed, A. A. Hill posits a blend with the term *buck(ing)* as the source for the first syllable. Watts also notes that the most widely known form, *buckaroo*, was used in the Northwest. In the Southwest *buckaree* was common. Blevins indicates that the term *buckaroo* was commonly used in "the desert basins of Northern Nevada, Northern California, Eastern Oregon, and Western Idaho." Hendrickson indicates that this word has become so integrated into the English language that it has been the model for over fifty American slang words. Among those referenced by Hendrickson are *stinkaroo* (a bad play or movie), *the old switcheroo* (the act of substituting one thing for another with the intention to deceive, 'bait-and-switch tactics'), *antsaroo* (refers to someone who is impatient or has 'ants in his pants'), *jugaroo* (jail), and *ziparoo* (energy). The original Spanish term is **vaquero**, a common name for a man who cares for cattle. *Alternate forms:* (some early forms were stressed on the second syllable) baccaro, bacquero, baquero, bucaroo, buccaro, buccaroo, buchario, buckara, buckaree, buckayro, buckeroo, buckhara, bukkarer, jackeroo. (2) Nevada: 1967. It may also be a verb meaning to work as a cowboy.

buckarooing:

According to Hendrickson, "working as a cowboy."

buckaroo saddle:

A kind of double-rigged saddle preferred by buckaroos. According to Blevins, it has narrow forks, bucking rolls, and a high cantle.

buckhara: *See* **buckaroo (1).**

buen pais:

(*buen país* [bwén] < *bueno* [see below] and [*país*] < French *pays*; good country). Carlisle: 1928. Carlisle refers to it as "a pretty good

country." Not referenced in Spanish sources. This term may have
been used contrastively with *mal pais* 'rough, treacherous region' to
describe terrain on long trail drives. *See* mal pais.

bueno:

(Sp. model spelled same [bwéno] < Latin *bonum* 'good'). Blevins
observes that it was used as a cattle term in the Southwest during the
open-range days. It referred to a cow that had not been claimed at a
roundup and whose brand could not be found in the brand book. Such
a cow was a good find because it could be slipped past brand inspec-
tors. This meaning is not referenced in Spanish sources.

buffalo:

(*búfalo* (búfalo] < Late Latin *bufalus* < Latin *būbulus* 'cattle;
beef'). West: 1848. The North American bison (*Bison americanus*).
According to Watts, Nuñez Cabeza de Vaca was the first to apply
erroneously the Spanish term *búfalo* to the American bison because it
was similar in appearance to the Indian or African wild ox or buffalo.
The buffalo played an important role in the exploration and settlement of the Old West. According to Josiah Gregg (*Commerce of the
Prairies*), it was a primary source of meat for early expeditions. It
was also widely hunted by Indians for its meat and hide. As a result
of the animal's importance in the Southwest, the term, originally
applied by the Spaniards, became highly integrated into English. This
is evidenced by its use as a verb (first referenced in English in central
Texas in 1896), meaning to frighten or confuse (or, by extension, to
strike on the head with the barrel of a gun), as well as by its use in
more than thirty compounds that refer to Southwestern plant life (buffalo berry, buffalo clover, buffalo pea) and animal life (buffalo fish,
buffalo wolf). Some compounds containing *buffalo* also pertain to the
history of the Southwest: "buffalo cider" or "buffalo gall" was a liquid found in the buffalo's stomach that could save a thirsty explorer,
"buffalo fever" was the excitement felt at the onset of a "buffalo
hunt," and "buffalo wood," "buffalo fuel" or "buffalo chips" referred
to dried buffalo manure, used to start fires. Santamaría and the *DRAE*
both point out the erroneous use of *búfalo* in North America to refer
to the American bison. *Alternate forms:* buff, buffler, bufler.

buffalo grass: *See* **grama grass** (1).

bukkarer: *See* **buckaroo** (1).

bunko:

(*banca* [báŋka] < Italian *banca* via French *banque* 'bank or bank-
ing'). (1) Chicago: 1921. According to Blevins, "a gambling game
played with dice or cards." He points out that this is not the same
game as the Spanish *banca*, but it may be related. (2) Hendrickson
glosses the term as "a swindler or cheat." Probably originally came
from the Spanish game *banca*. Blevins indicates that "the verb form
'to bunko someone' and the compounds that have come from bunko
(such as *bunko artist*, *bunko game*, and *bunko joint*) are not Westernisms." The *DRAE* describes the card game *banca* as a game in which
the dealer lays down a certain amount of money and the rest of the
players choose cards and make bets. Card games like this one were
popular diversions for the cowboy in saloons and cantinas throughout
the West. *Alternate form:* bunco.

burro:

(Sp. model spelled same [búřo] < *borrico* < Late Latin *burrīcum*
'little horse'). (1) New Mexico: 1844. A donkey. Sometimes referred
to a mule. According to Blevins, "also known as 'Arizona nightingale,' Colorado mockingbird,' 'desert canary,' 'mountain canary,'
'Rocky Mountain canary,' 'Washoe canary,' 'western nightingale'."
The *DRAE* references *burro* as an ass or solipede animal. (2) Among
cattlemen, the word also refers to a stand made for storing a saddle
when it is not in use. The *VCN* concurs. The stand has the appearance
of a pitched roof of a house, and Adams says that it is much better to
rest a saddle on a burro than to hang it or lay it on the ground. The
DRAE indicates that a *burro* is a type of adjustable sawhorse.

burro grass:

DARE: 1931. According to Hendrickson, a perennial range
grass found in the Southwest (*Scleropogon brevifolius*). It may
have been so named because it is so tough only burros will eat it.
Also known as needlegrass.

burro load:

DARE: 1944. A common unit of measurement in the Southwest. A
New Mexican informant for the *DARE* says that a *burro load* of wood
is "three ricks, two on [the] sides, one on the top [of the burro]."

burro milk:

Festive, expressive creation used by cowpokes and others meaning 'malarkey.'

burro trail:
Glossed by Bentley as "a pathway made by the repeated tramping of burro trains over certain routes, especially in the mountains."

burro train:
A drove of between six and fifty pack-burros for hauling goods through rugged terrain not generally accessible by rail or other modes of transportation.

pack-burro:
Bentley: 1909. A donkey for carrying goods and supplies.

buscadero:
(Sp. model spelled same [buskaδéro] < *buscar* 'to seek' (of uncertain origin) and the Spanish suffix *-dero*; loosely, 'seeker, searcher'). According to Adams and Blevins, this term originally referred to a lawman with a gun, and later to any gunman. It may have originally referred to a 'bounty hunter,' although this cannot be confirmed and the modern Spanish equivalent is *cazarrecompensas*. Spanish sources do not reference this term, although they do reference the root and suffix separately. The closest Spanish word is *buscador*, which means 'searcher' or 'seeker,' but does not denote a lawman or gunman.

buscadero belt:
A broad belt, four to six inches wide, with a slotted flap for a gun on each hip.

buscadero holster:
A holster inserted into a cartridge belt for carrying a gun. Used chiefly in Hollywood.

button:
(Possible calque of *botón* [botón] < Old Gascon and Old French *boton*, derived from *boter* 'to sprout, to bud'; Corominas indicates that the original term may have been Germanic). Glossed by Blevins as "a braided knot of leather or rawhide on tack." The *VCN* references a similar meaning for the Spanish *botón*, a woven ornament, or one of yarn, leather, or horsehair that adorns the halters, reins, quirt, and other gear used by the **charro**. *See also* **concha(s)**.

cabablada, caballáda, caballad, caballada, caballado, caballard: *See* **cavvy** (1).

caballero:

(Sp. model spelled same [kaβaǰéro] < Latin *caballum* 'nag, pack-horse' and the Spanish suffix *-ero* 'profession or occupation; 'horse-man'). (1) *DARE*, New Mexico: 1824; California: 1837. A horseman; a knight; a gentleman. The *DRAE* concurs. (2) Clark: 1950s. According to Clark, "a cowboy, especially one of Mexican descent or one who dresses himself and his horse in finery." (3) Bentley notes that the phrase *muy caballero* is sometimes used as an adjective to describe a person or action that is very gentlemanly or cavalier.

caballo:

(Sp. model spelled same [kaβáǰo]] < Latin *caballum* [see above]). Texas: 1843. General Spanish term for 'horse.' Clark indicates that this term was in common use "in Southwest Texas, Southern Arizona, and Southern California." Adams and Blevins note that it is often used "lightly or mockingly." This is due to a popular belief that things of Mexican or Spanish origin are substandard. *Alternate forms:* cavallo, cavoya.

cabarista, caberes, caberos: *See* **cabestro** (1).

cabase: *See* **cabeza.**

cabestro:

(Sp. model spelled same [kaβéstro] < Latin *capistrum* 'halter'). (1) *DARE*: 1805. Originally a halter or tether made of a hair rope. Watts notes that its original meaning was broadened to refer to any hair

34

rope, or even to a **reata**, which is generally a rope made of rawhide. This last application is not widespread, however, and can be confusing, since *cabestro* is often used to distinguish a rope made of hair from one made of rawhide or leather. The *DRAE* defines *cabestro* as a halter that is tied to the head or neck of a horse to lead or secure it. Islas's definition differs from the *DRAE*'s in that the horsehair *cabestro* need not be attached to a halter. According to Islas, it is the term most commonly used in Mexico to refer to a twisted horsehair rope used to restrain, lead, or train a horse. Its length is variable—it may be some sixteen feet long and serve as a halter, or about twenty feet long and function as a double-rein, or from twenty-six to thirty-three feet long and serve as a "false rein" (or halter and headstall used when breaking a horse). The thickness of the *cabestro* or *cabresto* also varies, depending on the function of the rope. Santamaría concurs with Islas, noting that *cabresto* is so common in Mexico that *cabestro* sounds strange to the ear. He cites Salvá as saying that *cabresto* is an antiquated form that appears in writing in the sixteenth century. (Linguistically, the fact that the /r/ appears to move from one syllable to the next and forms a consonant cluster with /b/ or /t/ is known as metathesis. Such variation is common in popularly transmitted forms and is evidenced in the history of both Spanish and English.) Cobos indicates that in New Mexico and southern Colorado *cabresto* can refer to a rope in general. *Alternate forms:* cabarista, cabaros, caberes, caberos, caboras, caboris, cabras, cabrass, cabressa, cabresse, cabresta, cabresto, cabris, cavraces. (2) According to Smith, *cabestro* can also refer to "one who might be led around by the nose." Spanish sources do not reference this term as a noun that can be applied to a person. However, the *DRAE* references *cabestrear* and Santamaría references *cabrestear* as verbs meaning to lead an animal around with a *cabestro* or *cabresto*. Santamaría indicates that the verb form can be used figuratively to lead a person "by the nose" or to coerce him or her to do something against his or her will. According to the *DRAE*, *llevar/traer del cabestro a alguien* has the same figurative meaning in Spain.

cabeza:
(Sp. model spelled same [kaβésa] < Hispanic Vulgar Latin **capitia* 'head'). Northern California: 1868. This General Spanish term for

'head' is often used jocularly by cowboys and others. See below for an example. *Alternate forms:* cabase, kerbase.

cabeza del fuste:

(Sp. model spelled same [kaβésaδelfúste] *cabeza* [see above] plus *del* 'of the' plus *fuste* < Latin *fūstem* 'stick, staff, club'). Watts glosses this term as the head part of a saddletree. Santamaría and Islas concur. Both reference *fuste* as the main part of the saddle to which other pieces are attached. It may also be called the frame of the saddle. The *cabeza del fuste* is the front piece or 'head' attached to the *fuste.* In English, *cabeza del fuste* may be shortened to "fuste" or "fusty," although these may also refer to the saddletree. *See also* **fuste.**

off one's cabeza:
Off one's head, or crazy.

caboras, cabras, cabressa, cabresse, cabresto, cabris: *See* **cabestro** (1).

cabron:

(cabrón [kaβrón] < Spanish *cabro* 'male goat' < Latin *caprum* 'male goat' plus the augmentative suffix *-ón*; literally, large (male) goat). Carlisle: 1930. A serious insult derived from Hispanic culture. It can refer to a cuckold or to an outlaw with no morals or principles. Spanish sources note that its principal meaning is 'male goat.' However, it has long been an insult as well. Originally, it referred to a man who allowed his wife to commit adultery. The *DRAE* notes that it can also refer to any coward who puts up with being the object of impertinence or mockery. In Mexico the insult has a broader meaning, and Santamaría indicates that it can mean ruffian, villain, rogue, rascal, loafer, wretch, or indecent person. No doubt a number of cowboys and cattlemen learned this term from the Mexicans they employed since it is an extremely common swearword among the lower classes in Mexico.

cachimilla:

(*cachanilla* [katʃaníʝa] < New Mexican Spanish *cachana* < Mexican Spanish *cachane* (*Senecio cardiophillus*, according to the *DM*)). *DARE*: 1911. A shrub (*Pluchea sericea*) with straight, tough stalks. The stalks were used by Indians to make shafts for their arrows. According to the

DARE, this plant ranges from western Texas to California and northern Mexico. The term *cachanilla* is referenced by Cobos as a plant with curative properties. He says the term derives from *cachana*, which he defines similarly. Its root is said to counteract the ill effects of curses, hexes and other forms of witchcraft. In English, it is *also known as* arrow weed, arrow wood. *Alternate forms:* cachanilla, cachinilla.

cacique:
(Sp. model spelled same [kasíke]; from the Taino word for 'chief or petty king'). A term used in the Southwest to apply to an Indian village chieftain or a local political boss. This term is used outside of the Southwest and originated in the West Indies, where it referred to a native chief or prince. The *DRAE* notes that the principal meaning of this term is a lord or chief in an Indian community. By extension, it may also be used in Spanish to refer to an influential political boss or to any person who abuses his authority over others. Cobos references it as a "Pueblo Indian chief and ceremonial leader." Santamaría indicates that in Mexico it is used contemptuously to mean a despot or no-account tyrant. *Alternate forms:* casick, casique.

cahon:
(*cajón* [kaxón] < *caja* 'box' < Latin *capsa* via Catalan *caixa* or Occitan *caissa* plus augmentative suffix *-ón*; literally, large box, trunk). (1) According to Clark, "a box canyon or a narrow basin of land nearly surrounded by steep sides." It is likely that the English equivalent is a calque from this Spanish term. The *DRAE* indicates that, especially in Chile, *cajón* may refer to a long canyon with an arroyo or river at its base. No Spanish source consulted provides a meaning for this term exactly like the one used in the Southwest, but Santamaría cites Beaumont, who uses *cajón* as a synonym for *cañón*. (2) Clark: 1860s. "A boxlike or squarish building constructed of adobe." Clark also notes that this term is frequently used in place names in the Southwest. Spanish sources do not reference this meaning.

calaboose:
(*calabozo* [kalaβóso] < Vulgar Latin *calafodium* < pre-Roman *cala* 'cave, protected place' and Vulgar Latin *fodere* 'to dig'; some variant forms may have been influenced by French *calabouse*). (1) Nevada: 1866. Town jail; its use today connotes a humorous or playful reference. The *DRAE* confirms that *calabozo* is used in Spanish to

refer to a jail or dungeon. Cobos attests to its use in Southwestern Spanish. *Alternate forms:* calabooza, calaboso, calaboz, calaboza, calabozo, calabózo, cattle boose. *See also* **carcel**. (2) Watts references a verb form to "calaboose," meaning 'to incarcerate.'

calf yard: *See* **cavvy** (1).

California:
(Sp. model spelled same [kalifórnja]; originally the name of an island in a Spanish romantic poem *Las Sergas de Esplandián*, written by Garci Ordóñez de Montalvo; the name is possibly a blend of the word *caliph* and the names of Spanish cities such as Calahorra. When Spanish explorers discovered Baja California, they assumed it was an island and called it California. The territory that is now the state of California was known as Alta California under Spanish and Mexican rule). (1) The thirty-first state in the Union. It became part of the United States in 1850. (2) Northwestern Texas: 1933. The *DARE* references *california* as a verb meaning to throw an animal by catching it with a rope around its neck and flank and tripping it with one's foot. A method used especially for large and unmanageable calves. Not referenced in Spanish sources. (3) An attributive adjective used in many combinations to denote animals (such as the California condor, California jay, California lion, California quail, California yellowtail, etc.), plants (California beeplant, California laurel, California lilac, California nutmeg, California sidesaddle flower), and items particular to California's history. The terms that are pertinent to the cowboy's era or trade are listed below.

California banknote:
California: 1840. A cowhide used as currency before and during the gold rush days. According to Hendrickson, it may also have referred to "silver used as a medium of exchange."

California bible:
According to Hendrickson, a pack of playing cards. *Also known as* California prayer book.

California bridle:
Watts notes that this term referred to one that was often made of horsehair and elaborately decorated.

California collar:

Wyoming: 1842 (probably earlier in oral form). Glossed by Hendrickson as "a joking term given to the hangman's noose when vigilante justice ruled in early California."

California drag rowel:

A spur with a rowel that dragged along the ground when its wearer was not on horseback. Spanish caballeros and vaqueros preferred the larger spurs and rowels.

California fever:

Hendrickson: 1844. The fervent wish to be in or travel to California.

California Jack:

Carlisle: 1903. A card game.

California moccasins:

Watts: 1934. Flour sacks worn on the feet and tied at the ankles in place of shoes or socks. Watts indicates that they provided some defense against exposure to extreme cold. *Also known as* California socks.

California pants:

DARE: 1927 (Clark says the term has been in oral use since the 1870s). Clark indicates that these were heavy woolen pants with a double weave worn when riding horses for long periods of time. They were generally brown or tan and usually of a striped, checked, or plaid design, and may have been reinforced with buck or antelope skin.

California reins:

DARE: 1961. According to the *DARE*, reins tied together at the ends or made of a single piece of leather.

California rig:

Referenced by Watts as "a saddle with a single cinch-ring in a central position directly below and on either side of the saddle tree." Also referred to as a "center-fire rig."

California sight:

Clark: 1880s. A near sight on a rifle with a series of notches for shooting at various distances.

California skirts:
DARE: 1968. Round skirts on a stock saddle. Said by Adams to be the preferred style in the state of California.

California sorrel:
DARE: 1968. Watts indicates that this term refers to a palomino horse of a red-gold color; an older term for any palomino.

California toothpick:
Clark: 1850s. A bowie knife or a similar large knife.

California trail:
According to Blevins, a trail that branched off the Oregon Trail and led to California. Especially used by the Forty-niners.

California twist:
DARE: 1961. A roping technique during which the cowboy did not twirl his rope but cast it with a single overhand twist.

Californio:
(Sp. model spelled same [kalifórnjo] < *California*). A resident of California. According to Blevins, this term originally referred the Spanish or Mexican colonizers of Alta and Baja California in the 1800s. The *DRAE* concurs.

calzone:
(*calzón* [kalsón]< *calza* 'stocking' < Vulgar Latin **calceam* 'trousers'). Carlisle: 1912. Carlisle indicates that the Spanish model is *calzones*, referring to a particular style of pants. According to her, it means pants or trousers in the Southwest. A popular Mexican song "Allá en el rancho grande," recorded by Gene Autry as well as other country and western singers, includes the lines: *Te voy a hacer los calzones como los usa el ranchero. Te los comienzo de lana y los acabo de cuero.* (I'm going to make your *calzones* like the ones the *ranchero* wears. I'll start them off in wool and I'll finish them in leather.) *Alternate form:* calzon. *See also* **calzoneras** below.

calzoneras:
(Sp. model spelled same [kalsonéras]< *calzón* 'pants' [see above] plus the Spanish derivative suffix *-era*). Southwest: 1844. Blevins correctly observes that this term refers to Mexican or Spanish-style

pants that are split along the outside seam, usually to reveal cotton or linen underwear. The edges of the split may be decorated with buttons, braids, or silver **conchas**. This term is referenced in the *DRAE* and the *DM*. Santamaría indicates that it refers to pants made of cloth or soft leather, left open from top to bottom on both sides. They had buttons and buttonholes so that the wearer could partially or completely close the splits. They were more common in earlier periods, especially for riding horseback.

cama:

(Sp. model spelled same [káma] < Hispanic Latin *cama* 'bed or couch on the ground,' probably of pre-Roman origin). Nevada: 1940. This General Spanish term for bed sometimes refers to a buckaroo's bedroll. The Spanish term may connote a jocular or pejorative meaning, since a bed on the hard ground next to the campfire is not likely to be very comfortable or fancy. Spanish sources do not reference this particular meaning for the term.

camisa:

(Sp. model spelled same [kamísa] < Late Latin *camisia* (possibly influenced by Anglo-Saxon and Celtic) < Germanic *hemidi* 'shirt'). New Mexico: 1831. According to Blevins, "a shirt or chemise," especially one that is loose and blousy. It is often referred to as a type of blouse worn by Indian women and Latinas, similar to a "peasant dress." The *DRAE* indicates that in Spanish the term refers to any shirt with a collar, sleeves, and buttons, and not specifically to one that is loose and blousy or worn by women.

campomoche:

(*campamocha* [kampamótʃa]; of uncertain origin, probably from Nahuatl *campa-mo-chan* 'where your house is' via Spanish). California: 1919. Bentley references this term as an insect known as a 'praying mantis' (*Mantis religiosa*), so called because its folded wings resemble a clerical garment and its front two legs resemble hands clasped in prayer. The insect is *also known as* the "praying insect," "devil's horse." The term *campomoche* is also applied to a smaller green or gray-colored insect with a sticklike body, sometimes called a "walking-stick." The walking-stick is difficult to distinguish from the plants that it inhabits, and it is said to be fatal to cattle when they ingest it along with grass. Islas confirms that the insect is poisonous and kills numerous cattle in Chihuahua, Mexico, when they accidentally eat it. Santamaría references *campamocha* as an orthopterous insect of the mantis family that deposits its eggs in a multicolored capsule that is also called a *campamocha*. He provides the genus and species *Stagmomantis limbata*. Cobos indicates that the *campamocha* is the common praying mantis. Islas and Cabrera describe a different insect that blends in with foliage because of its sticklike appearance.

canelo:

(Sp. model spelled same [kanélo] < *canela* 'cinnamon' < Old French *canele* < Italian *cannella*, diminutive of *canna* 'cane,' because of the canelike shape of dried cinnamon bark). A red-roan or cinammon-colored horse. Watts notes that this term generally "applies to a horse of California or Spanish stock." Smith indicates that this term can also refer to a brown or cinammon-colored cow. The *DRAE*, *DM*, and *VCN* all reference this term as a color for horses. Islas specifies that the color is a mixture of sorrel and white and that horses of this color have muzzle, mane, tail, and points of a reddish-brown color. Santamaría also says that the color is similar to sorrel mixed with white, but that the horse's muzzle, mane, tail, and points are black.

cantina:

(Sp. model spelled same [kaŋtína] < Italian *cantina* 'wine cellar, wine shop'). (1) Watts: 1875. In the Southwest, especially Texas, a saloon or tavern; a Mexican wineshop. (2) According to Watts, "a pocket of a **mochila**." Blevins notes that the Pony Express used **mochilas** with pockets, or *cantinas*, to carry mail. (3) Southwest: 1844. A saddlebag or other container hung from the saddle. Blevins references *cantina* as "a leather box packed by a mule." *Alternate form:* cantiness. (4) Watts: 1942. A receptacle used to heat liquids; a coffeepot. This definition is similar to the English canteen, a tin or wooden container used to hold water or liquor used by travelers, soldiers, or workmen. It is unknown whether this meaning derives from Spanish or whether the Spanish term has been extended to be synonymous with canteen. The *DRAE* gives several definitions for *cantina*, among them a shop where liquor and other provisions are sold; a box made of wood, metal, or cork and covered with leather and divided into various compartments for carrying food; and (especially

in Mexico) two squarish leather bags with lids that are hung from
either side of a saddletree, similar to the more antiquated **alforjas**.
They are used for carrying foodstuffs. Islas and Santamaría concur
with the definitions in the *DRAE*, with a few exceptions. Islas indicates that the bags may be round or square, they hang from the cantle
rather than the saddletree, and they are used to carry all sorts of provisions for the rider, not just food. He also mentions that the term is
generally used in the plural. Santamaría notes that the *cantinas* have
replaced the older *alforjas*, *árganas* (wicker baskets used as packsaddles), and *cojinillos* (another name for saddlebags, these were generally bags or small wicker baskets). Cobos states that in New Mexico
and Colorado a cantina can be either a bar or tavern or a large wallet
or leather box. None of the Spanish sources consulted concurred with
senses (2) and (4). Perhaps (2) is an extension of (3), and (4) did not
come from Spanish but was later used as an alternate term for the
English *canteen*.

canyon:

(cañón [kaɲón], origin uncertain; either a figurative application of
the augmentative form of *caño* 'pipe, conduit' < *caña* 'cane' < Latin
cannam 'reed,' or since *callón* is an older form, it may derive from
calle 'street' < Latin *callem* 'narrow path'). Bentley: 1805. According
to Blevins, a steep-sided valley, gorge, or ravine formed by a stream
or river that has cut through the landscape. Water may or may not be
flowing through it. The *DRAE*, *DM*, and *VCN* provide concurring
definitions. In Spanish, a *cañón* is a narrow pass or valley between
two mountains, generally with a river running through it. *Alternate
forms:* cañon, kanyon, kenyon. (2) According to Blevins, canyon can
be used as a verb, meaning to lead into a canyon (as a stream). The
verb form is not referenced in Spanish sources. *Alternate forms:* canyon
out, canyon up.

box canyon: *See* **cahon.**

canyon country:

Glossed by Blevins as "the country of Southern Utah and
Northern Arizona, with adjacent portions of Colorado and New
Mexico," so named because a significant portion of the landscape
was fashioned by the Colorado River.

canyoned:
Confined or trapped in a canyon.

cañada:
(Sp. model spelled same [kaɲáða] < Latin *cannam* 'cane' and the Spanish derivational suffix *-ada* 'abundance or content.' Corominas indicates that *cañada*, meaning receptacle or measurement for water, comes from *canna*, in the sense of 'a tube through which liquid flows out of the receptacle or instrument for measurement'). Bentley: 1836. A valley or dale between mountains. Bentley says that this term is synonymous with **arroyo** and **canyon** in the Southwest. Hoy notes that it may also refer to a drainage or tributary forged by a spring; alternately, it may have as its referent a water- and soil-filled basin of arable land. This term is not common in English, where, according to Bentley, it is used more in writing than in speaking. The definitions found in English sources correspond to those found in Spanish sources. The *DRAE* defines *cañada* as a narrow piece of land between two higher points. Islas adds that the higher points are generally hills or hillocks. Santamaría indicates that in Mexico it refers to a cornfield just after a harvest, and in Cuba it is a small **arroyo** or waterway that is dry during part of the year. According to Cobos, in New Mexico and southern Colorado, a *cañada* may be "a dry riverbed or a small canyon in the **sierra**."

canadian:
(Spanish *cañada* [see above]). Carlisle: 1841–42. Glossed by Carlisle as an adjective, meaning of or pertaining to the Canadian River. Its primary meaning 'of or pertaining to Canada,' however, does not derive from Spanish. According to Falconer's *Texas Santa Fe Expedition*, the Canadian River was not named for the nation of Canada but received its name from its steep riverbanks, which are similar to the sides of a **cañada**, or ravine.

capador:
(Sp. model spelled same [kapaðór] < *capar* 'to castrate' < *capón* 'gelded animal' < Vulgar Latin *cappo* 'capon' plus agentive suffix *-dor*; 'one who castrates'). The cowboy who castrates male calves, making them steers. He is also responsible for marking each animal by nicking a piece off its ear. The *capador* keeps the ear pieces in his pocket so

that they can be used later for counting purposes. The *DRAE* confirms that a *capador* is a man whose responsibility it is to castrate animals.

caponera:

(Sp. model spelled same [kaponéra] < *capón* 'gelded animal' [see above] plus the collective suffix, *-era*). (1) A group of geldings, or castrated horses. (2) Southwest, according to Dobie: 1929. The "bellmare" or mare chosen to lead a herd of horses when they are not being ridden. Spanish sources reference *caponera* as a wooden coop used to house castrated animals when they are being fattened or as a lead mare in a herd of horses or mules.

caporal:

(Sp. model spelled same [kaporál] < Italian *caporale*). Texas: 1892. A foreman, usually of Mexican origin, on a ranch. He was employed by the owner of the ranch to direct the cowhands. Dobie gives *straw boss* as a synonym. May also refer to the foreman of a sheep operation. *Alternate form:* corporal (by association with the military rank). The *DRAE* defines *caporal* as a caretaker of cattle. Santamaría and Islas note that in Mexico it refers to the boss among cowboys on a ranch. Cobos references *caporal* as a foreman who reports to a *mayordomo* (a boss or manager).

carajo:

(Sp. model spelled same [karáxo], of uncertain origin. Cognate terms exist in Spanish, French, and Galician). (1) Clark: 1840s. A strong expletive used especially by Mexicans to express disgust or frustration. (2) A base fellow, or one who would use an expletive like *carajo*. Often applied derisively to mule drivers, cowboys, outdoor workers, and Mexicans. (3) *DARE*: 1880. In the Southwest, "the tall, upright stem [of the *maguey* plant], used as a goad" or walking stick. Blevins suggests that the stem of the **maguey** received this name because of its similarity to the virile member. *Alternate forms:* caracho pole, carajo pole. (4) As a verb, meaning to use the expletive. The *DRAE* concurs with definition (1). The other three are not attested to in most Spanish sources, but derive from (1). Santamaría describes it as an expletive with folkloric color used in Spain as well as Latin America. It is very common and has prompted the creation of a number of euphemisms, including *carancho, caramba, carache,* and *caray.* Sobarzo concurs with this definition and adds that *carajo* can be used to refer to a malevolent, perverse, or base individual. *Alternate form:* caraho.

carajoing:
According to Adams, "shouting *carajo!*"

carcamen:
(*carcamán* [karkamãn], origin not found). According to Smith, a card game similar to keno or lotto that was popular among Mexicans and Anglos in the early period of the Southwest. The cards used in the game had pictures on them instead of numbers, and the pictures were often given facetious nicknames by the announcer, such as *amigo del borracho* ('the drunkard's friend') for the card portraying a bottle of liquor. The game was often played in Mexican-style fiestas and on Mexican holidays. Santamaría, Islas, Sobarzo, and Cobos all reference a game by the name of *carcamán.* Sobarzo describes a card game using cards with pictures on them similar to the game explained by Smith. Santamaría, Islas, and Cobos, however, provide a different definition. Cobos glosses *carcamán* as "a game of chance involving the use of dice in order to guess the lucky number in a raffle."

carcel:
(*cárcel* [kársel]< Latin *carcerem* 'jail'). West: 1840. General Spanish term for jail. Not frequent in English, and not as widely used as **calaboose**. *Alternate form:* caracel.

carga:
(Sp. model spelled same [kárɣa] < *cargar* < Vulgar Latin **carricāre* 'to carry' < Celto-Latin *carrus* 'cart or wagon'). *DARE:* 1844. (1) A cargo or load to be transported. (2) A unit of weight that varied depending on the product or the way in which it was carried. Hoy notes that a *carga* carried by an Indian was equivalent to two *arrobas* (approximately fifty pounds), but one carried by a mule (a *carga de mulas*) was the same as eight *arrobas* (about three hundred pounds). The *DRAE* references *carga* as something that can be transported on one's shoulders, on one's back, by pack animal, or on any vehicle. The *DRAE* also indicates it can refer to a variable unit of weight for wood, fruit, grains, and other items. Santamaría also references *carga*

as a variable unit of measurement, which may refer to two hectoliters (a measurement roughly equivalent to two-and-a-quarter dry gallons), two boxfuls, or the quantity that can be transported on the back of a pack animal. It is also used as a measurement for dry goods that is roughly equivalent to the weight of four hundred cocoa beans. Islas concurs, adding that another equivalent measure is that of ninety-six *cuartillos* (equal to two hectoliters).

carga de mulas:

(Sp. model spelled same [kárɣaðemúlas] *carga* 'load' plus *de* 'of' plus *mulas* 'mules'). Eight *arrobas* or three hundred pounds. See above definition.

cargador:

(Sp. model spelled same [karɣaðór] < *cargar* plus agentive suffix *-dor*; 'one who carries.') (1) According to Blevins, a porter, generally a Mexican or Indian, employed by traders or by the army to pack loads on his back. (2) *DARE*: 1811. A freighter who reports to the pack master of a mule train. The *DRAE* references *cargador* as one who loads merchandise or one who transports cargo. In America, the term refers to a porter or errand boy. Santamaría concurs and adds that a *cargador de hatajo* is the foreman of a pack train or the leader among muleteers.

carne:

(Sp. model spelled same [kárne] < Latin *carnem* 'meat'). (1) Carlisle: 1846–47. General Spanish term for meat, also common in the Southwest. (2) A short form for chili *con carne*, a favorite dish among cowboys and settlers in the West. Spanish sources concur with the first sense, but not the second.

carne asada:

(Sp. model spelled same [kárne] 'meat' and [asáða] < *asar* 'to roast' > Latin *assare* 'to roast' plus the nominalizing suffix, *-da*; 'roasted meat'). According to Watts, jerky. Clark also references this term as meat cooked over a fire (roasted or grilled). *See* **jerky**.

carne fresca:

(*carne* [kárne] 'meat' and *fresca* [fréska] 'fresh' < Germanic *frisk*). Carlisle: 1903. Glossed corectly by Carlisle as 'fresh meat.'

Santamaría indicates that *carne fresca* refers to the meat of an animal the day that it is killed, as opposed to aged, refrigerated meat.

carne seco:

(*carne* [kárne] 'meat' [see above] and *seca* [séka] 'dry' < Latin *siccum* 'dry'). Clark: 1890s. Beef that is sliced into long strips, salted, and dried. *See also* **jerky**. *Alternate form:* carne seca (technically, the correct form, since *carne* is assigned feminine gender). Santamaría references *carne seca* as meat that is salted and sundried. It is also known in Spanish as *cecina* or **tasajo**. Pioneers, explorers, as well as cowboys on long trail drives, frequently carried stores of dried beef, venison, or buffalo meat as part of their provisions.

caronie: *See* **corona.**

carpieta:

(probably from Spanish *carpeta* < French *carpette* < English *carpet*). Glossed by Blevins as "a Mexican saddle blanket." Spanish sources do not reference this term. In General Spanish *carpeta* refers to a table cover. The Royal Academy also notes that it can refer to a blanket, curtain, or piece of cloth hung on a tavern door.

carrera del gallo:

(Sp. model spelled same [kařéraðelɣáǰo] < Vulgar Latin **carraria*, an abbreviation of *via carraria* 'path for carts' plus *del* 'of the' plus *gallo* < Latin *gallum* 'rooster'). According to Blevins, a cowboy pastime in which a rooster is buried up to its neck, and a rider tries to pull or jerk it out of the ground while riding a horse. The rooster seldom survives the game. Islas references a similar game, known in Mexico as *carrera del pollo* or *carrera del gallo*. He says it is common at parties held on ranches and in communities in the northern and central regions of Mexico. In the Mexican version of the game, one rider holds a rooster in his right hand and a second rider pursues him, trying to grab the rooster.

casa:

(Sp. model spelled same [kása] < Latin *casam* 'hut or cabin'). Clark: 1840s. The General Spanish term for 'house' was used in the Southwest to refer particularly to a Mexican- or Spanish-style house made of adobe with a tiled roof.

casa grande:

(Sp. model spelled same [kása] 'house' and [ɣráŋde] 'large' < Latin *grandis* 'big'). (1) Carlisle: 1850. Referenced by Carlisle and Hendrickson as a large house. (2) Clark: 1910s. On a Spanish-American ranch or **hacienda**, the owner's home. According to Adams, this is where "all the hands gathered for fun and frolic." Bentley notes that it was without exception painted white and generally had a large veranda along the entire front. He also indicates that it was the "hub of the universe" for the laborers of the ranch. Although this term was more common in earlier times, it continues to be widely recognized in the Southwest. Santamaría says that a servant or laborer of a ranch or hacienda refers to the owner's home as the *casa grande* or *casa principal*. (3) Clark: 1840s. Clark glosses it as "an extensive pueblo in the Southwest." Not referenced in Spanish sources, but common in toponyms in the Southwest and Mexico: Casa Grande, Arizona, and Nuevo Casas Grandes, Chihuahua, for example.

cascabel:

(Sp. model spelled same [kaskaβél] < Occitan *cascavel* 'bell' diminutive form of Vulgar Latin *cascabus < Latin *caccabus* which was anciently used to mean bell, and it evolved into its modern form by onomatopoeic influence). According to Watts, "The enlargement at the loose end of the *reata*, which, after the dally around the saddlehorn was made, could be caught under the right leg of the roper." This meaning is not referenced in Spanish sources, and it is uncertain how the Spanish word for 'small bell or jingle bell' gained this meaning in the Southwest. Perhaps the southwestern definition came from another meaning in American Spanish, where *cascabel* can also refer to the rattle on a rattlesnake.

casick: *See* **cacique.**

cattalo:

(Combination of English *cattle* and *buffalo* < Spanish *búfalo* [see citation]). Watts: 1944. A cross between a cow (longhorn or fully domesticated one) and a buffalo. Adams says that Charles Goodnight was the first to produce a hybrid between these species, but Watts indicates that Spanish colonists attempted to breed cattle and buffalo as early as 1750 and that the idea was suggested in 1598. The original reason for breeding the two animals is disputed. Hendrickson cites Ferber, who suggests it was to make cattle more resistant to heat and ticks. Watts says that it was to produce a new kind of meat, which unfortunately proved to be inferior to beef. These hybrid animals are said to be difficult to domesticate and often sterile, but some believe there may yet be a market for them. *Alternate forms:* catalo, cattlo. *See also* **beefalo**.

cattle boose: *See* **calaboose** (1).

cavalade, cavalgada, cavallada, cavalry yard, cavayado, caviada, caviya, cavoy, cavvy-avvi: *See* **cavvy** (1).

caverango: *See* **wrangler.**

cavoya: *See* **caballo.**

cavraces: *See* **cabestro (1).**

cavvy:

   (*caballada* [kaβaǰáδa]< Spanish *caballo* 'horse' plus thé collective suffix *-ada*; 'a herd of horses'). (1) Texas: 1821 (*caballada*); Southwest Texas: 1937 (*cavvy*). A band of saddle horses; refers to the mounts owned by a ranch when they are not being ridden. Although Adams indicates that this term refers exclusively to domesticated horses, Watts notes that in literature it has been applied occasionally to a band of wild horses. The *DARE* indicates that it may have meant a grouping of horses or mules, and Clark says that in rural areas it referred to a group of stray cows, perhaps because some associated the sound of "cavvy" with "calfie." Watts mentions that *cavvy* and other forms were commonly used to refer to a group of saddle horses on northern ranges in the early days of cattle herding in the West. **Remuda** was more common in the Southwest and Texas. Later, the variant *cavieyah* became the standard on northern ranges, while *remuda* continued to be used on southern ranges. Both the *DRAE* and Santamaría reference *caballada* as a herd of horses, both stallions and mares. Although *cavvy* is considered the most common variant, there are many *alternate forms:* caavy, cabablada, caballad, caballada, caballado, caballard, caballáda, calf yard, cavalade, cavalgada, cavallad, cavallada, cavallado, cavallard, cavalry yard, cavalyard, cavayado, cavayard, cavayer, caviada, caviard, caviarde, caviata, caviya, cavoy, cavvayah, cavvayard, cavvie, cavvieyah, cavvieyard, cavvie-yard, cavviyard, cavvieyeh, cavvoy, cavvy yard, cavvyard, cavvy-avvi, cavvyiard, cavy, cavyard, cavyyard, cavy-yard. Some of these alternate forms, such as calf yard, cavalry yard, and other formations that include the term *yard* are folk etymologies. *See also* **manada**, **mulada**. (2) By extension from (1) a "ca(a)vy"[*sic?*] was "a pony or saddle horse used on a round-up," according to Hendrickson. (3) Hendrickson indicates that the term might also refer to "a stray horse or steer." Neither (2) nor (3) are referenced in Spanish sources, but may represent extensions from the original meaning.

cavvy-broke:
According to Watts, an adjective to describe a horse that was not necessarily tame enough to ride, but was able to run with the rest of the *cavvy* or **remuda**.

cavvy-man:
As Watts notes, another name for the wrangler, or the man who cares for a ranch's horses when they are not being ridden. *Also known as* the horse rustler, the horse wrangler, the **remudero**.

shotgun cavvy:
According to Adams, a *cavvy* that consists of horses from several different ranches brought together at a round-up.

cencerro:
(Sp. model spelled same [senséřo] onomatopoeic formation of uncertain origin, probably < Basque *zinzerri*, 'dog's bell'). Carlisle: 1876. A mare that wears a bell to help locate the herd. *Also known as* bell-mare. Spanish sources, including the *DRAE* and the *VCN*, gloss *cencerro* as a type of small, crude bell. The *DRAE* indicates that it is attached to the necks of cattle; Islas notes that it is most often used for animals that tend to stray from the herd, or for those that serve as guides or **caponeras**.

cenizo:
(Sp. model spelled same [seníso] probably < *ceniza* 'ashes' [due to the color of the plant's leaves] < Vulgar Latin *cinīsia* 'ashes mixed with hot coals,' a collective noun derived from Latin *cinerem* 'ashes'). (1) Texas: 1892. A salt-bush, including the *Atriplex canescens*. (2)

Texas: 1936. A silverleaf, including the *Leucophyllum frutescens.*
Alternate form: ceniza. The *DRAE* references *cenizo* as a wild plant
of the Chenopodiaceae family that has an erect, herbaceous, white-
colored stalk that is approximately two to two-and-a-half feet in
height. The plant's leaves are rhomboidal in shape, serrated, green on
top, and ash-colored on the undersides. The flowers are greenish and
form an irregular spreading cluster. Santamaría also references *cenizo*
and gives three distinct meanings. In northern Mexico and Texas, it
refers to a scrophulariaceous bush that is used as a home remedy to
reduce fever. It is also known in Spanish as *palo cenizo* and *yerba de
cenizo*; in Texas as *cenicilla* or *cenicillo.* The Latin name is *Leucophyllum texanum.* In Tabasco, Mexico, and southeastern Mexico,
cenizo is a melastomaceous plant (*Miconia argentea*) that is native to
tropical climates and is especially common on the isthmus. In northeastern Mexico and New Mexico it is a chenopodiaceous plant
(*Atriplex canescens*) whose seeds are used for food by some native
tribes. It is *also known as chamiso* (along the border) and *costillas de
vaca* (in Zacatecas, Mexico). Its leaves, which have a salty flavor, are
used as fodder. Cf. (2). Watts gives *chamiso* and *chamizo* as alternate
forms, but the *DARE* indicates that these are generally different
plants.

chaparral:
   (Sp. model spelled same [ʧaparál] < *chaparro* 'short, stubby'
probably of pre-Roman origin, and apparently related to the dialectal
Basque term *txapar(ra)*, a diminutive of *saphar(ra)* 'thicket' or
'hedge' plus the Spanish collective suffix *-al*). Texas: 1842. As Watts
observes, it appears that this term originally applied exclusively to the
scrub oak. It now refers to a number of thicket-forming, often thorny
shrubs or small trees, and to a large dense thicket formed by these
plants. It may also refer to a plain covered with such unruly brush
(*see also* **brasada**). Clark indicates that this term applies especially
to shrubs and trees of the genera *Acacia, Ceanothus, Condalia,
Forestiera*, and *Quercus.* Hendrickson notes that this term has
become recognized throughout the United States because of its use in
western films. The *DRAE* references *chaparral* as a place covered in
chaparros, which may be either a variety of shrublike oak trees with
many branches, or a Central American malpighiaceous bush with

clustered flowers, round fruit, and opposite leaves that are thick and petiolate. This second plant grows on dry plains and has thick, knotty, resistant branches used to make walking sticks. Santamaría defines *chaparral* as either the common name of a wild rhamnaceous plant native to central and northern Mexico (*Condalia obovata*), or a place abounding in *chaparros*. Santamaría gives several definitions for *chaparro*. It is generally a bush found in tropical regions in the Americas whose rough-textured leaves are sometimes used as sandpaper and whose bark is rich in tannin. On the southern coast of Mexico, it refers to several varieties of oak trees of the genus *Quercus*. In Tabasco, Mexico, it is an isolated mass of vegetation formed by vines and short trees, and in all of Mexico it is the common name given to the *Aythia collaris*, a plant native to the northern part of the continent. Islas concurs with the definition given by Santamaría for *chaparro* in Tabasco, Mexico, but he says that it is a low-lying thicket. *Alternate forms:* chaparrelle, chaparro, chaperelle, chapparal, chapparall, chapparo, chapparral, chapperell, chapporal.

Black chaparral:
   Glossed by Watts as a type of live-oak brush native to southwest Texas. *Chaparro prieto* is glossed in the *DM* as a plant of the genus *Mimosa*. *Also known (in English) as* chaparro prieto.

chaperajos: *See* **chaps.**

chaparro:
   (Sp. model spelled same [ʧapáɾo] see above). Texas: 1892. (1) Any of various undergrown evergreen oaks or similar plants. A thicket formed from such plants, or brush in general. *See* **chaparral.** (2) *See* **chaps.**

chapo:
   (Sp. model spelled same [ʧápo], of disputed origin. May be from Nahuatl *tzapa* 'dwarf' or from Spanish *chaparro* 'short, stubby person.' Sobarzo suggests it is the shortened form of the past participle *chapodado*, meaning 'cut off' [as the branches of a tree]). Clark: 1850s. Short and stocky, chubby, or a person with those characteristics. Clark indicates that this term may also refer to a horse. Not referenced in the *DRAE*. Santamaría and Sobarzo gloss *chapo* as a noun or adjective that describes a short, fat person. Cobos indicates that the meaning is the

same in New Mexico and southern Colorado and that *chopo* exists as
an alternate form in Spanish. *Alternate forms:* chopo, chupo.

chaps:

   (*chaparreras* [ʧapařéras] < *chaparro* [see above] plus the Spanish
suffix *-era* 'utensil'; the preferred pronunciation in English is [ʃǽps];
this pronunciation was probably influenced by the Spanish spoken
along the border, where speakers often pronounce the digraph {ch} as
[ʃ] or {sh}). Wyoming: 1884 (chaps); *DARE*: 1887 (*chaparajos*);
Texas: 1892 (*chaparreras*). Leather leggings worn by cowboys over
regular trousers to protect their legs from brush or **chaparral**. They
are generally made from the hides of goat, sheep, calves, bulls, and
deer, but they can be made from any type of leather. They also come in
many lengths and varieties, ranging from simple and practical ones to
highly decorated ones with silver ornaments and animal hair left on
the outside. Spanish sources reference *chaparreras*, but only Cobos
references *chaparejos* (he says the word is a blend of **chaparro** 'shrub'
and **aparejo** 'gear' and refers to leather leggings or *chaps*). However,
the *DARE* suggests that *chaparejos* may be a blend of *chaparreras* and
aparejo. The *DRAE* defines *chaparreras* as a type of tanned leather
breeches used in Mexico. Santamaría adds that they are a type of pants
without a seat consisting of two separate coverings for the legs that are
attached to the belt by straps. They are often made of goatskin with the
hair left on, and as such are *also known as* **chivarras**. They are worn
over the pants and serve as a protection against rain and mud. They
may also be made of puma or jaguar skin, chamois, or canvas. Islas
adds that they are often open along the seams and are fastened to the
legs with buckles. *Alternate forms:* chaparajos, chaparejos, chapareras,
chapareros, chaparraros, chaparras, chaparreros, chaparro, chaparros,
chaperajos, chapparejos, schapps, schaps, shaps.

   bat wing chaps:
      Clark: 1930s. A variety of *chaps* with short, wide leggings. *Also
   known as* buzzard wings.

   chapping:
      DARE: 1910. (1) A competition of sorts in which two cowpokes
   take turns slapping each other with leather chaps. The first to give

up is the loser. (2) A punishment in which a man is beat with leather chaps.

chap guard:

Glossed by Watts as "a small knob or hook on the shank of a spur to prevent the chaps from catching on the rowel."

chap string:

According to Adams, "a short string which holds the legs of the chaps together in front at the waist."

dude chaps:

Glossed by Adams as ornate or Hollywood-style chaps that are not worn by real cowboys.

pinto chaps:

Spotted chaps made of several pieces of leather with hair remaining, according to Adams.

shotgun chaps:

Chaps that go all the way around the legs (giving the appearance of a double-barreled shotgun, according to Adams). Watts indicates that they were popular between the 1870s and the 1890s. *Also known as* Texas leg chaps, shotgun leg chaps, stovepipe chaps.

winged chaps:

According to Watts, a popular style of chaps from the 1890s. *Alternate term:* Texas wing chaps.

chaqueta:

(Sp. model spelled same [ʧakéta] < French *jaquette* 'morning coat' or 'long jacket' such as those worn in earlier times by peasants). Texas: 1892. A jacket made of heavy cloth or leather worn by cowboys along the border between Texas and Mexico. Spanish sources gloss this term as a jacket in general.

chaquira:

(Sp. model spelled same [ʧakíra], of American Indian origin). Colored beads made of mock pearl or glass. Glossed in the *DRAE* as rosary beads or other beads made of various materials that the Spaniards traded with the American Indians. It may also refer to jewelry

Sombrero

Barbiquejo

Chaqueta

Armitas

Botas

made from such beads. Santamaría concurs, adding that in Mexico it refers to small colored beads used in making embroidery, purses, cigar cases, baskets, and other things. He notes that at the time of publication of the *DM*, the term was still very common in Mexico. Cobos references *chaquira* as a "glass bead or beadwork." *Alternate form:* chaquina.

charco:

(Sp. model spelled same [ʧárko], of uncertain origin, possibly pre-Roman). *DARE*: 1890. A pond, pool, or puddle; a watering hole. This term generally refers to standing water after a rain, but is occasionally applied to a spring. Referenced in the *DRAE* as water or another liquid retained in a hole or cavity in the ground. A source of drinking water was always a concern for the cowboy on long trail drives.

charqui: *See* **jerky.**

charreada:

(Sp. model spelled same [ʧaɾeáða] < *charrear* < *charro* [see below] and the Spanish derivative suffix *-ada* 'an event in which the techniques of *charros* are practiced'). Clark: 1890s. This competitive event was the precursor of the modern rodeo. According to Clark, it is still popular throughout the United States and involves traditional events, including wild riding tricks by women and horse-tripping. Santamaría notes that *charreada* comes from the verb *charrear*, which he defines as to act like a **charro** or to carry out the practices and exercises of the *charro*. The *DRAE* references *charreada* as a Mexican *charro* festival, and Islas indicates that it is a Mexican-style rodeo (*jaripeo*).

charro:

(Sp. model spelled same [ʧáɾo]'coarse, crude, rustic, or in bad taste'; probably from Basque *txar* 'bad, defective' or from a related Iberian term). (1) Clark: 1890s. A Mexican horseman or cowboy, particularly one in the traditional costume consisting of a large sombrero decorated with gold or silver embroidery; a loose-fitting white shirt; a short, tight-fitting jacket; and tight-fitting, flared pants that are also decorated with embroidery, buttons, and braids. Carlisle notes that *chario* is an alternate spelling in the Southwest. (2) The costume worn by the cowboy described in (1). (3) Clark: 1930s. A coarse, mean person; a churl. (4) More recently, a Mexican cowboy who competes in the Mexican rodeo circuit that is popular in southern California. According to the *DRAE*, *charro* originally referred to a resident of Salamanca, Spain, especially the region surrounding Alba, Vitigudino, Ciudad Rodrigo, and Ledesma, and to things of or pertaining to this region, such as the *charro* dress and manner of speaking. It is also an adjective used to describe a thing that is in poor taste or something decorated with bright, clashing colors. In Mexico, a *charro* is a horseman who dresses in a special costume as described above. Santamaría defines *charro* as an expert rider who is skilled in taming horses and other animals. Islas concurs, adding that *charros* are skilled in using rodeo-style rope-throws. He also notes that although the term *charro* and the clothing and customs pertaining to the *charro* originated in Salamanca, Spain, they have evolved considerably in the New World, and the *charro* has become a representative figure for the Mexican people. This term had reference to upper-class horsemen and **hacendado**s (owners of the large Spanish land-grant **hacienda**s) and contrasted with the term **vaquero**, which indicated much humbler origins.

chato:

(Sp. model spelled same [ʧáto] < Vulgar Latin *plattus 'flat or flat-nosed'). Glossed by Smith as "flat-nosed." Although this term refers to any person with a pushed-in or flat nose, Smith notes that in the Southwest it refers to Apache women whose noses were mutilated or cut off because they were unfaithful to their husbands. Referenced in the *DRAE* as a person with a flat nose, or the nose itself. Santamaría notes that in Mexico the term *chata* may be applied affectionately to any woman, regardless of the shape of her nose. For example, a family's most spoiled daughter may be called *la chata*. It is generally considered a compliment. No Spanish source references this term as applied to an Apache woman with a mutilated nose.

chicote:

(Sp. model spelled same [ʧikóte], of disputed origin; either from French *chicot* 'piece of a trunk or cut root emerging from the ground,' 'splinter embedded in a horse's hoof,' or 'root of a tooth' [*DRAE*, Corominas]; or from Nahuatl *xicotli* 'wasp with a loud buzz and a painful sting' [Cabrera]). A whip; horsewhip. Referenced in the *DRAE*, *DM*, and *VCN* as a whip. Also called **latigo**, **azote**.

chigaderos: *See* **chinks.**

Chihuahua:

(Sp. model spelled same [ʧiwáwa] (a place name)). (1) Southwest: 1930. A mild expletive common in the Southwest. Also *Ay, Chihuahua.* Santamaría references *Ay, Chihuahua* as an exclamation used as a euphemism for *chingar* 'to copulate.' Galván also references *Chihuahua* as an interjection of varying intensity of meaning. He says that in Chicano Spanish it can mean everything from 'Goodness gracious!' to 'Hell!' (2) West: 1936. A spur with a large rowel, often intricately decorated with silver. Known as a Chihuahua spur. (3) According to Hendrickson, a slang term used on the frontier for "a little town with a large number of saloons and dancehalls." *See also* **Chihuahua town** below. (4) A freighting wagon or large cart with two solid, wooden wheels. Also Chihuahua cart. No Spanish sources reference meanings (2), (3), and (4), but it is probable that (2) and (4) originated in the state of Chihuahua, Mexico.

Chihuahua town:

DARE: 1966–67. As glossed by Watts, a derisive term for a section of a town primarily populated by persons of Mexican ancestry. *Also known as* Chihuahua hill or little Chihuahua.

chileno:

(Sp. model spelled same [ʧiléno] < *Chile* (place name) plus the derivative suffix, *-eno*). *DARE*: 1946. A ring bit; a type of bridle bit made from a steel ring that fits into the horse's mouth. It is said that in the hands of a gentle rider it is an acceptable bit, but many find it to be cruel and harmful to a horse's mouth. Not glossed in Spanish sources.

chimayo:

(*Chimayó* [ʧimaǰó] < Tewa *tsimajó* 'obsidian flake'). Glossed by Carlisle as a kind of Indian blanket made of colorful cotton-warp, machine-twisted yarn finely woven into intricate patterns. They are not as valuable as Navajo blankets. Cobos refers to Chimayó as a New Mexico place name and *chimayó* as a type of Indian blanket.

chinks:

(Spanish source uncertain; the original etymon may have been *chincaderos* [ʧiŋkaδéros] or *chigaderos* [ʧiɣaδéros]). *DARE*: 1936. A short variety of **chaps** that extended only to the knees. Not glossed in Spanish sources. *Alternate forms:* chigaderos, chinkaderos. Also called **armitas**.

chivarras:

(Sp. model spelled same [ʧiβár̃as] < *chivo* 'goat'; originally a call used in herding goats, and in this sense it is an expressive creation common to many languages). Texas: 1892. Chaps made of goatskin with the hair left on the outside. The *DRAE* references *chivarras* as pants made of hairy goatskin. Santamaría concurs. *Alternate form:* chivarros.

cholla:

(Sp. model spelled same [ʧóǰa] 'head' or 'good judgment,' a popular and affective term of uncertain origin, perhaps from antiquated dialectal French *cholle* 'ball' < Frankish *keula* 'mace' [weapon]). California: 1846. (1) A common cactus, known for its long sharp spines that are so loosely attached to the plant that they seem to jump onto any person or thing that brushes them. Adams notes that the cactus can grow to up to eight feet; he indicates that the branches of the cactus, rather than the spines, are easily detached from the plant and seem to jump onto passersby. The *OED* defines *cholla* as one of several species of *Opontia* cacti. The *DARE* says that it is the prickly pear cactus. Santamaría glosses *cholla* as the common name used in northern Mexico for various native cacti of the same genus. He gives *O. cholla* and *O. thurberi* as examples. Cobos glosses it as the "buckhorn or cane cactus." Sobarzo describes the plant as a cactus with a vascular, pulpy stalk divided into sections about four inches in length and covered with very sharp spines. Its fruit is like that of the prickly pear, but quite small. It grows to a height of approximately four feet. Sobarzo suggests that the plant gets its name from the shape of its fruit. This variety of cactus is also commonly depicted in western films. *Alternate form:* choya. *Also called* jumping cholla, staghorn cholla, tree cholla, deer brush. (2) The term also has figurative meanings in the Southwest. Smith notes that it may be a colloquial term for 'skull,' or it may refer to a dull or stupid person. No Spanish source references the latter meaning.

cane cholla:

DARE: 1909. The prickly pear cactus. *Also called* cane cactus, walking stick cholla.

cholla gum:

A sticky substance exuded by the *cholla* cactus. It is generally found on aging or diseased cacti.

chonchos: *See* **conchas.**

chongo:

(Sp. model spelled same [ʧóŋgo], of uncertain origin. Cabrera hypothesizes that it comes from the Nahuatl *tzónyoc* 'hair on top' < *tzontli* 'hair' plus *yoh* 'abundant' plus *c* 'place'). (1) *DARE*: 1967. "A woman's bun; a top-knot." (2) Carlisle: 1913. Carlisle glosses it as "a pigtail worn by the older Isleta Pueblo Indians." (3) New Mexico: 1893. Apparently by extension from (2), a steer with a drooping horn; the horn itself. Glossed in the *DARE* and the *DM* as a hairstyle in which the hair is twisted into a ball and secured on the back of the head. The *DRAE* also notes that in the Dominican Republic it can mean a common or poor-quality horse. No Spanish source references (3), however.

choya: *See* cholla (1).

chuchupate:

(Sp. model spelled same [ʧuʧupáte], of unknown origin). (1) *DARE*: 1937. A lovage, especially the *Ligusticum porteri*. (2) California: 1961. A biscuit root (including *Lomatium californicum*), a plant of the genus *Lomatium*; also the root of the plant. *Also called* parsley, hog fennel, prairie fennel, whiskbroom parsley, wild carrot, wild parsley. Carlisle glosses *chuchupate* as a plant that Mexicans use for relief from indigestion. Smith also references *chucupate* as "a bitter root of a Southwest plant used as a tonic, particularly for flatulence." He notes that Indians often carried a piece of this root to be used for medicine and to ward off rattlesnakes. It is unclear whether Smith and Carlisle are referring to (1) or (2). According to Cobos, *chuchupate* is a variety of wild celery, *also known as* oshá (in northern New Mexico).

chupadero:

(Sp. model spelled same [ʧupaðéro] < Spanish onomatopoeic *chupar* 'to suck' plus the Spanish agentive suffix -*dero*; 'sucker, one who sucks'). A cattle-tick found in the Southwest. Cobos concurs.

cibola:

(*cíbolo* [síβolo], abbreviation for *ganado de Cíbola* or *toro de Cíbola*. Cíbola was a territory in Arizona and New Mexico < Zuni *šiwona*). (1) Carlisle: 1888. A buffalo, or American bison. Santamaría concurs, adding that in Mexican Spanish the term *cíbolo* may also refer to the hide of the animal, which is so thick and soft that travelers use it in place of a mattress. Cobos indicates that in New Mexico and southern Colorado Spanish, the animal is also called *vaca de Cíbola* 'cow from Cíbola.' (2) A land of great wealth, or seven golden cities, searched for by Coronado and other early Spanish explorers. Blevins and Hendrickson indicate that the area later proved to be a region in western New Mexico inhabited by Zuni Indians. Santamaría glosses *cíbolas* (also *cíbolos*) as inhabitants of an imaginary city, country, or kingdom called Cíbola, which the Spaniards searched for in vain. He also notes a fissure in a mountain range in Coahuila, Mexico, that is known as Cíbolo. In addition, members of an ancient Indian tribe in Coahuila are known as *cíbolas*.

cibolero:

(Sp. model spelled same [siβoléro]< *cíbolo* and the agentive suffix -*ero* 'profession or trade'). Carlisle: 1928. A buffalo hunter. Watts indicates that the term refers to the mestizos who hunted buffalo with lances or bows and arrows. He indicates that these were the precursors of the unpopular **Comancheros.** Spanish sources do not reference this term, but it follows typical morphological patterns.

cigarro:

(Sp. model spelled same [siɣáɾo], of uncertain origin; either < Maya *siyar*, or < Spanish *cigarra* 'cicada,' due to a perceived similarity in shape and color to the insect). Carlisle: 1928. Correctly glossed by Carlisle as a cigar. The *DRAE* concurs. In Mexico, *cigarro* refers to a cigarette; Santamaría indicates that a cigar is invariably called a *puro*. Among his vices, the cowboy often demonstrated a fondness for (if not an addiction to) tobacco in its various forms. Smoking was associated with the tough **hombre** and was depicted in commercials (Marlboro Man), western literature, and film.

cigarito:

(*cigarrito* [siɣaɾíto]< *cigarro* see above). A cigarette or small cigar. *OED:* 1844. Not referenced in Spanish sources; however, the *DRAE* references *cigarrillo* as a small cigar made of shredded tobacco wrapped in a piece of smoking paper, *i.e.*, a cigarette. *Alternate forms:* cigarillo, cigarrillo, cigarrito, segarrito.

cigarron:

(*cigarrón* [siɣařón] < *cigarro* plus the augmentative suffix *-on*). Carlisle: 1932. Referenced by Carlisle as a "big cigar." The *DRAE* indicates that *cigarrón* is the augmentative form of *cigarra* 'cicada'. No Spanish source references *cigarrón* as a large cigar, but the term follows typical morphological patterns.

cimarron:

(*cimarrón* [simařón], probably < *cima* 'summit, top' because *cimarrones* fled to the mountaintops < Latin *cȳma*). (1) Southwest: 1844. A bighorn or mountain sheep (*Ovis canadensis*). (2) According to Watts, the *cimarrones* were "the wild black cattle of Texas." (3) Texas: 1892. Any wild or solitary creature. Blevins notes that it sometimes referred to a runaway slave or a person who separated himself from civilized society. This term is often used in place names in the Southwest. The *DRAE* gives several meanings for *cimarrón*. It is used in America to mean a tame animal that has escaped and become wild or a wild animal that has never been domesticated. It also means a runaway slave. Santamaría notes that it means wild or untame in general and that it is used in Mexico to refer to a wild plant or animal when there is a domesticated breed of the same name. For instance, a wild duck is called a *pato cimarrón*. *Alternate forms:* cimmaron, simarron.

cinch:

(*cincha* [sínʧa] < Latin *cingulam* 'belts; girdles'). Noun *forms:* (1) Colorado: 1859. The saddle girth or strap used to hold a saddle on an animal. It is generally made of braided horsehair, leather, canvas, or cordage, and has a metal ring on either end. *Alternate forms:* cincha, cinche, cincher, cincho, sinche. (2) New York: 1888. A sure bet; an easy thing. *Alternate forms:* cincha, cincho, sinch. (3) *DARE*: 1889. A four-player card game *also known as* Double Pedro *or* High Five. *Alternate form:* Sinch. *Verb forms:* (4) *DARE*: 1871. To tighten the strap on a saddle; to secure the saddle on a horse's back. *Alternate form:* cinch up (Adams says that *cinch up* is the proper term and that *cinch* alone was never used in Old West). (5) California: 1968. To secure or fasten something. (6) Nebraska: 1905. To secure a deal, to make certain. *Alternate form:* cinch up. (7) California: 1875. According to the *DARE*, "to squeeze into a small place." This was also used figuratively. For instance, a person caught committing a dishonest act was cinched. Spanish sources reference only the first of the above definitions. The rest are extensions. The *DRAE* glosses *cin-cha* as a band made of hemp, wool, horsehair, leather, or *esparto* grass with which one secures the saddle on an animal. It fits behind the front legs or under the belly of the horse and is tightened with one or more buckles. Santamaría and Islas give similar definitions to that found in the *DRAE*, but they indicate that in Mexico the term is commonly spelled *cincho*.

busted cinch:
A broken cinch strap or a figurative expression for any failed venture.

cinch binder:
Washington: 1916. According to Watts and Adams, a horse that bucks and falls backward when the cinch on its saddle is pulled too tightly.

cinch hook:
Blevins glosses this term as a hook on a spur that attaches to the cinch to prevent an animal from throwing its rider.

cinch ring:
The ring on a cinch, according to Blevins.

double cinch:
As Clark notes, this term refers to the two straps on a western-style saddle; one in the front and the other at the rear.

flank cinch:
Carlisle: 1912. According to Carlisle, a saddle strap that fits "between the ribs and the hips of the horse."

hind cinch:
Carlisle: 1930. The rear strap on a western saddle.

lead-pipe cinch:
OED: 1898. A sure thing; something that is easy. Hendrickson suggests that the term comes from a combination of *cinch* (*see* 2) and a reference to the underworld where criminals used lead pipes as weapons because they were a surefire way to dispose of their victims. He goes on to say the lead pipes were easy to get rid of if the criminals were approached by police. His etymology is unsup-

ported by other English sources consulted, and appears fanciful, to say the least. Also referenced in the *OED* as "a complete certainty."

cocinero:

(Sp. model spelled same [kosinéro]< Latin *coquinarium* 'cook'). Texas: 1845. According to Watts, a cook on a ranch or trail drive. Spanish sources gloss this term as a cook. *Alternate forms:* cocenero, **coosie**, coosy, coshinera, cosi, cosinero, cusi, cusie.

cocinera:

(Sp. model spelled same [kosinéra] see above). Carlisle defines this term as a female cook. Spanish sources concur.

cusi segundo:

(cocinero [kosinéro] see above and *segundo* [seɣúŋdo] < Latin *secundus* 'second'). Carlisle: 1903. Glossed by Carlisle as a "second cook," or one of lower rank than the *cocinero*.

cojinillo:

(Sp. model spelled same [koxiníǰo], probably < Italian *cuscino* 'cushion, pillow' plus the Spanish dimunitive suffix -*illo*). Blevins notes that this term refers to a pocket on a saddle or a small box or case fastened to a saddle. Used to carry small objects, including bottles of liquor. Santamaría indicates that in Mexico it can also refer to one of two pockets or wicker baskets that hang from the head of the saddle. They are used to carry letters, lightweight goods, provisions, and other items. Santamaría notes that the term is generally used in the plural. Islas glosses *cojinillo* as each of the two detachable round leather bags that hang from the front part of the saddle and are used in a similar fashion. *See also* **cantina**.

colache:

(*colachi* [koláʧi] from a Yaqui term). A dish made from boiled pumpkin or squash. Blevins notes it was used by the Californios. Santamaría indicates that it is a regional dish eaten in northwestern Mexico that consists of tender squash, corn, and cheese. Sobarzo concurs.

colear:

(Sp. model spelled same [koléar] < *cola* < Vulgar Latin *cōda* 'tail' < Latin *cauda*; the /l/ may result from a blend with the Spanish *culo* 'bottom or backside'). New Mexico: 1844. Used as a verb, it means "to throw an animal by the tail," according to the *DARE*. As a noun, it refers to the act of throwing an animal in such a way. The *DRAE* defines *colear* as a transitive verb (used in the context of a bullfight) meaning to throw a bull by the tail, especially when the bull is about to charge a fallen picador. The *DRAE* also notes that in Mexico and Venezuela, it means to catch a bull by the tail while riding by on horseback and then, holding the animal's tail under the right leg against the saddle, to throw the bull with a lunge by the horse. Santamaría concurs. *Alternate forms:* to colear (verb), coleo (noun), colliar.

coleada:
(Sp. model spelled same [koleáða] < *colear* [see above]). Glossed by Smith as an equestrian sport in which competitors throw bulls by grabbing them by the tail while riding at full speed. Spanish sources gloss *coleada* as the act of throwing a bull by grabbing the tail. Santamaría references *coleadero* as the Mexican term for the sport in question. Islas describes a similar game by the name of *colear*, and Cobos says it is called *coleo*. *Also called* colea de toros.

collote: *See* **coyote (1).**

colonche:
(Sp. model spelled same [kolóntʃe], of uncertain origin; possibly from Nahuatl *coloa* 'to twist or turn'). California: 1846. Referenced in the *DARE* as "a fermented drink made from the *tuna* plant." The *DRAE* glosses it as an intoxicating drink made from the juice of the red prickly pear plant mixed with sugar. Santamaría and Cabrera indicate that it is a type of *tepache*. Islas says that it is a regional drink in San Luis Potosí, Mexico, but Santamaría indicates that it is consumed principally by the Tarahumara and Yaqui Indians in Chihuahua and Sonora, Mexico, and by American Indians in Arizona and California. *Alternate form:* calinche. No doubt a few buckaroos got drunk on such a concoction when other preferred alcoholic drinks were unavailable.

Colorado:
(Sp. model spelled same [koloráðo], perfective participle of Spanish *colorar* 'to color; to give color to' < Spanish *color* < Latin *color* 'color'). (1) The thirty-eighth state of the union, named after the Colorado River. Hendrickson indicates that Spanish explorers named the river after the red color of its water. (2) Carlisle: 1929. Red. (3)

As Clark observes, it is used as an attributive adjective in many combinations to denote animals (such as the "Colorado potato beetle" and the "Colorado turkey"), plants ("Colorado blue spruce," "Colorado fir," "Colorado grass," "Colorado River hemp") indigenous to the state. It often has a jocular connotation, as in "Colorado turkey," which can be either the great blue heron or the wood ibis, and "Colorado mockingbird" (see below). The combinations pertinent to the cowboy's era or profession are listed below.

Colorado bluestem:

According to the *DARE*, a wheatgrass *also known simply as* bluestem.

Colorado (bottom) grass:
DARE: 1884. Texas millet.

Colorado mockingbird:
DARE: 1968. A jocular term for a burro. *Also called* Arizona nightingale, Rocky Mountain canary, according to the *DARE*.

Colorado ranger:
A dappled horse, resembling an Appaloosa.

Colorado (River) hemp:
DARE: 1900. According to the *DARE*, "a tall annual legume (*Sesbania exaltata*) of the Southwestern and Gulf States which produces long tough fibers formerly used like hemp by the Indians." *Also called* bequilla, coffee bean, coffeeweed, indigo, siene bean, **zacate**.

comadre:
(Sp. model spelled same [komáðre] < Latin *commātrem* 'godmother'). *DARE*: 1834. A godmother; one who serves as a sponsor at a Catholic baptism. The *DRAE* concurs. More loosely, a close female friend of a family. Cobos indicates it is the form of address a godmother uses with the mother of her godchild and vice versa. In the Southwest as well as in Andalusia and Mexico, a *comadre* may be a ranchwoman's close friend or neighbor.

Comanche:
(Sp. model spelled same [komán̟tʃe], from a Shoshonean word). *OED:* 1806. An Indian nation of the Shoshonean family. Comanche

Indians were known for their horsemanship and bellicose nature and are also linked in the popular mind with the cowboy and the Old West. The *DRAE* notes that the Comanches live in tribes in Texas and New Mexico. Santamaría adds that in past eras they were nomads who wandered in New Mexico and west Texas, continually waging war against the Apaches. They frequently invaded Mexico, sometimes committing atrocities as far south as the state of Durango, up until several years after Mexican independence. *Comanche* is also used as an attributive adjective in English (see below). *Alternate forms:* Camanche, Cumanche.

a la Comanche:
Southwest: 1844. According to the *DARE*, riding while hanging off one side of a horse. *Alternate form:* à la comanche.

Comanche moon:
Texas: 1952. A full moon. According to Watts, the full moon in September, under which Comanche raids were said to take place.

Comanche pill:
Texas: 1969. As the *DARE* notes, "a laxative."

Comancheros:
(Sp. model spelled same [komán̪t͡ʃéros] < *comanche* plus the agentive suffix *-ero* 'profession or trade'). Traders, generally mestizos, who traded between Indians and Mexicans. Watts indicates that these traders were liaisons for the Comanche Indians and the Anglos. The Comanches would raid Mexican and Anglo towns and sell their spoils to each party through the *Comancheros*. The *Comancheros* were generally hated by Texans. Sometimes this term referred to mestizos in general. Cobos glosses *Comanchero* simply as an "Indian trader."

Comanche Trail:
The trail that led from the Staked Plain to Old Mexico, so named because it was the path used by Comanches on their raids into Mexico.

comanche yell:
According to Hendrickson, a frightening war whoop that the Comanches used in combat.

Comancheria:

(*comanchería* [komanˌʧería] < *comanche* plus -

ería, a Spanish collective suffix). According to Blevins, "the area of the Central and Southern Great Plains claimed by the Comanches, 400 miles wide and 600 miles from north to south."

compa: *See* **compadre.**

compadre:

(Sp. model spelled same [kompáðre] < Latin *compatrem* 'godfather'). *DARE:* 1834. A godfather or, more loosely, a close male friend. The *DARE* notes that it is common as a familiar term of address. Adams specifically notes that, among cowboys in the Southwest, it referred to a "close friend, partner, companion, or protector." The *DRAE* glosses it as a godfather and, in Andalusia, Spain, and other parts of Latin America, a way to address friends and acquaintances. Santamaría references it as a form of address between friends or persons of the same social class. Commonly used as a form of address in western literature, films, and songs like "Compadres in the Old Sierra Madres," sung by the CowDaddies, among others. *Alternate form:* compa.

conchas:

(Sp. model spelled same [kónˌʧas] < Late Latin *conchulam*, diminutive of *concha* 'shell'). Ornaments, usually made of silver, used to decorate saddles and other pieces of riding gear, including the chaps, saddleskirt, spurs, etc. *Concha* is Spanish for 'shell.' Cobos notes that in New Mexico and Southern Colorado Spanish, a concha may be a disc made of nickel or leather that serves as a washer for saddle strings, or a shell-shaped disc made of silver or copper used on Navajo Indian belts. With the exception of Cobos, Spanish sources do not reference the term as a silver decoration; it is evident that the southwestern definition is an extension of the meaning of 'shell' and refers to the shape of the decorations. *Alternate forms:* chonchos, conchos.

string conchos:

According to Blevins, saddle decorations that come in sets of eight.

concho grass:

(*concho* [kón̪ʧo]< Spanish concha [see above]). *DARE*: 1884. Texas millet (*compare with* Colorado grass). According to the *DARE*, the name of this grass probably comes from the *Concho River* in Texas, but it may derive from Spanish *concho*, meaning cornhusk (the *DRAE* confirms that *concho* has this meaning in Ecuador). Cobos notes that in New Mexico and southern Colorado, *maíz concho* is a type of large grain corn.

conquain: *See* **cooncan.**

cooncan:

(*conquián* [koŋkján], the name of a card game). Arizona: 1889. According to the *DARE*, "a card game similar to rummy" played in the Southwest and the South. The *DARE* also indicates that this term is mistakenly thought to derive from *con quién*, in Mexican Spanish. The term actually derives from Spanish *conquián*, which Santamaría and Cobos gloss as a card game. *Alternate forms:* conquain, coon can, councan.

cooney, coonie: *See* **cuna.**

coosie:

(1) Western Texas: 1933. *See* **cocinero.** (2) *DARE*: 1895. *See* **cuna** (2).

coosy: *See* **cocinero.**

corazon:

(*corazón* [korasón] < Vulgar Latin **coraceum* 'heart' plus the augmentative suffix -*on*. Corominas notes that the term perhaps originally referred to brave men and enamored women who were said to have large hearts). Carlisle: 1908. Glossed by Carlisle as either 'heart' or 'sweetheart.' The poem "A Border Affair," written by Badger Clark and later set to music and retitled "Spanish Is the Lovin' Tongue" by Bill Simon, an Arizona cowboy, contains the refrain: "(*Adios*) mi amor, mi *corazon*," '(Goodbye) my love, my sweetheart.' The Spanish sources consulted do not reference *corazón* as a term of endearment; however, it is heard commonly in many varieties of Spanish.

cordillera:

(Sp. model spelled same [korðiȷ́éra] < Spanish *cuerda* 'visible summit of a mountain' < Latin *chorda* 'string of a musical instrument' or 'rope, cord' plus the diminutive *-illo* and derivative suffix *-era* 'place where the summits abound'). Clark: 1880s. A mountain range; especially the Rocky Mountains of the western United States and Canada. Clark notes that there is an adjective form, *cordilleran*, and Hendrickson indicates that the term is frequently seen in the plural, *cordilleras*. The *DRAE* glosses it as a series of mountains that are connected to one another. *See also* **sierra**.

corona:

(carona [karóna], evolved along with the ancient locative adverb *a la carona* 'in direct contact with the skin of an animal or person' from an earlier, probably pre-Roman, term, **carón* or a similar form). Southwest (west Texas, New Mexico, and Arizona): 1892. A saddle pad placed between the saddle and the animal's back. Watts notes that it was often form-fitted to the saddle and left open on top to allow ventilation. The *DARE* indicates that it was sometimes highly decorated and may have been made of "pigskin, embroidered broadcloth, brightly-colored Navajo blankets, woven horsehair," or other materials. Southwestern sources, including Watts, Adams, Blevins, Smith, Carlisle, and the *DARE* say that this term derives from Spanish *corona*, meaning 'crown.' This is inaccurate. Actually, the term derives from *carona*, a Spanish term that the *DRAE* defines as a piece of thick, padded fabric that fits between the saddle blanket and the (pack)saddle and serves as a protection for the horse. It may also refer to the interior part of a packsaddle or, according to both the *DRAE* and Islas, the part of the horse's back on which the *carona* sits. Islas glosses it as a thick saddle blanket or **sudadero** that fits between the saddle and the horse's back. It may also refer to a piece of canvas under a saddle or saddle blanket. Cobos indicates that a "saddle blanket used on donkeys and mules" is known as a *carola* in New Mexico and southern Colorado. He suggests that the term derives from Spanish *escarola* 'ruffled collar,' but it is more likely a variant form of *carona*. *Alternate form:* caronie.

corral:

(Sp. model spelled same [koṝál], a term of uncertain origin common to Spanish, Catalan, Portuguese, Galician, and Occitan. It is related to Spanish and Portuguese *corro* 'enclosure' or 'circle of people,' but it is uncertain which of the two terms derives from which. Corominas notes that *corral* was probably the original term; if so, it derives from Vulgar Latin *curralem 'race track' or 'place where vehicles are enclosed' < Latin *currum* 'cart'). (1) *DARE*: 1829. A pen or enclosure for horses or livestock. Such pens were generally made of wooden posts and slatting or other fencing material, but they could be constructed of rope or adobe walls (Watts notes that the latter was used to protect herds from pillaging Indians). (2) Rocky Mountains: 1848. A group of wagons drawn into a circle for defense. (3) *DARE*: 1859. According to a quote included in the *DARE*, a correll was a hedge built around a campsite to protect travelers from the wind. (4) *OED:* 1847. As a verb, *corral* means to herd animals into an enclosure, or (5) to draw wagons into a circle. (6) *OED:* 1860. Blevins notes that, by extension from (4), to corral is to gain control of anything. Hendrickson includes a quote from the *New York Times* (1867) that demonstrates the variety of meanings the term *corral* had in the West at that time: "If a man is embarrassed in any way, he is 'corraled.' Indians 'corral' men on the plains; storms 'corral' tourists. The criminal is 'corraled' in prison, the gambler 'corrals' the dust of the miner." The *DRAE* references *corral* as an enclosed, uncovered place in a home or a field that serves as a pen for animals. The additional meanings above are not referenced in Spanish sources, but are extensions of the original meaning. *Alternate forms:* coral, corel, corell, corrale, correll, coural.

corral bar:
Carlisle: 1914. One of the wooden bars that make up the gate to a corral.

corral boss:
Glossed by Adams as "the man in charge of stock and corrals on a dude ranch." *Also called* corral pup.

corral branding:
According to Adams, "branding calves in a corral."

corral dust:
A tall tale or a yarn, in cowboy vernacular.

count corral:
A corral in which cattle are counted.

trap corral:

According to Adams, "a corral for trapping wild horses or cattle." Characterized by a gate that swings inward easily and then closes behind an animal, trapping it.

corrida:

(Sp. model spelled same [koříða] < *correr* 'to run' < Latin *currere* 'to run' plus the derivative suffix *-ida*). (1) *DARE*: 1929. A cattle ranching outfit. Only Cobos references this meaning. (2) A shed built on the side of a **corral**. No Spanish source provides a similar gloss. In Southwestern and Mexican Spanish (according to Santamaría, Islas, and Sobarzo), a *corrida* is generally a roundup in which cowboys gather grazing cattle together for a variety of purposes.

corrido:

(Sp. model spelled same [koříðo], perfective participle of *correr* 'to run' [see above]). A ballad, usually one that narrates a local legend, historical event, or love story. Blevins notes that such ballads are a significant part of the oral tradition of the border region. Santamaría glosses *corrido* as a popular ballad that relates some story or adventure. It may be recited or sung and is usually accompanied by music and even dance. Cobos points out these ballads are patterned after eighteenth century Spanish romances. It is quite likely that a few **vaquero**s, **charro**s, and cowpokes were immortalized in these border ballads. A number of cowboy classics such as "Streets of Laredo" or "(Out in the West Texas Town of) El Paso" are somewhat similar in form and content to the *corrido*.

corriente:

(Sp. model spelled same [kořjéŋte] imperfective participle of < Latin *currere* 'to run'). A Spanish term meaning "ordinary" or "common" that has been adopted into the cowboy lexicon. Among southwestern cowboys, it means "ordinary" or even "inferior" when referring to cattle or commodities. The *DRAE* glosses it as average, common, ordinary, or not extraordinary. Santamaría references it as something of common quality, not fine or distinctive. Sobarzo says that it refers especially to people and merchandise and indicates poor quality or little value.

corus:

(*coraza* [korása] < *coracha* < Latin *coriaceam* 'leathery' or 'made of leather,' via Mozarabic). Adams provides the following gloss: "The covering of a saddle, at first made of two pieces of leather stitched together through the middle, with a hole cut for the fork and a slit for the cantle. It was worked and shaped to fit the tree, and, after the rigging was in place, was slipped down over the saddle and buckled or laced in front of the horn." The *DRAE* glosses *coraza* as the part of the mount that covers the saddletree. It is made of embroidered leather. Santamaría indicates that it is generally part of a cowboy's saddle and consists of a wide mantlelike piece of leather that hangs from both sides of the saddle and protects the rider's legs from the animal's sweat. Cobos references it as an "ornamental saddle covering popular in Territorial New Mexico."

cosi: *See* **cocinero.**

coural: *See* **corral.**

cowboy:

A man who is employed by a ranch to care for grazing cattle. The origin of the term is a matter of some discussion. The first cowboys of the American West were the Mexican vaqueros. It is likely that the term *cowboy*, like its synonym **buckaroo**, derived from **vaquero**. The fact that the earliest *cowboys* were the Mexican herders and that cowboy is so similar to *vaquero* in its formation lends credence to this theory. The use of "boy" in the term rather than "man" may be explained by the fact that it was originally used (before the Civil War) to refer only to young, inexperienced drovers who herded cattle. It may also have been a derisive or condescending term, similar to the use of 'boy' as a form of address (from whites to black males) in the Deep South. By the 1870s, *cowboy* became a general term to refer to anyone who tended cattle. Somewhat later (after the 1880s), the term came to connote a wild or uncouth individual. For instance, the Clanton gang, who battled the Earps, are sometimes referred to as such. The term *cowboy* has become widespread in English and is used extensively as an attributive adjective. Its usage today frequently connotes an impulsive individual who, through a show of force, attempts to resolve a conflict.

cowboy bible:

Arizona: 1980. The *DARE* provides a quote from *Arizona Highways*: "Roll-your-own cigarettes were so popular that the little books of paper were called 'cowboy bibles.' They hated pipes and couldn't afford cigars or expensive manufactured cigarettes."

cowboy boot:

(1) The cowboy's footwear. (2) The mail and baggage rack on a stagecoach. Blevins is the source for the definitions that follow. (3) "A horseshoe calked at both heel and toe." (4) "The scabbard for a saddle gun." (5) A rawhide covering on a **honda** to keep it from wearing out prematurely. (6) An extra value, traded with a horse, to make it an even deal.

cowboy-broke:

DARE: 1946. According to Jo Mora (as cited in the *DARE*), a horse that can be saddled, fitted with a bridle, and mounted without too much difficulty is considered cowboy-broke.

cowboy change:

DARE: 1968. According to Adams, gun cartridges that were used as small change because the silver fifty-cent piece was the smallest coin in circulation.

cowboy cocktail:

DARE: 1968. Straight whiskey.

cowboy coffee:

DARE: 1967. Very strong coffee. *Also called* Indian coffee.

cowboy leg:

Colorado: 1967–70. According to the *DARE*, "a bowleg."

cowboy lily:

(1) North Dakota: 1938. "A stickleaf," including *Mentzelia decapetala*, according to the *DARE*. (2) *DARE*: 1959. An evening primrose found in the West, including *Oenothera caespitosa*.

cowboy of the Pecos:

According to Adams, a "salty and efficient" cowboy, named after the Pecos River, a symbol of wildness and lawlessness. A cowboy of the Pecos was either an expert cowboy and rider or a rustler.

cowboy pants:

Colorado: 1967–68. Strong work trousers made of heavy fabric.

cowboy pen:

DARE: 1961. A stick used for writing in the soil.

cowboy potatoes:

Texas: 1967. As the *DARE* notes, this term referred to a variety of fried potatoes favored by cowboys.

cowboy preacher:

Colorado: 1967. Generally, "an unprofessional, part-time lay preacher," according to the *DARE*.

cowboy's delight:

Wyoming: 1960. A variety of mallow from the herb family *Malvaceae*.

cowboy stew:

Texas: 1967. Either a dish "made from the head and innards of an animal" (*DARE*) or from beef or pork haslets. *Also known as* son-of-a-bitch stew, son-of-a-gun stew.

coyote:

(Sp. model spelled same [kojóte] < Nahuatl *cóyotl* '*coyote*'). Noun *forms:* (1) Clark: 1820s. A small American wolf (*Canis latrans*). Spanish sources provide the same genus and species. Santamaría indicates that it is a wolf about the size of a large dog. It has yellowish-gray fur and is endowed with instincts and cunning, making it similar in behavior to the fox. *Alternate forms:* cayeute, cayota, cayote, cayute, collote, coyoto, cuiota, cyote, kiote, otie. *Also called* barking wolf, brush wolf, cased wolf, medicine wolf, prairie wolf. (2) Southern California: 1872. An Indian or a person with one Indian parent. Santamaría says that *coyote* sometimes refers to a *criollo*, or a person of Spanish descent born in the Americas, or to his/her parents. Cobos concurs, pointing out that in southern Colorado and New Mexico it also means the offspring of an Anglo-American, Indo-Hispanic marriage. Sobarzo indicates that it is a synonym for *mestizo* or *mestiza*, a mixture of European and Indian blood, and is common in the feminine. Galván provides a similar meaning for the term in Chicano Spanish, namely "half-breed." (3) A contemptible person; a liar or cheat; one who sneaks around like a *coyote*. Also a squatter. (4) According to Blevins, a person from the Dakotas. (5) *DARE* (Adams): 1903. A dun-colored horse with a dark strip down its back. *Also called* coyote dun. (6) Verb *forms:* to clear out; run away. *See also* **vamoose**.

coydog:

DARE (Missouri, New York, Vermont): 1966–68. A hybrid of a coyote and a wild dog. Blevins notes that they are common in South Dakota. *Also called* **coyote dog**.

coyote around:

According to Hendrickson, to prowl about; to slip away furtively.

coyote around the rim:

According to Adams, to hint or "talk around" a subject.

coyote cactus:

New Mexico: 1936. As the *DARE* notes, this term refers to a prickly pear cactus (of the genus *Opuntia*).

coyote days:

The era in which the West was settled, according to Hendrickson.

coyote dog:

Clark: 1860s. A dog with coyote bloodlines or one exhibiting traits of a coyote. *Compare* **coydog**.

coyote dun:

See coyote (5). *Compare* **bayo coyote**.

coyote house:

Utah: 1870. According to Hendrickson, A dugout or excavated cellar covered with boards.

coyotero:

(Sp. model spelled same [koĵotéro] < *coyote* plus the agentive suffix -*ero*, 'profession or office'). According to Hendrickson, a member of various Apache tribes in Arizona. Sobarzo concurs, but does not indicate that the Apaches who are called *coyoteros* are limited to the state of Arizona.

Coyote State:

South Dakota.

coyote tobacco:

Southern Arizona: 1912. A species of wild tobacco. Blevins notes that the Indians in Mexico and the Southwest smoked it during religious ceremonies.

coyote well:

California: 1933. According to Blevins, a small, usually hidden, desert spring.

coyotey:

Nebraska: 1937. An adjective synonymous with 'mangy,' according to Hendrickson.

out-coyote:

To outsmart someone.

cristianos:

(Sp. model spelled same [kristjános] < Latin *cristianum* 'Christian'). According to Watts, Christians or "civilized people." Santamaría indicates that *cristiano* is a name used by some as the antonym of Indian, savage, or animal. The *DRAE* does not reference this meaning, but glosses *cristiano* as an adjective that makes reference to aspects of the Christian religion. Colloquially, it refers to a person or a living soul.

cuidado:

(Sp. model spelled same [kwiðáðo], imperfective participle of *cuidar* < Latin *cōgitare* 'to think,' and, by extension 'to pay attention' or 'to attend to'). New Mexico: 1846. An exclamation meaning 'watch out' or 'beware,' also common in General Spanish. Buckaroos and **bandidos** who ran afoul of the law may have found themselves "on the *cuidado*" 'hiding out from the law.' *Alternate forms:* ciudado, cuidáo, quidow.

cuiota: *See* **coyote (1).**

cuna:

(Sp. model spelled same [kúna] < Latin *cūna* 'cradle'). According to Watts, a cowhide stretched under a wagon to carry fuel and equipment. Spanish sources do not reference this meaning, but this carrying device likely received its name because it is similar in shape to a *cuna* or child's cradle. *Alternate forms:* cooney, coonie, cuña. *Also called* bitch, caboose, **coosie**, possum belly.

cuñado:

(Sp. model spelled same [kuɲáðo] < Latin *cognātus* 'blood relative' < *natus* 'born' and *con* 'together'. The term originally meant any kind of relative, and later came to mean 'brother-in-law'). Bentley: 1836. The General Spanish term for a brother-in-law. It was also used jocularly for the suitor of one's sister, or future brother-in-law. Bentley says that it "is well-known by Southwesterners with a knowledge of Spanish." Galván notes that in Chicano Spanish it is used to address a friend who has a sister and to imply that the speaker is interested in dating her. Cobos indicates that in New Mexico and Southern Colorado Spanish it means a "pal, chum, friend, or protégé." A cowboy with a Mexican girlfriend would have received this form of address from her brothers and others.

curandero:

(Sp. model spelled same [kuraŋdéro] Spanish < *curar* 'to cure' < Latin cūra 'help provided for a sick person' plus the *-nd(o)* suffix '-ing' and the derivative suffix *-ero* 'profession, occupation'). A healer or medicine man; often connotes a charlatan or quack. The *DRAE* glosses *curandero* as a person who, although not a doctor, practices ritual healings and home remedies. By extension, the term may also refer to one who practices medicine without a license. Cobos indicates that a *curandero* is a healer or one who practices herbal or folk medicine. Injured or sick cowboys who found themselves far from civilization or wanted to avoid a visit to the doctor in town may have enlisted the help of a *curandero*.

cusi, cusie: *See* cocinero.

dale: *See* **dally** (1).

dalebuelta: *See* **dally** (1).

dally:

(*dale vuelta* [dáleβwé]ta]< *dar* 'to give' < Latin *dare* 'to give' plus dative pronoun *le* and *vuelta* [bwé]ta] 'a turn,' nominalized participial form of *volver* 'to return' < Latin *volvere* 'to roll, turn around'; the theory that this term derived from the infinitive form *dar la vuelta* 'to take the turn' is less plausible). (1) West: 1921. As a verb, to pass the rope around the saddlehorn after making a throw in order to bring an animal down; to snub. This is an early technique, associated with the Mexican vaqueros. Blevins notes that in Texas the more popular technique was the "hard-and-fast" method, in which ropers would secure one end of the rope to the saddlehorn before making a throw. *Alternate forms:* dale, dalebuelta, dally welta, dolly, dolly welter. (2) Arizona: 1915. As a noun, a turn of the rope around the saddlehorn. Neither of these meanings is referenced in Spanish sources. In Spanish, *dale vuelta* has the general meaning of 'give it a turn.' Clark provides a third meaning for the term: to move slowly, "as if a brake had been applied." Clark's suggestion that this is an extension of one of the above meanings is unfounded; the *OED* references *dally* with this meaning and attests to its use in English as early as 1538.

dally man:

Clark: 1930s. According to Blevins, a man who employs the dally technique for roping animals (as opposed to the "hard-and-fast" method). *Also* dally roper.

dally your tongue:

Glossed by Adams as "a command to stop talking."

del norte:

(del norte [delnórte] < *del* 'of the' and *norte* < French *nord* < Anglo-Saxon *north*). Blevins indicates that this was "a name for the Rio Grande River until the mid-19th century." Two Spanish names for the river are the *Río Bravo del Norte* (on the Mexican side) or the *Río Grande del Norte* (on the U.S. side).

desperado:

(*desesperado* [desesperáðo], perfective participle of *desesperar* 'to despair, discourage' < Latin *desperāre* 'to despair, to lose hope'). Carlisle: 1899. An outlaw. *Desesperado* is glossed in the *DRAE* as an adjective meaning 'possessed with desperation.' A cowboy or ranch hand might become a desperado, if the law was after him. The form cited here represents a feature common in Popular Spanish, the deletion (syncope) of one of two similar contiguous syllables.

diablo:

(Sp. model spelled same [djáβlo] < Late Latin *diabolum* 'he who slanders or causes discord'). Carlisle: 1925. An exclamation meaning 'the devil!' Bentley says that it is often preceded by *qué* 'what a.' *Diablo* is also included in place names, such as Mount Diablo in northern California. The *DRAE* references *diablo* as 'devil.' It also glosses *¡diablo!* as an exclamation expressing surprise, admiration, disbelief, or disgust and *¡qué diablos!* as an expression of admiration or impatience. No doubt the borderlands cowhands learned such expressions from the **vaquero**s.

dinero:

(Sp. model spelled same [dinéro] < Latin *denarium*, originally a Roman silver coin < *dēni* 'each ten' < *decem* 'ten'). (1) California: 1856. General Spanish term for money; its usage in the Southwest is frequently considered slang or colloquial. (2) Texas: 1920. A cook on a ranch or trail drive. The *DARE* suggests that this term is a play on *dine* or *dinner*. The Spanish term for cook, *cocinero*, which shares the ending *-inero*, probably contributed to this wordplay.

dob, 'dobe, dobie: *See* **adobe.**

dogal:

(Sp. model spelled same [doɣál] < Late Latin *ducālem* 'halter for leading horses'). Referenced by Watts as a verb meaning to place a rope around the neck (of cattle). The *DRAE* glosses *dogal* as a cord or rope with which one makes a knot and forms a loop to secure horses by the neck.

dogie:

(origin uncertain, see below). (1) West: 1888. A motherless calf; a young, scrawny calf; a runt. *Alternate forms:* doge, dogee, dogey, doghie, dogie calf, dogy, doughie. (2) Arizona, California: 1921. By extension, a motherless lamb. *Also* dogie lamb. (3) Adams indicates this term sometimes means a laced shoe. (4) According to Blevins, also used adjectivally in a humorous way for anything doomed to failure or "unlikely to survive." The origin of this term is uncertain, but there are many theories. Hendrickson provides several possibilities. The term may be from "dough-guts," referring to the swollen bellies of orphaned calves, or it may derive from "doggie," a playful way to refer to young calves. This latter etymology does not explain why the stem vowel of *dogie* is never pronounced [ɑ] (as in doggie) but as [o]. Hendrickson, among others, also claims that it derives from the Spanish *adobe* or "dobie." Both he and Blevins also note that it may have derived from Bambara *dogo* or African Creole *dogi*, both of which mean 'short' or 'small.' Hendrickson hypothesizes that the term was originally applied by black cowboys. Blevins cites Owen Wister, who believes that the term comes from *doga*, a term meaning 'trifling stock.' Dale Jarman (personal communication) presents the most convincing etymology. He derives the term from **dogal** (see above), since these young orphaned calves could be led by a rope tied around the neck. It is possible that some cowpoke who knew enough Spanish to mistakenly identify *-al* as the common collective suffix, may have coined the blend: supposed Spanish root *dog* plus the English diminutive. Spanish sources do not reference a similar term.

bucket dogie:

According to Adams, orphaned or stray calves purchased by stockmen to restock a rancher's range.

dogied:
Orphaned (animals).

dogieman:
DARE (Adams): 1944. Either a small rancher who gets his cattle from other farms or a farmer or rancher who takes in dogies.

dolly, dolly welter: *See* **dally** (1).

Doña:
(Sp. model spelled same [dóɲa] < Latin *dominam* 'female owner'). The wife of a rancher, usually one of some importance in the community. Glossed in the *DRAE* as a respectful way to address a woman. It precedes her Christian name. Recently, the term has been limited to married and widowed women. Some varieties of Mexican Spanish apply this term only to older, respected women.

doughboy: *See* **adobe.**

dulce:
(Sp. model spelled same [dúlse]< Latin *dulcem* 'sweet'). (1) *DARE*: 1844. A piece of candy, sweetmeat, or other refreshment. *Alternate form:* dulcy. (2) Texas: 1897. According to the *DARE*, "a sweetheart, girlfriend." *See also* **novia.** Glossed in the *DRAE* as an adjective meaning 'sweet.' It also refers to a fruit or other treat that is baked or prepared with syrup or sugar.

El Dorado:

(Sp. model spelled same [eɪdoráδo], consisting of the definite article, and the perfective participle of *dorar* 'to gild' < Latin *deaurāre* 'to gild'; the gilded one'). (1) Clark: 1900s. "A nickname for California." *Also* El Dorado State. (2) Clark: 1840s. The West; a place in the West where gold is believed to abound. This name refers to a treasure city that Spaniards searched for in Cíbola. Blevins notes it originally referred to a sixteenth-century Indian chief in Colombia who covered his body in oil before sprinkling himself with gold dust; however, this may be more legend than fact.

El Paso del Norte:

(Sp. model spelled same [elpásoδelnórte], consisting of the definite article, *paso* 'pass' < Latin *passum* 'step,' *del* 'of the' and *norte* < Anglo-Saxon *nord*, 'north'). Carlisle: 1888. According to Carlisle, a pass or trail adopted by eastern and Santa Fe traders. The city of El Paso is named for this trail.

en pelo:

(Sp. model spelled same [empélo] *en* 'in; on' and *pelo* 'hair' < Latin *pilum* 'hair'). Bareback (a style of riding). Santamaría and Islas confirm that *en pelo* describes a horse without a saddle.

enramada:

(Sp. model spelled same [enȓamáδa], nominalized perfective participle of *enramar* 'to branch; fill with branches' < *ramo* 'branch'< Latin *rāmum* 'branch'). (1) "A shady grove or bower," according to Watts. (2) According to Smith, a temporary shelter that consists of a framework of light poles and a makeshift roof of leafy branches. Referenced in the *DRAE* as a covering made of naturally intertwining branches or an ornament made from tree branches for a party or festival. It also refers to a covering made of tree branches. Santamaría glosses *ramada* as a term used in Tabasco, Mexico, for an adornment or canopy of branches placed in front of the entrance to a church during a town festival. Cobos notes that in New Mexico and southern Colorado Spanish *enramada* refers to a fence made of tree branches or a corral used to trap wild horses. He indicates that the term is related to *ramieda* (from Spanish *rama* 'branch'), a term used in Territorial and Colonial New Mexico for a fence, stockade, or palisade erected as a defense against attacking Indians. *Alternate form:* ramada.

escopeta:
(Sp. model spelled same [eskopéta] < antiquated Italian *scoppietta* or *scoppietto*, diminutive of *schioppo* 'explosion' < Late Latin *stloppum* 'noise of a slap on the cheek,' of onomatopoeic origin). Bentley: 1912. A muzzle-loading musket or an old-fashioned shotgun. The *DRAE* describes it as a portable hunting firearm with one or two barrels that are twenty-four to thirty-two inches long.

estampido:
(Sp. model spelled same [estampíðo] < *estampida*, probably from Old Occitan *estampida* < *estampir* < Gothic **stampjan* 'to crush, to pound'). Carlisle: 1841. Glossed by Carlisle as a "shot, crack, or crash." The *DRAE* defines it as a strong, sharp noise like that produced by the firing of a cannon. *See* **stampede**.

estancia:
(Sp. model spelled same [estánsja] < *estar* < Latin *stāre* 'to stand' or 'to be firm or immobile' plus the nominalizing suffix *-ncia*). Carlisle: 1897. A ranch in the Southwest, especially a large one. Hoy glosses it as a colonial term meaning "a Spanish land grant for running cattle or sheep." The *DRAE* references it as a residence or dwelling-place and its surrounding land. The *DRAE* also notes that in Argentina, Chile, Peru, and Uruguay it refers to a country ranch (**hacienda**) dedicated to farming and raising livestock. Islas defines it as the portion of a ranch in which the **caporal** and the cowboys are established, along with the head of cattle in their charge. Cobos indicates that in New

Mexico and southern Colorado it is a small farm or a permanent homestead attached to a pasture.

estanco:

(Sp. model spelled same [estáŋko] < *estancar*, of uncertain origin, probably pre-Roman, perhaps from Celtic **tankō* 'I fix' or 'I secure'). According to Blevins, "a government trading post or a store." The *DRAE* gives several meanings for this term in Spanish, including a store that sells liquor or a store where state-controlled merchandise— especially stamps, tobacco, and matches—is sold. Cobos glosses it as "a government-owned store" in Colonial and Territorial New Mexico.

estanque:

(Sp. model spelled same [estáŋke] < *estancar*, of uncertain origin, probably pre-Roman, perhaps from Celtic **tankō* 'I fix' or 'I secure'). Southwest: 1930. Glossed by Carlisle as a "pool, pond, or reservoir." The *DRAE* glosses *estanque* as a hole dug into the ground to collect water. The pool generally has a utilitarian purpose, such as to raise fish or irrigate land, but it may be purely ornamental. Another in a series of terms that refers to that ever important commodity in the desert Southwest, water. *See also* **tank**.

estribo:

(Sp. model spelled same [estríβo], of uncertain origin, possibly Germanic, perhaps from Gothic **striup[s]*). According to Watts, "a stirrup-iron." Glossed in the *DRAE* as a piece of metal, wood, or leather that hangs from a stirrup-leather and supports the foot of a rider. Not a particularly common term among most riders.

estufa:

(Sp. model spelled same [estúfa] < *estufar* 'to heat a room or object' Vulgar Latin **extūfāre* 'to scald; heat with steam'). (1) Rocky Mountains: 1887. A stove or a room containing a stove, according to Watts. (2) New Mexico: 1844. Among Pueblo Indians, an underground council chamber housing a sacred fire. Glossed in the *DRAE* as a fire enclosed in a metal or porcelain chamber that is placed in a room in order to provide heat. It also refers to a room or chamber that is closed-in, insulated, and heated artificially. The use of the term to describe a Pueblo Indian council chamber is an extension of the first meaning and is not referenced in Spanish sources.

fandango:

(Sp. model spelled same [faŋdáŋgo], of uncertain origin, perhaps < *fado*, a popular Portuguese song and dance < Latin *fātum* 'destiny; prophetic utterance' because it was a lyrical commentary about a person's fate). (1) New Mexico: 1807. A lively Spanish or Spanish-American dance in triple time accompanied by castanets. (2) *DARE*: 1843. The music that accompanies such a dance. (3) New Mexico: 1774. A social party or celebration where dancing is a principal activity. (4) *DARE*: 1848. Any boisterous, disorderly get-together. (5) Texas: 1890. A dance hall. The *DARE* notes that this usage is obscure. (6) As a verb, to throw a celebration for someone. (7) California: 1928. As an attributive adjective, it relates to prostitution (according to the *DARE*, dance halls were commonly associated with prostitution). Thus, a fandango house was a brothel, and fandango girls were prostitutes. *Fandango* is glossed in the *DRAE* as an old Spanish dance that is still common today in Andalusia, Spain. It is a dance in triple time with lively and passionate movements accompanied by guitar playing, singing, castanets, and sometimes violins and cymbals. In Spanish the term may also refer to the music and verses that accompany a fandango dance or, figuratively, to a brawl or uproar. Cobos glosses *fandango* as a dance or "shindig."

fiador:

(Sp. model spelled same [fjaðór] < *fiar* 'to guarantee' < Vulgar Latin *fidere* plus the agentive suffix *-dor*; 'guarantor'). According to Watts, a cord made of rawhide, hair, or white cotton that attaches to a "hackamore" and fits around the neck of the animal, converting the

hackamore into a strong halter. The *DARE* quotes Grant, who provides a more detailed description: "The *fiador* is a small doubled rope
of either horsehair or sashcord that runs through the loops of the
hackamore's brow band at the point just below and behind the ears.
Then it goes around the neck, is knotted under the throat, and ends in
another and lower knot, so tied that it will not slip over the heel button
of the bosal." The *DRAE* gives several definitions for this term, one
of them describing a leather strap worn by the outside front animal in
a team from the harness to the cheek piece of the bit. As a general
term in Spanish, *fiador* refers to any cord or other item that secures
something and assures that it does not slip or fall out of place. Islas
glosses the term as the part of the hackamore; a harness strap that
secures the hackamore. It is passed around the nape of the animal's
neck and tied behind the jawbone. *Alternate forms:* feador, fiadore,
theodore (the latter is a folk-etymology).

fierro:
(Sp. model spelled same [fjér̄o] < Latin *ferrum* 'iron'). New
Mexico: 1844. According to the *DARE*, this is an obscure term that
means "a brand affixed to an animal upon purchase." The *DRAE* confirms that it has this meaning in the Americas, and that *hierro* is a
synonym. Santamaría and Islas concur. Cobos indicates that it can
refer to a branding iron, a brand burned onto an animal's hide, or
scrap iron. *See also* **vent**.

filaree, fileree: *See* **alfilaria.**

fofarraw:
(*fanfarrón* [faɱfar̄ón], an expressive creation that has passed from
Spanish into other Romance varieties). (1) Clark: 1850s. Trinkets or
baubles worn by a vain or bawdy woman; also excessive makeup. (2)
According to Clark, a term of contempt for a "fancy woman," by
extension from (1). (3) West: 1848. As an adjective, vain or conceited
(obscure). (4) *DARE*: 1940. As an adjective, gaudy or tawdry. (5)
DARE: 1943. An uproar or hoopla. The *DRAE* glosses *fanfarrón* as an
adjective describing a person who claims to be something that s/he is
not. It especially refers to a cowardly person who boasts of his own
bravery. It also refers to things that are showy or trashy. *Alternate
forms:* fofaraw, fofarrow, foforrow, foofarar, foofaraw, foofarraw,

Freno

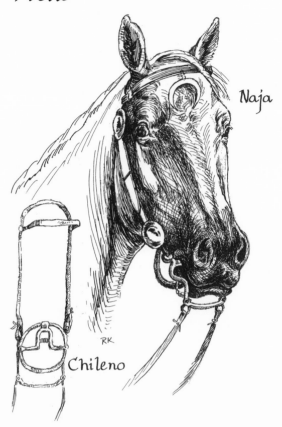

Naja

Chileno

RK

fooferaw, foofooraw, forfarrow, forforraw, forforrow, froofraw, froufraw, frufraw, fuforaw, fufurraw.

free-holy, freeholies: *See* **frijole.**

freno:

(Sp. model spelled same [fréno] < Latin *frēnum* 'horse's bit'). West: 1933. A horse's bit or bridle. Glossed in the *DRAE* as an iron instrument made up of a mouthpiece, cheek piece, and curb strap; it is used to train and lead horses. It was also applied to (horseless) carriages or buggies and the iron horse with the meaning 'brake,' an extension of its original meaning.

frigolito: *See* **frijolillo** (1).

frijole:

(*frijol* [frixól] < Latin *faseolum* 'bean' via Galician-Portuguese *freixó*, and possibly influenced by Mozarabic). *DARE*: 1831. A kidney or pinto bean, or any similar bean. It may refer to a dried bean or (generally in the plural) to beans prepared with lard and refried until they form a paste. The *DRAE* indicates that *frijol* is an Americanism and that the standard spelling is *fréjol*. Santamaría notes that *frijol* is the only variant used in the Americas, except in Colombia, where *frísol* may be heard. Santamaría also indicates that *frijol* is a general term to describe many varieties of beans. In Mexico, the plural form *frijoles* refers to a meal made from beans. Cobos concurs. Cecilia Tocaimaza (personal communication) indicates that the singular form refers to dried beans whereas the plural form has reference to the cooked, prepared beans. *Alternate forms:* freeholies (plural), free-holy, frejol, fricole, frijol, frijole bean. *Also called* Mexican strawberry. Beans were a common staple in the diet of many a ranch hand and cowboy.

frijole diet:

Carlisle (Dobie): 1929. A meager diet consisting only of Mexican beans.

frijole-eater:

DARE: 1963. A derisive term for a Mexican.

frijolillo:

(Sp. model spelled same [frixolíǰo] < *frijol* [see above] plus diminutive suffix *-illo*; 'little bean'). (1) Texas: 1886. According to the *DARE*, "an evergreen shrub or tree (*Sophora secundiflora*)." *Alternate forms:* frigolito, frijolilla, frijolito, frijollito. Also called big-drunk bean, coral bean, mescal bean, mountain laurel, whiskey bean. (2) *DARE*: 1947. A locoweed (including *Oxytropis lambertii*). *See* **locoweed**. Santamaría references many plants by this name, including various leguminous plants native to Mexico. One of these is the *S. secundiflora*, a northern variety of *colorín* known as the *frijolito* in Texas. The seeds of this plant contain a pungent, highly poisonous alkaloid that Indians ingest in small doses to induce intoxication, delirium, and finally, a deep sleep that lasts for several days. It is probably because of its narcotic properties that the plant is known in the Southwest as the whiskey bean or big-drunk bean. Cobos references *frijolillo* simply as another name for locoweed.

fuke: *See* **fusil.**

fusee, fuzee: *See* **fusil.**

fusil:

(Sp. model spelled same [fusíl] < French *fusil* < Vulgar Latin **focīle* 'flint' < *focus* 'fire.' In the Middle Ages, the French term meant 'flint' or 'piece of steel for starting a fire'; later, it referred to the flint that, when struck by the hammer, causes a firearm to discharge. The term finally came to refer to the firearm itself). According to Blevins, "a muzzle-loading musket; a trade musket." Blevins indicates that it refers to a firearm similar to those the Hudson's Bay Company and Northwest Fur Company traded to the Indians. He also notes that it was seldom a musket of fine quality. This term may have come into American English from Spanish or French. It is glossed in the *DRAE* as a portable firearm designated for use by infantry soldiers in place of a *(h)arquebus* or musket. It consists of an iron or steel barrel, generally from twenty-four to thirty-two inches long, a firing mechanism, and an encasement that holds the barrel and firing mechanism together. Modern versions of this firearm are of a lesser caliber than earlier models; they may be automatic or semiautomatic, and include a clip. *Alternate forms:* fuke, fusee, fuzee.

fuste:

(Sp. model spelled same [fúste] < Latin *fūstem* 'stick, staff, club'). Blevins: 1844. A Mexican saddle or its wooden saddletree over which a cloth is thrown. It is sometimes used to differentiate between an American and a Mexican saddle. The Mexican saddle uses less leather than the American and can be damaging to a horse's back. Glossed in the *DRAE* as the framework of a riding saddle. The *DRAE* also notes that this term may refer poetically to a saddle. Santamaría references it as a saddletree that consists of two inclined planes that leave an opening in the center. At the front is the **cabeza del fuste**, or head of the saddle, and at the other end is the *teja*, or cantle. Islas concurs and provides the names of the various parts of the *fuste* and the several varieties of saddletree that are used in Mexico. *Alternate form:* fusty.

gaieta: *See* **galleta** (1).

galleta:

(Sp. model spelled same [gaɣéta] < French *galette*). (1) Southwestern California: 1856. According to the *DARE*, a stiff, dense grass used in the Southwest for forage. It includes several varieties of the genus *Hilaria*, especialy *H. jamesii*. Bentley says that it grows to a height of two to four feet and thrives in even the driest of soils. Spanish sources do not reference this meaning. *Alternate forms:* gaieta, galleta grass, gietta grass. *Also called* tobosa. (2) A kind of hardtack cracker. The *DRAE* glosses *galleta* a cookie or cracker, or a kind of unleavened bread used on ships. Cobos glosses it as a biscuit.

galon:

(Possibly Spanish *galán* [galán] < French *galant*). According to Hendrickson, a big horse used for hauling. He quotes Edna Ferber, who suggests that the term is a Mexican adaptation of the American English phrase 'G'long!' used to urge the horses along. However, the Spanish sources listed below provide a much more credible derivation for this term. Sobarzo notes that in Sonora a *galán* is a lively, graceful, well-proportioned horse. The *DRAE* defines *galán* as a good-looking, well-proportioned man who carries himself in an elegant or graceful manner. A Spanish origin for this term is much more plausible, since it was the Mexican/Spanish vaqueros who taught the Anglos cowboying and ranching.

gama grass:

(Possibly < *grama* [gráma] < Latin *gramina* 'grass[es]'). Texas: 1894. According to Watts, a tall grass of the genus *Tripsacum* used for grazing cattle. The *DARE* notes that it usually refers to *T. dactyloides*. The origin of this term is uncertain; it may derive from *grama grass*. Not referenced in Spanish sources. *Alternate form:* gamma grass, gemma grass. *Also called* sesame grass. *See also* **grama grass**.

ganado:

(Sp. model spelled same [ganáðo] < nominalized perfective participle of *ganar* 'to earn' or 'to win,' probably from Gothic **ganan* 'to covet.' *Ganado* originally meant 'goods,' 'gain,' or even 'money'). A general term for cattle or livestock. The *DRAE* glosses *ganado* as a group of animals that belong to the same herd and graze together. Santamaría notes that in Mexico the term does not necessarily refer to animals of the same herd, animals that graze together, or even a group of animals of the same species. Rather it is a general term to describe any group of four-legged animals controlled by man and providing a benefit to him. The animals may be wild or tame and may wander over a great space of land. He further notes that, although this term may refer to any sort of animal that is used for man's benefit, it is generally applied to cattle.

ganadero:

(Sp. model spelled same [ganaðéro] < *ganado* [see above] plus agentive suffix *-ero* 'profession or trade'). Blevins correctly glosses this term as referring to a cattleman. Referenced in the *DRAE* as a person who cares for cattle or other animals.

ganado red:

A bright red color made with analine dye. Blevins notes that it is named for Ganado, Arizona.

gancho:

(Sp. model spelled same [gán̪ʧo], of uncertain origin, probably pre-Roman, possibly from Celtic **ganskio* 'branch'). Texas: 1892. According to Blevins, "a shepherd's crook." *Alternate form:* gaucho. (2) Texas: 1892. An iron bar with a crook. The quotes included in the *DARE* indicate that it was used to brand horses and to lift heavy lids off of hot cooking vessels. *Alternate forms:* gauch hook, gauch iron, gaunch hook. The *DRAE* glosses *gancho* as a curved instrument, generally pointed on one or both ends, used to grasp, seize, or hang an object.

garanon:

(*garañón* [garaɲón] < Germanic *wranjons* 'breeding animal, stud'). According to Carisle, a male jackass. Referenced in the *DRAE* as a large ass that mates with mares and female donkeys. Santamaría glosses it as an uncastrated horse used for breeding.

garbancillo:

(Sp. model spelled same [garβansíǰo] < Spanish *garbanzo* 'chickpea' < Mozarabic *arvanço* 'chickpea' plus the diminutive *-illo*). Kansas: 1887; Texas: 1970. Referenced in the *DARE* as "a milk vetch," including the *Astragalus mollissimus* and the *A. wootonii*. Santamaría glosses it as a bush (*Brongniartia parryi*) that grows on the Mexican altiplano. In Baja California, the name *garbancillo de buey* is given to the *A. leucopis*. Cobos references *garbancillo* as **locoweed**. *Alternate form:* garbanzilla.

gateado:

(Sp. model spelled same [gateáðo] < *gato* 'cat' < Late Latin *cattum*, 'undomesticated cat' plus the derivative suffix *-eado*). A dun-colored horse with stripes on its legs and shoulders, similar to the zebra dun. Santamaría indicates that it refers to a light or blond-colored horse with a blackish stripe along the ridge of its back and similar transversal stripes on its ribs and hindquarters. Islas defines it as a pattern observed on the legs of many bay-colored mules that consists of dark transversal stripes on the shoulders, knees, thighs, and hocks. The pattern is similar to that on many brown-colored cats, which is the origin of the term. *See also* **bayo tigre**.

gauch hook, gaunch hook, gauch iron: *See* **gancho** (2).

gaucho: *See* **gancho** (1).

gemma grass: *See* **gama grass**.

gerga:

(*jerga* [xérɣa], of uncertain origin; Corominas suggests that it may be from Latin *sērica* 'cloth or clothing of silk,' although he admits that this etymology presents semantic as well as phonetic difficulties). Carlisle: 1930. According to Watts, a coarse cloth sometimes used as a saddlecloth. Also the saddlecloth itself. The *DRAE* references *jerga* as thick, coarse cloth. Islas says that it refers to a coarse woolen cloth of which there are many specific varieties that serve a number of purposes. Santamaría glosses it as a piece of material that fits between two saddle blankets on the back of a horse. Cobos indicates that *jerga* is often used to cover floors. He notes that in New Mexico and Southern Colorado Spanish, it may also be spelled *xerga* or *gerga*. *Alternate forms:* jerga, xerga, zerga.

get a halo gratis:

(*grátis* [grátis] < Latin *gratīs*, a contraction of *gratiīs* 'by the graces' or 'freely'). Hendrickson references this phrase as "a cowboy expression meaning to be killed."

gietta grass: *See* **galleta** (1).

good man:

(*hombre bueno* [ómbre] < Latin *hominem* and [βwéno] < Latin *bonum*). Glossed by Hendrickson as an old term in the Southwest for "an arbitrator in a dispute." He indicates that it is a calque from Spanish. The *DRAE* references *hombre bueno* as a legal term for a mediator in proceedings for conciliation. *See* **hombre bueno**.

gotch:

(*gacho* [gátʃo], probably a postverbal adjective derived from *agachar* 'to lower, bend; squat' of uncertain origin). Kansas: 1905; Arizona: 1910. As Clark notes, drooping or askew, as an ear on a horse or donkey. The *DRAE* references *gacho* as an adjective meaning curved or drooping downward. It also describes a cow or ox that has one or both horns drooping downward; in Spanish the term may also refer to the horn itself. Santamaría concurs and adds that in Mexico the adjective is also used to describe an animal that, because of an accident or illness, has lost the ability to move one or both ears, hence the ears are always drooping. Cobos notes that in New Mexico and Southern Colorado Spanish *gacho* means bad or lousy, and Galván references it as ugly or ridiculous.

gotch-eared:

According to Hendrickson, an adjective that describes an animal that has had its ear clipped for identification.

gotch-eyed:

Having crossed eyes, or having one eye looking askew, as Hendrickson notes.

grama grass:

(*grama* [gráma] < Latin *gramina* 'grass[es]'). (1) *DARE*: 1828. A grass of the genus *Bouteloua*, especially *B. oligestachya*. *Alternate forms:* gramma, gramma grass, grammar grass, gramme grass. *Also called* buffalo grass, **mesquite grass**. (2) Arizona: 1872. A muhly grass, especially *Muhlenbergia porteri*. *See also* **black grama** below. The *DRAE* glosses *grama* as a general term for grass; however, in southwestern English it has developed specific meanings.

black grama:

Any of a variety of species of grasses including the dark purple grama grass *Bouteloua eriopoda*, the muhly grass *Muhlenbergia porteri*, and the galleta grass *Hilaria jamesii*. *See* **galleta**.

mat grama:

DARE: 1950. A variety of grama grass (*Bouteloua simplex*).

grammar grass: *See* **grama grass** (1).

grande:

(Sp. model spelled same [gráŋde] < Latin *grandem* 'grandiose' or 'aged'). (1) The General Spanish term for big or great, extremely common in southwestern place names. (2) A nickname for the Rio Grande. This meaning is not referenced in Spanish sources.

gringo:

(Sp. model spelled same [gríŋgo], of disputed origin). A term used derisively in the Southwest to refer to Anglos, newcomers, and strangers. The *DRAE* references *gringo* as a foreigner, generally one who speaks a language other than Spanish, and especially one who speaks English. It is also an adjective for any foreign language. Santamaría notes that in Mexico it refers to a person from the United States and adds that the term has been extended to refer to any fair-skinned person, or even a white animal with blue eyes and light-colored lashes. There have been many theories, some of which do not reflect careful, serious study as to how this term came into Spanish. Some wordsmiths have suggested it derives from 'green coat,' referring to the uniforms of United States soldiers. Another theory holds that the term comes from a song sung by American soldiers that contained the verse "green grow the rashes, O" ("rashes" was sometimes replaced by "rushes" or "lilacs," depending on the version). Hendrickson suggests that the term derives from the name of Major Samuel Ringgold (pronounced with a trilled /r̄/ and apocope of the final consonant cluster; a plausible Mexican Spanish adaptation). Ringgold was a United States officer and strategist who faced the Mexicans during the Mexican War. However, since the term is attested to as early as 1787 with reference to the Irish brigades in Spain (who may have worn green coats and sung the verse cited above), the preceeding explanations cannot be entirely correct. Far more likely than any of these theories is the distinct possibility that the term comes from *griego*, meaning Greek in Spanish. It is comparable to the English phrase "it's all Greek to me."

gringa:

(Sp. model spelled same [gríŋga]). The feminine form of *gringo*.

grulla:

(Sp. model spelled same [grúǰa], probably derived from the older form *gruya* or *grúa* < Latin *grŭem* 'crane.' Corominas indicates that there is no good explanation for the appearance of the grapheme {ll} in this term). (1) A crane bird. The *DRAE* defines it as a long-legged bird that grows to some four feet in height and has a prolonged, conical beak, a head partially covered in red and brown feathers, a long black neck, large round wings, a small tail with long bristly coverts, and gray plumage. It flies high and rests on one leg. (2) Central Texas: 1866. Mouse-colored or dark-colored, said of a horse or mule. Spanish sources reference *grullo* as an adjective to describe an ash-colored or mouse-colored horse. *Alternate forms:* gruller, grullo, gruya, gruyay, gruyer, gruyo.

grulla mare:

A dark-colored horse.

gruya, gruyay, gruyer, gruyo: *See* **grulla** (2).

guaco:

(Sp. model spelled same [gwáko], of American Indian origin, perhaps from a native Caribbean or Nicaraguan language). (1) New Mexico: 1844. According to the *DARE*, "the Rocky Mountain bee plant." Sources for the *DARE* give the family *Capparidacae* for one variety of this plant and the Latin name *Cleome serrulata Pursh* for another. (2) An extract from the Rocky Mountain bee plant that is used as a black pigment for Pueblo pottery designs. The *DRAE* describes it as a composite plant with vinelike stalks from sixteen to twenty-two yards long; large oval-shaped leaves that have heart-shaped bases and pointed tips; and bell-shaped, noxious-smelling white flowers in groups of four. It is a *liana* native to intertropical America and its leaves, when boiled, are considered protection against venomous animal bites, intestinal obstructions, rheumatism, and cholera. Santamaría concurs with the definition provided by the *DRAE* and adds that *guaca* and *huaco* are alternate forms in Mexico. He also provides *Mikania genoclada*, *M. guaco*, *M. houstonis*, *M. coriacea*, *M. repanda*, *M. angulata*, *M. aristolochya*, and *Eupatorium mikania* as various genera and species for the plant. Cobos glosses *guaco* as either a stinkweed or a name for the Rocky Mountain bee plant, whose roots are used to make a black paint.

guancoche:

(Sp. model spelled same [gwaŋkóʧe] < *vanchoche*, in Tarascan [a Meso-American Indian language of Southwestern Michoacan, Mexico], a net in which loads are carried, and in Sinaloa, Mexico, a blanket or bag made of the most ordinary sort of fiber). A gunnysack or large basket used in the Southwest and Mexico to carry items on a mule, horse, or burro. Santamaría glosses it as a thick, coarse, woven fabric used for lining and packing and in making gunnysacks. He indicates that the term is common in nearly all Latin-American countries, with some variations in spelling and meaning. *Related forms:* gancoche, gangocho, gangochi, guangochi, guangocho; all share the fundamental meaning of a coarse, crude, sparse cloth or loose robe; or a large sack, blanket, wrapped package, or container for heavy things made from such a fabric, all of which may be oversized or loose-fitting. It was probably influenced by the Mexicanism *guango* 'loose-fitting,' and has emigrated from Mexico to other countries. Whether or not cowboys or ranchers used such an artifact to transport goods, they probably knew some individuals who did and were aware of the term.

guayave:

(*guayabe* [gwaǰáβe] < Tewa *buwayabe* 'paper bread'). New Mexico and Texas: 1850. Blevins references this term as a cornbread made by

Pueblo Indians. Carlisle glosses it as cake, or hot cake in New Mexico. Hendrickson says that the term was also used in the Southwest to refer to rolls of money because of their similarity in shape to the Pueblo Indian bread. The only Spanish source to reference this term is Cobos, who indicates that it is a sort of "waferlike bread made with blue cornmeal." He also notes that the bread is called *piki* by the Hopi Indians and *hewe* by the Zuni.

guia:

(*guía* [gía] < *guiar* 'to guide, lead,' a term common to all Western Romance languages; the initial consonant indicates that it is of Germanic origin, but no similar term exists in known Germanic lexicons. Corominas suggests it is from Gothic **widan* 'to gather together,' since the original meaning in Romance was 'to escort someone and guarantee his safety'). Bentley: 1844. Referenced by Watts as a custom pass or manifest. Blevins indicates it was a written permit to allow American merchandise into Mexico, especially during the time of the Santa Fe Trail. The *DRAE* provides a similar definition. Cobos references it as an invoice or a bill of lading (according to the *OED*, it is an official receipt given by the master of a merchant vessel to the person shipping the goods; the document makes the master of the vessel responsible for the safe arrival of the goods; it may be used as legal proof of ownership of goods, and may be deposited with a creditor as security for a loan).

hacienda:

(Sp. model spelled same [asjéŋda]< Latin *facienda* 'things that must be done,' plural neuter form of the future passive participle of *facere,* which originally meant 'affairs; matters,' then 'goods, riches,' then 'the administration of the goods and riches belonging to the state'; *compare* **ganado**). (1) New Mexico: 1810. The central compound or main building located on a large ranch or estate. This central compound consisted primarily of the rancher's living quarters. By extension, the term is used in the Southwest to refer to any large Spanish-style home. (2) Texas: 1825. The ranch or estate itself, particularly if it was large or extensive. The *DRAE* gives several meanings for *hacienda,* among them a piece of land dedicated to agriculture, or a collective term for the livestock owned by a farmer. Santamaría notes that in Mexico a *rancho* is a farm of little importance, and a *hacienda* is a larger, more important agricultural venture.

hacendado:

(Sp. model spelled same [aseŋdáðo], perfective participle of *hacendar < hacienda* [see above]). According to Watts, the owner of a large ranch or estate. *Alternate forms:* haciendero. According to the *DRAE*, it usually refers to an individual who owns a large or particularly lucrative *hacienda*. Cobos glosses *haciendado* as a rich landowner, or a person who owns land or sheep.

hackamore:

(*jáquima* [xákima] < Arabic *šakîma* 'halter'). California: 1850. A headstall or rope halter with reins and a lead rope. It may also be constructed of rawhide or horsehair. Adams describes it as a headpiece

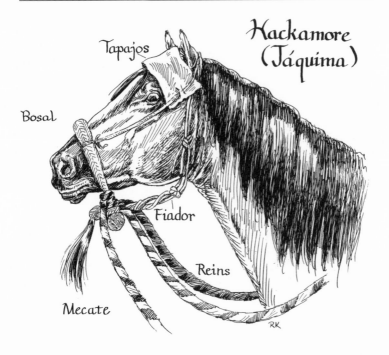

Tapajos

Hackamore
(Jáquima)

Bosal

Fiador

Reins

Mecate

RK

similar to "a bridle with a *bosal* in place of a bit." It has no throat-latch, and its brow-band is about three inches wide and can be used to cover the horse's eyes. The hackamore is especially useful for inexperienced horses in the process of being broken because it has knots that fit close to the horse's nostrils and cause pain when the horse does not submit to its rider. This term comes from the Spanish *jáquima*, which the *DRAE* defines as a rope headstall that is used to tie and lead horses. *Alternate forms:* hackamer, jakoma, jaquima, stockamore.

hackamore bit:
    According to Watts, a bit lacking a mouthpiece. It is used with a hackamore and usually has a padded noseband.

hackamore colt:
    A colt trained using a hackamore and a hackamore bit, according to Watts.

hackamore rope:
    A rope fastened to a hackamore; generally a lightweight hair rope.

hackel: *See* **jacal.**

hindu: *See* **honda** (1).

hombre:
(Sp. model spelled same [ómbre] < Latin *hominem* 'man'). (1) New Mexico: 1846. An individual of Mexican or Spanish ancestry. The *DARE* notes that this usage is somewhat old-fashioned. (2) Southwest: 1854. By extension from (1), any male. It is often used jocularly or colloquially. Watts, quoting Adams, indicates that it is often used with an adjective, as in big hombre, good hombre, tough hombre, or bad hombre. Both Adams and Blevins say that it sometimes, but not always, denotes a man of low character. Spanish sources gloss it as a general term for a man.

hombre bueno:
(Sp. model spelled same [ómbre] [see above] and [βwéno] < Latin *bonum*). An arbitrator. The *DRAE* concurs. *See also* **good man.**

hombre del campo:
(Sp. model spelled same [ómbreðelkámpo] *hombre* [see above] and *del* 'of the' and *campo* < Latin *campus*, 'flat land or battle field'). Referenced by Watts as a term used in Mexico, Texas, and the Southwest for a man who is an expert at living in the wilds, meaning that he is knowledgeable about tracking and trapping animals. It may also refer to a man who, according to Watts, "possessed a great store of wild lore."

hombrote:
(Sp. model spelled same [ombróte], augmentative of *hombre* [see above]). New Mexico: 1912. Carlisle references the term in New Mexico as an "industrious or courageous man." Cobos defines it as a macho or "he-man," or a term applied affectionately to a boy who does his chores willingly and quickly.

seldom hombre:
Blevins references this term as "an unusual man."

honda:
(? probably from Spanish *hondón* [oŋdón] 'eyelet' or 'bottom of a hollow object,' augmentative of *hondo* < Latin *fundum* 'bottom, depth.'

As the *DARE* notes, *hondón* may have crossed paths with Spanish *honda* 'slingshot,' giving rise to this commonly attested form). (1) West: 1887. A metal or leather ring at one end of a rope through which the other end is looped; also refers to the piece of rope attached to the ring. Whether one ties hard and fast or dallies, the *honda* forms the slip knot or noose which tightens around the animal that is roped. *Alternate forms:* hindu, hondo, hondoo, hondou, hondu. (2) Texas: 1894. According to the *DARE*, the term also refers to a parbuckle (a device consisting of a looped rope to lower or hoist cargo shipboard). Often used to secure casks, spars, and other heavy items. Neither of the above definitions is glossed in Spanish sources. *Alternate forms:* hondoo, hondou.

hondo:
(Sp. model spelled same [oŋdo] < Latin *fundum* 'bottom, depth'). (1) A deep arroyo. The *DRAE* indicates that this term may apply to ground lower than the surrounding terrain. (2) *See* **honda** (1).

hoosecow: *See* **hoosegow** (1).

hoosegarden: *See* **hoosegow** (1).

hoosegow:
(*juzgado* [xusɣáðo], also popularly [xusɣáo] or [xusɣáy̯], perfective participle of *juzgar* < Latin *jūdicāre* 'to judge'). (1) *DARE*: 1909. According to the *DARE*, "a jail, prison or courthouse." Hendrickson's claim that the slang word *jug*, meaning jail, may come from *juzgado* is unsubstantiated and cannot be explained, given Spanish phonology. *Alternate forms:* hoose, hoosecow, hoosegarden, hoosegaw, hoosgow, hoozegow, housgau, jusgado. (2) Western Montana, western Wyoming: 1931. An outhouse or restroom. The *DRAE* glosses *juzgado* as a group of judges who concur in a sentencing, a territory under the jurisdiction of such judges, or a place where judgment is entered. Hollywood and pulp fiction writers have greatly exaggerated the lawlessness of cowboys and ranchers in the Old West—however, the term in question was well known among them; no doubt, at least a few buckaroos had a first-hand experience with the hoosegow, regardless of their guilt or innocence.

housgau: *See* **hoosegow** (1).

hua!:

(*gua* [gwá] < *¡guarda!* 'watch out!' imperative of *guardar* < Germanic *wardôn* < *warôn* 'to attend to; to pay attention'). Carlisle: 1850. Blevins suggests that this command, used to urge a team of animals along, comes from the Spanish *¡Gua!*, meaning the same. Corominas is the only Spanish source to reference this term, and he glosses it briefly as an expression of admiration or fear. Perhaps this cry would have identified the trail driver as Spanish or Mexican to the cowboy who came across him on a long cattle drive. *See also* **wagh!**

huarache:

(Sp. model spelled same or *guarache* [warátʃe] from Tarascan). Carlisle: 1899. A crude open-toed sandal made of rawhide or leather strips, commonly worn by poor mestizos or Indians. The *DRAE* references *guarache* and *huarache* as Mexicanisms for crude sandals made of leather. Santamaría gives a similar definition for *guarache*. Cobos refers to *guarache* as "a sandal with a tire-casing sole," which is how they are manufactured today. Cowboys may not have worn these, but would have been familiar with this footgear among the poorer Mexicans they dealt with. *Alternate forms:* guarache, guarrache, huaracho. *See also* **teguas**.

hueco tanks:

(*hueco* [wéko] < *ocar* or *aocar* 'to dig; to dig up; to hollow out' < Latin *occāre* 'to rake the ground' plus *tank*). Holes in rock where rainwater accumulated and provided welcome moisture for travelers. Smith notes that these holes could be found along the overland trail near El Paso, Texas, and served as a well-known landmark to pioneers and convoys. *See also* **estanque**, **tank**.

huevosed:

(*huevo* 'egg' < Latin *ovum* 'egg'). Bentley: 1917. Bentley indicates that this term was probably confined to 1846–1848, the duration of the Mexican-American War. During this time, the verb 'to *huevo*' meant either to purchase or steal the eggs from a ranch, farm, or poultry yard. The phrase "*huevosed* the ranche" was coined during this time, and he suggests that it was formed by analogy from "vamoosed the ranche."

Indio:

(Sp. model spelled same [íŋdjo] < *India* (country)). The Spanish word for Indian, common in the Southwest. The *DRAE* indicates that it refers to someone indigenous to America or the West Indies. It also applies to a thing belonging to or related to American Indians.

> **he had his Indian up:**
>
> (A calque from the Spanish *se le subió el indio*, meaning the same). He was angry or lost his temper. The *DRAE* confirms that *subírsele a uno el indio* is a figurative expression used in the Americas that means to lose one's temper. Among mestizos it could be interpreted as a racist expression because it implies that one allowed the allegedly uncivilized and uncontrollable Indian side to get the best of him.

istle, ixtle:

(*iscle* [ískle] < Nahuatl *ichtli*; also *ixtle* < Nahuatl *ixtli*). *OED:* 1883. A fiber obtained from an agave or yucca plant, used to make carpets, nets, ropes, and other items. The *OED* indicates that it comes from *Bromelia sylvestris* and several species of agave, such as *Agave ixtli*. Santamaría glosses two related terms. He indicates that in Mexico *iscle* refers to the filament of the **maguey** plant before it has been rinsed. After the rinsing process, it is called **pita**. It is also the common name of several **agave** plants that produce the fiber, such as *Agave rigida* and *A. endlichiana*. *Ixtle* is a related Aztequism that has become a universal name for any vegetable fiber, especially the ones produced by plants of the genus *Agave*. By extension, it refers to several ropes made of such fiber used by *charros*. *See also* **lechuguilla**.

iztle:

(etymology not found). According to Blevins, a southwestern term for a kind of obsidian used by Indians for arrowheads. The term appears to be from Nahuatl but is not referenced by Cabrera or Santamaría or any other Spanish source.

jacal:

(Sp. model spelled same [xakál] < Nahuatl *xacalli* 'hut; cabin; house made of straw'; either from *xacámitl* 'adobe' and *calli* 'house' or from *xalli* 'sand'). Texas: 1838. A primitive hut or shelter, especially one owned by a Mexican or Indian. The *OED* describes it as a hut built of poles or stakes plastered over with mud. It also indicates that such huts are common in Mexico and the Southwest. The *DARE* notes that the term may also refer to the method or material used to construct such a hut. It is referenced in the *DRAE* as a term used in Mexico for a hut or hovel. Santamaría adds that it commonly refers to a hut made of **adobe**, with roof made of straw or thin strips of wood. *Alternate forms:* hackel, jacel, jackall, jeccal.

jackeroo: *See* **buckaroo** (1).

jakoma: *See* **hackamore.**

jaquima: *See* **hackamore.**

jarro:

(Sp. model spelled same [xáⁱo] < *jarra* < Arabic *ğárra* 'jar; jug; pitcher'). Glossed by Watts as a term used in Mexico and the Southwest for "an earthen pot." The *DRAE* references it as a clay, earthenware, glass, or metal vessel made in the shape of a jug or pitcher with a single handle. These jugs or pots might be used to transport drinking water, to heat water for coffee, or even to cook beans on the trail. They were also used by the Indians and Mexicans in the Southwest and most likely made their way into kitchens on the **haciendas** or **ranchos.**

jeccal: *See* **jacal.**

jerga: *See* **gerga.**

jerky:
(*charqui* [ʧárki] < Quechua *ch'arki*). California: 1848. According to Watts, strips of meat, especially beef, but also venison or buffalo meat, which are dried in the sun or over the smoke of a fire. Of course, this was a preferred way of preserving meat in the Old West. The *DRAE* glosses *charqui* as a South American synonym for *tasajo* or dried meat that is cured or salted to preserve it. *Alternate forms:* **carne asada,** carne seca, **carne seco,** charqui, jerk, jerkie, jerkmeat, jerky beef, tassajo. *See also* **tasajo.**

jerk:
(1) *See* **jerky** above. (2) South Carolina: c. 1770; Western Tennessee: 1835. As a verb, to preserve meat by cutting it into strips and drying them in the sun. The *DARE* notes that, with this meaning, *jerk* may be either a back formation from *jerky*, or it may have derived directly from the Spanish verb *charquear*, which has the same meaning.

jerked buffalo:
Carlisle: 1903. Buffalo meat that has been salted and dried.

jicara:
(*jícara* [xíkara] < Nahuatl *xicalli* 'cup made from a gourd'). Clark: 1900s. Usually a vase or bowl, but Watts notes that it can also refer to tightly woven containers made and used by Apache Indians. Carlisle defines it as "a drinking cup made by cutting a gourd in half." Santamaría defines *jícara* as the fruit of the *jícaro* or calabash tree. It is a hard, solid fruit whose flesh and seeds are similar to those of a squash. He also notes that the term is also applied to a wide-mouthed hemispherical vessel made from the *jícara* fruit. It is generally painted with many colors, polished and engraved, and often blackened with smoke. By extension, the term is also used in Mexico to refer to any vessel primarily used for drinking hot chocolate. The *DRAE* concurs and adds that in Spain *jícara* often refers to an earthenware vessel used for drinking hot chocolate. Cobos glosses it as a chocolate mug or a cup made from cutting a gourd shell in half.

jicarilla:
(Sp. model spelled same [xikaríǰa], diminutive of *jícara* [see above]). (1) Carlisle: 1867. A small cup used for drinking hot

chocolate, or a small, tightly woven basket. Cobos concurs with both of these definitions. *See* **jicara** *above*. (2) *OED:* 1850. An Apache tribe found primarily in New Mexico. Hendrickson suggests that the tribe takes its name from a hill in southeast Colorado or northern New Mexico shaped like an upside-down chocolate cup, a place where they once lived. He also notes that the tribe may have been named for the baskets woven by its members. *Also known as* Jicarilla Apaches.

jinete:
(Sp. model spelled same [xinéte] < Arabic *zanāti* or Vulgar Arabic *zenêti* 'an individual from Zeneta'). This term originally referred to a mounted soldier who fought with a lance and shield and used a saddle with short stirrups). According to Adams, an excellent horseman or a man who breaks horses for riding. Glossed in the *DRAE* as a man who is skilled in riding horses.

jornada:
(Sp. model spelled same [xornáδa], from another Romance language, probably Occitan, where it meant the same as in Spanish. The root *jorn* is from Latin *diurnum* 'diurnal, taking place during the daytime,' an adjective nominalized in Late Latin, meaning 'daytime'). (1) A day's journey, or the distance that could be traveled in one day. (2) A long cattle drive or wagon trip, often one in which water is not encountered for many hours. The *DRAE* glosses *jornada* as the distance normally traveled in one day or an entire journey, even if it is one that takes longer than a day.

junta:
(Sp. model spelled same [xúŋta] < Latin *junctūra* 'meeting, assembly'). Among cattlemen, a business meeting. The *DRAE* and Simon and Schuster's International Dictionary confirm that 'meeting' or 'conference' is one of the meanings of *junta* in Spanish. Neither source makes specific reference to the use of this term in the cattle industry, but it is obviously an extension or specific application.

jusgado: *See* **hoosegow** (1).

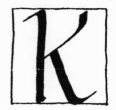

kenyon: *See* **canyon** (1).

kerbase: *See* **cabeza.**

ladino:

(Sp. model spelled same [laðíno] < Latin *latŕnum* 'Latin.' In the Middle Ages it meant Romance, as opposed to Arabic, and referred to a Moor who could speak Latin; with reference to books, it applied to 'fine, learned, Latinlike' languages (according to Corominas), and later came to mean 'skillful,' 'astute,' or 'wise'). Texas: 1892. Originally, a wild longhorn, but more recently, a horse or cow that is vicious, wild, and unmanageable, and seems to possess a certain crafty intelligence. The *DARE* indicates that this term may be used as a noun or as an adjective. Clark notes that it is sometimes applied to a "crafty or wily person." In Spanish, this term originally applied to a person who knew Latin or was wise or learned in general. It has since come to mean 'clever' or 'knowledgeable.' Santamaría confirms that in Coahuila, Mexico, the term is used to refer to a bull that, having been at one point confined to a corral, on its return to the field is not only wild again but seems to possess a certain knowledge of humans that allows it to evade all the cowboys who attempt to capture it.

ladino (clover):

DARE: 1925. According to the *DARE*, white Dutch clover (*Trifolium repens*).

largo: *See* **latigo** (1).

lariat:

(*la riata* [laȓjáta], derived from the definite article *la* plus *riata*, variant form of *reata* 'rope' [refers especially to a rope used to tie horses or mules in single file] < *reatar* < Latin **reaptāre* 'to tie'). (1) Oklahoma:

El Ladino

1832. A long rope, usually with a *honda* at one end to form a loop or noose, used for catching, throwing, and tethering animals. The *DRAE* glosses *reata* as a cord, strap, or belt used to fasten or tie something. It is also a rope or cord used to tie animals in single file. *Alternate forms:* lareat, lariat rope, lariet, lariette, larreyette, laryetto. *See also* **lasso**, **reata**. (2) Southwest: 1846. In English, this term can also be used as a verb, meaning to catch or tether using a lariat. The *DARE* notes that when followed by "out," it can mean to purchase land from the government without occupying it. *Alternate form:* larriet.

hair lariat:

Watts refers to this as a lariat made with horsehair. It is used for tying, but is too lightweight to be used for throwing animals. *Also called* hair reata, hair rope.

lariat pin:

According to Watts, a stake to which horses are tethered. *Also called* a picket pin, stake pin, hitch pin.

larigo:

(*látigo* [see latigo]). (1) Another name for the cinch ring on a saddle. (2) *See* **latigo** (1). Watts presumes correctly that it is a variation of *latigo*.

laryetto: *See* **lariat** (1).

lass rope: *See* **lasso** (1).

lasso:

(*lazo* [láso]< Vulgar Latin *lacium*, simplification of Latin *laqueum* 'loop; knot'). (1) *DARE*: 1891. A long rope, generally one made of rawhide, with an adjustable loop or noose on one end for snaring and securing animals. *Alternate forms:* lass rope, lassoo, lazo. *Also called* **reata**, string. (2) West-central California: 1831. As a verb, to catch an animal (or other object) using a lasso. (3) Figuratively, to snare. The *DRAE* gives several definitions for *lazo*, among them a braided rope with a running knot on one end, used to snare bulls, horses, and other animals by throwing them by the legs or the head.

latigo:

(*látigo* [látiɣo], a term of uncertain origin, common to Spanish and Portuguese; given that the oldest meaning is 'strap used for tying something,' it is probable that the term derives from Gothic **laittug*, which would also be related to the Anglo-Saxon *lâttêh* 'halter rope'). (1) Clark: 1880s. A piece of leather three to five feet long and two inches wide used to fasten the cinch onto the saddle. One end is fastened to the cinch ring on the saddle and the other passed through the ring on the end of the cinch and the saddle ring and secured with a knot once the desired adjustment is obtained. *Alternate forms:* ladigo, largo, larigo, latigo strap. The form *larigo* is a spelling pronunciation; English speakers seeing the term in its written form would have pronounced the intervocalic {t} (or {d}) in the first variant form as a flap, which is how an intervocalic {r} in Spanish is pronounced. *Largo* is a later term that evolved from *larigo* via schwa deletion. Bentley notes that *largo* is extremely common today on ranches where a western-style saddle is employed. (2) Hendrickson indicates that the term also refers to a rawhide thong that secures a gun holster to the leg. The *DRAE* glosses it either as a long, thin, flexible whip made from rope, leather, baleen, or another material used principally to discipline horses, or as a cord or strap used to secure and adjust the cinch of a saddle.

lechuguilla:

(Sp. model spelled same [letʃuɣíʝa], diminutive of *lechuga* < Latin *lactūca* 'lettuce'). Texas: 1834. Any of a variety of agave plants, especially *Agave lechuguilla*, native to the Southwest. Santamaría indicates that *lechuguilla* is a name given to several plants, including various species of agave. It also refers to ropes made from the fibers of the plant. Cobos glosses it as "sand verbena, Indian hemp, or dogbane." *Alternate forms:* lechugilla, letchugia. *See also* **maguey**.

legaderos:
(possibly a blend < English *leg* and *rosaderos*). According to Watts, "stirrup straps." Not referenced in Spanish sources.

leppy:
(*lepe* [lépe] < *lépero* [lépero], of uncertain origin; probably derived by process of epenthesis from *lepra* 'leprosy' or from English *leper*). Carlisle: 1923. According to Hendrickson, a motherless calf, or by extension, an orphaned lamb or colt. Santamaría indicates *lepe* is used in northwestern Mexico and glosses it as an orphaned calf that suckles from another mother. *Alternate terms:* bum, bum calf, bummer, bummie, **dogie**.

llano:
(Sp. model spelled same [ǰáno]< Latin *plānus* 'plain' or 'flat'). Carlisle: 1844. A plain or prairie. Glossed in the *DRAE* as an adjective meaning level or flat, and by extension, a level field, plain, or prairie. *Alternate form:* yarner.

llano estacado:
(Sp. model spelled same [ǰáno] [see above] plus [estakáðdo], nominalized perfective participle of *estacar* 'to enclose or fence in' < *estaca* 'stake,' perhaps of Germanic origin [such as < Gothic *stakka]; in this case, *estacado* should be glossed as 'fenced, barricaded or stockaded'). Texas: 1883. A wide plateau in Texas and New Mexico, the site of a trail from San Antonio, Texas, to Santa Fe, New Mexico, used by early Spanish explorers. Cobos indicates that 'Stockaded Plain' or 'Palisaded Plain' would be a more appropriate translation of the Spanish *llano estacado* than 'Staked Plain,' which is how the name of the region is generally translated into English. He notes that Spanish explorers named the plain after a rimrock formation that resembled a stone fortress. The assumption by English speakers that the plain was named for a trail marked by stakes driven into the earth is a misconception or simply the product of a poor translation.

loafer, loafer wolf, lover wolf: *See* **lobo** (1), (2).

lobo:

(Sp. model spelled same [lóβo] 'wolf' < Latin *lupum*). (1) A wolf in general. *Alternate forms:* loafer, loafer wolf, lobo wolf, lobos wolf, loper, lover wolf. (2) *DARE*: 1852. The combination *lobo wolf* generally refers to the gray or timber wolf (*Canis lupus*). Also loafer wolf. (3) Texas: 1967. A coyote (*C. latrans*). (4) West: 1907. An outcast or loner. *Also called* lobo wolf. Spanish sources gloss **lobo** as a general term for a wolf. Santamaría gives *C. mexicanus*, *C. occidentalis*, and *C. lupus* as the three most common species by this name.

lobo stripe:

West: 1941. As Watts notes, a dark stripe running down the middle of the back of some animals, including Texas and Mexican longhorn cattle. *See also* **bayo coyote**.

loco:

(Sp. model spelled same [lóko], a term of uncertain origin, found in both Spanish and Portuguese; it comes from an earlier form *laucu, which may be from Arabic *láu̯qa*, *láu̯q*, the feminine plural form of the adjective *álwaq* 'foolish; crazy'). (1) West: 1887. As an adjective, crazy or obsessed, according to Hendrickson. (2) *See* **loco-weed**. (3) *DARE*: 1889. Often applies to a person or animal whose mind has been affected by locoweed. In this latter sense, *locoed* is also used. The *DARE* glosses this as a distemper caused by ingesting noxious plants that afflicts cattle. Its symptoms are erratic behavior, often characterized by lethargy and impaired coordination. *Also called* loco disease, locoism. (4) *DARE*: 1852. As a noun, a crazy or obsessed individual. *Also called* loco blossom. (5) West: 1884. As a verb, to craze or derange. Spanish sources concur with definitions (1) and (4), although the association of (1) with the effects of a poisonous plant does not figure in Spanish definitions.

locoweed:

(*loco* [lóko] [see above]). Missouri: 1844. Any of several poisonous leguminous plants that cause a sort of distemper in cattle known as *loco* (disease). The *DARE* notes that the two most common plants of this name are the milk vetch (a plant of the genus *Astragalus*), and *Oxytropis lambertii*. *Also called* loco, loco grass, loco plant, loco vetch. Santamaría references *loco* as a plant commonly called *acacia* in Mexico. However, he notes that this plant belongs to the genus *Robinia*, while English sources indicate that most plants known as locoweed are of the genera *Oxytropis* and *Astragalus*.

melon loco:
> Texas: 1886. Referenced in the *DARE* as "a cucurbitaceous plant (*Apodanthera undulata*) native from southern Arizona to western Texas."

purple loco:
> A variety of locoweed that produces purple blossoms.

scarlet loco:
> Carlisle: 1927. A variety of locoweed found in arid regions.

white loco:
> A variety of locoweed native to the Rocky Mountains. It produces dark green leaves and white blossoms. *Also known as* crazy weed.

loper: *See* **lobo** (1).

los muertos no hablan:
> (Sp. model spelled same, [los̠mwértos̠nóə́βlan] consisting of the masculine plural definite article *los* and *muertos*, plural of *muerto* 'dead person, corpse' < Latin *mortuus*, perfective participle of *morīre* 'to die' plus adverb *no*, and *hablan*, third person singular conjugation of *hablar* 'to speak' < Vulgar Latin *fabulare* 'to converse; to talk'). Correctly translated by Hendrickson as "dead men don't talk." Hendrickson notes that the expression in English is likely to be a calque from Spanish. Slatta (personal communciation) provides the English version "dead men tell no tales" as an equivalent. Another common English saying "three can keep a secret if two of them are dead" conveys essentially the same message.

macardy, macarte, mecarte: *See* **mecate.**

macheer, machere: *See* **mochila.**

machero:

(*mechero* [meʧéro] < *mecha* 'wick,' probably from French *mèche* < **mecca*, probably of pre-Roman origin). Referenced by Watts as a portable fire-making instrument used for lighting cigars and cigarettes. He suggests that the form used in the Southwest resulted from a blend with the English *match*. 'Pocket cigarette lighter' is among the definitions given by the *DRAE* for *mechero*.

madrina:

(Sp. model spelled same [maðrína] < Latin *matrīna* 'godmother' < *matrem* 'mother'). The bell-mare, or the mare that serves as the lead in a herd. The *DRAE* concurs, although it also lists several unrelated definitions. Santamaría glosses *madrina* as a tame horse that is tied with another in order to aid in the breaking of the new horse. It also refers to a tame horse on which a rider sits and leads an unbroken horse on which an **amansador**, or horse-breaker, rides. Islas indicates that the term *madrina* may refer to the rider of a tame horse or to the team consisting of a horse and its rider.

maguey:

(Sp. model spelled same [maɣéi̯], of Taino origin). (1) *DARE*: 1830. Another name for the agave plant. Both Blevins and Hendrickson reference *agave*, Hendrickson noting that the term derives from the name of "the daughter of the legendary Cadmus who introduced the Greek alphabet." While many species make up the Agave genus, the most remarkable one is the so-called century plant (*A. americana*). According to legend, the plant earned its name because it only blooms once every one hundred years. However, it actually blooms any time after fifteen years, usually in twenty to thirty years. Both Blevins and Hendrickson state that the plant dies after blooming, but no Spanish source reaffirms this. According to the *DRAE* and Blevins, it is originally from Mexico (although introduced into Europe in the sixteenth century and naturalized on the Mediterranean coast). The agave, maguey, or century plant is a light green succulent with fleshy leaves and yellowish blooms. The leaves are similar in arrangement to a triangular pyramid or a rosette; the edges as well as the tips of the leaves are covered with sharp spines, and the plant may grow up to some twenty to twenty-three feet in height. This particular plant and related species are used as hedges or fences in dry, hot areas and they produce fiber (thread), alcoholic beverages (mescal, tequila and pulque), soaps, and foodstuffs. In Mexico, the term *maguey* is used much more frequently to refer to these same plants. The *DARE* notes that this name is limited to the Southwest and the Gulf states. *Also known as* amole, century plant, **lechuguilla**, **mescal**. (2) New Mexico: 1899. A rope, such as a lasso, made from the fibers of a *maguey* plant. Santamaría and the *DRAE* concur with the first definition, but no Spanish source glosses the term as a kind of rope. *Alternate forms:* maguay, McGay (the latter is a folk etymology).

major domo:

(*mayordomo* [maĵorðómo] < Late Latin *major domus* < Latin *maior* 'higher; highest' and *domus* 'domestic'). (1) California: 1834. The foreman on a ranch or farm or the overseer of a mission. By extension, the supervisor over any group or project. (2) New Mexico: 1885. In New Mexico, the manager of an irrigation system. *Alternate forms:* majordomo, mayor domo, mayordomo. *Mayordomo* is glossed in the *DRAE* as the head servant in a household. Santamaría references it as the employee of a ranch who is second in command to the administrator or boss (*jefe*), is superior to the overseer or foreman (*capataz*), and is responsible for supervising and directing the activities of the workers. Cobos gives several definitions in use in New Mexico and southern Colorado, including a foreman or manager, an overseer, or a 'ditch boss.'

mal pais:

(*malpaís* [malpaís] < *malo* 'bad' < Latin *malum* and *país* 'country' < French *pays* 'rural territory' < Latin *pagensim* 'country dweller' < Latin *pagum* 'agricultural district'). (1) *DARE*: 1844. Rugged terrain, bad country, especially if the ground is composed of eroded basaltic lava. *Alternate forms:* malapai, malapais, malipi, mallapy, malpais, malpiar. Santamaría references *malpaís* as arid, desertlike, and unpleasant terrain. It lacks water or any type of vegetation because it is generally covered with volcanic rock. Cobos glosses it as "lava beds" or "badlands." (2) Arizona: 1881. Basaltic lava, or a piece of volcanic rock. Sobarzo concurs with this definition. *Alternate form:* malley.

maleta:

(Sp. model spelled same [maléta] < Old French *malete* 'suitcase; valise'). A bag used with a saddle, generally one made of rawhide. The *DRAE* glosses it as a general term for a suitcase, but Cobos indicates that it may also refer to a lady's handbag, a wallet, or a saddlebag.

malipi, mallapy, malpiar: *See* **mal pais** (1).

malley: *See* **malpais** (2).

manada:

(Sp. model spelled same [mãnáδa] < Spanish *mano* 'hand' < Latin *manum* and suffix *-ada*, indicating capacity; literally, 'handful'). (1) California: 1842. In general, a herd of wild or tame horses, but more specifically, a herd consisting of a stallion and several mares and colts. (2) Carlisle: 1848. By extension from (1), any herd of horses or cattle. *Alternate form*: manather. *Manada* is referenced in the *DRAE* as a herd or flock of livestock cared for by a herder. It also refers generally to a grouping of animals of the same species that stay together, such as ducks or wolves.

manadero:

(Sp. model spelled same [mãnaδéro] < *manada* [see above] and suffix *-ero*, 'profession or trade'). The stallion in a *manada* of horses. Santamaría, Sobarzo, and Islas note that in Mexico this term refers to a male donkey that mates with a number of females. The *DRAE* references it as the herdsman who cares for a *manada*.

manather: *See* **manada** (2).

manga:

(Sp. model spelled same [mą́ŋga] < Latin *manicam* 'sleeve' < *manum* 'hand'). Clark: 1834. A **poncho** or cloak used to protect the upper body against rain and cold weather. Referenced in the *DRAE* as a piece of cloth that covers the body from the shoulders almost to the feet. It may also refer to a rubber cape used to protect one from the rain while riding horseback. Santamaría concurs with the latter definition, and notes that it generally is fastened at the front and is known more commonly as a *manga de hule* in Mexico. A cowpoke needed some protection against the sudden cloudbursts or soggy days when the rain, wind, and mud created difficult working conditions. A *manga*, poncho, or waterproof jacket served that purpose.

mangana:

(Sp. model spelled same [mą̃ŋgána] < *manganilla* 'trick, ruse' < Vulgar Latin **manganellam*, plural diminutive form of *manganum* 'war machine'). Texas: 1929. A rope throw used by a cowboy to catch an animal by its forefeet. The *DRAE* glosses it as a loop thrown at the front feet of a horse or bull while it is running with the intention of making it fall and catching it.

mangana de pie:

(Sp. model spelled same [mą̃ŋgánaðepjé] *mangana* [see above] and *de* 'of' and *pie* 'foot' < Latin *pedem*). A variation of the *mangana*, in which the cowboy forms a loop on the ground and throws it with his foot as the animal passes by. Adams calls this a "fancy throw" and notes that it is seldom used in actual work.

manko:

(*manco* [mą́ŋko] < Latin *mancum* 'disabled; maimed; incomplete'). Crippled, as an animal with an injured forefoot. The *DRAE* indicates that it describes a person who has lost an arm or a hand or an animal that has lost a forefoot. It also refers to an animal or person that has lost the use of one of these members. Santamaría glosses it as a four-legged animal that limps because of an impaired forefoot, even if the injury is temporary and the animal has not lost complete use of the member. In the movies, a *manco* horse was frequently put out of its misery by a shot heard but not seen. In real life, depending on the seriousness of the injury, the horse might be nursed back to health, particularly if the outfit was short on working mounts.

La Mangana

(The forefoot catch)

Vaquero

Reata

Orejano

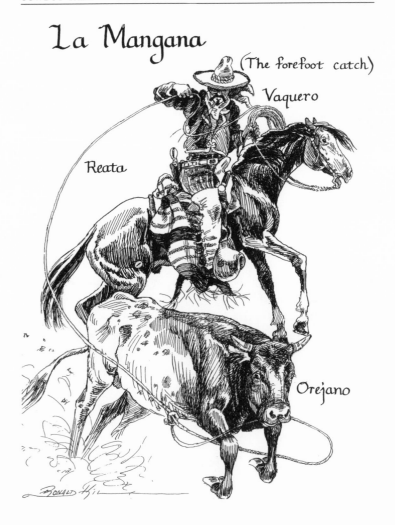

mano:

(Sp. model spelled same [máno] < Latin *manum* 'hand'). (1) The General Spanish term for 'hand,' sometimes heard in the Southwest. (2) Clark: 1890s. The stone used to grind corn by hand on a **metate**. Santamaría and the *DRAE* confirm that this term applies to a stone used to grind corn, cacao, and other grains or foodstuffs into a fine powder (*masa*). Both the American Indians and the Mexicans prepared food this way. No doubt a few buckaroos became familiar with the implement and term, having enjoyed a meal thus prepared.

manso:

(Sp. model spelled same [mãnso] < Vulgar Latin *mansum* 'meek' < Latin *mansuētum*). *OED:* 1836. An Indian who has been converted to Christianity. Santamaría glosses *indio manso* as a term still used in Mexico (at the time of publication) to refer to an Indian who lives in a settlement or Indian encampment and submits himself to the government, as opposed to one who is still considered 'savage' or 'wild.' The diminutive form, *mansito*, is also common. Such Indians posed little threat to pioneers, traders, trappers, and ranchers and their hands.

manta:

(Sp. model spelled same [mãŋta] < *manto* 'mantle; cloak' < Late Latin *mantum* 'short cloak'). Arizona: 1887. A pack cover, generally a large cotton or canvas one (approximately nine feet by twelve feet), laid over the top of a loaded packsaddle to protect the goods from rain or snowstorms. It may also have been wrapped around a load of goods before setting it on the packsaddle. Among the several definitions given by the *DRAE* for this term is a one describing piece of ordinary cotton fabric used in Mexico or a piece of cloth used as protection for the horses. Santamaría defines it as an ordinary piece of cotton cloth used primarily for everyday clothing. No Spanish source gives a definition identical to the southwestern meaning of 'pack cover.' It is possible that the first *manta* was an improvised one and the name simply stuck. *Alternate form*: manto.

manzana:

(Sp. model spelled same [mãnsána] < *mazana* < Vulgar Latin [*malam*] *mattianam*, the name of a popular type of apple, probably named for the agriculturist Caius Matius). Carlisle: 1846–47. Glossed by Carlisle as an apple, but in the Southwest it refers to the saddlehorn, which is shaped like an apple cut in half. Santamaría confirms that the term also has this meaning in Mexico. *See also* **apple—apple-horn**.

marrons:

Wild horses. An aphæresis of cimarrones. *Alternate form*: maroons.

masketo: *See* **mesquite** (1).

matanza:

(Sp. model spelled same [matánsa] < *matar* 'to kill; to slaughter,' probably from Vulgar Latin **mattāre* 'to strike, to knock down' <

mattum 'stupid; brutalized'). The slaughtering of cattle, or the slaughterhouse itself. Blevins indicates that in Spanish California this term referred especially to "the killing of cattle for hides and tallow." The *DRAE* defines it as the process of killing pigs, extracting the bacon, making use of the loin and other parts, and the making of blood sausage. It also refers in Spanish to the portion of livestock that is set apart for slaughtering. A Spanish synonym that shares the same root is *matadero*.

McCarthy, McCarty: *See* **mecate.**

McGay: *See* **maguey.**

mecate:

(Sp. model spelled same [mekáte] < Nahuatl *mécatl* 'rope or cord' < *metl* 'maguey'). California: 1849. According to Blevins, a rope made of horsehair or **maguey** used for leading and tethering horses, or as reins with a **hackamore**. The *DRAE* defines it as a type of twine, cord, or rope made of agave fibers. Santamaría defines it as any rope made of vegetable fiber used for tying. By extension, it also refers to any rope made from twisted or braided fibers, provided it is thin and is used for tying. *Alternate forms:* macardy, macarte, McCarthy, McCarty, mecarte. The supposed surnames are folk etymologies. No doubt some ranch hand who knew little or no Spanish pronounced the term with English phonology, having convinced himself that McCart(h)y (a cowboy legend in some distant region?) was the inventor or master craftsman of the *mecate*.

mecheer: *See* **mochila.**

mesa:

(Sp. model spelled same [mésa] < Latin *mensam* 'table'). (1) Northwestern Texas: 1840. A hill or mountain with a flat top or a steep-sided plateau. (2) Nebraska: 1927. According to the *DARE*, this term has a specific meaning in Nebraska; it refers to "a steep gully along a river." The *DRAE* defines *mesa* as an extended piece of elevated flat land surrounded by valleys or cliffs. This geographical term, along with a few others such as **arroyo** and *(box) canyon*, is linked in the popular mind with gunslingers, rustlers, sheriffs, ranchers and cowboys, thanks to Hollywood and pulp fiction. In fact, many outlaws hid out in the badlands.

cloud mesa:
A reflection or other duplication of a mesa, according to Hendrickson.

mesilla:
(Sp. model spelled same [mesíʝa], diminutive of *mesa* [see above]). According to Blevins, this diminutive of *mesa*, was heard sometimes in the Southwest.

mescal:
(*mexcal* or *mezcal* [meskál] < Nahuatl *metl* 'maguey' and *(i)xcalli* 'stew' < *ixcalhuia* 'to cook or boil something.' The original meaning of this term refers to an intoxicating drink obtained from the maguey or agave plant). (1) New Mexico: 1831. Another name for the agave plant. Also refers to the root or the young bud stalk of the plant used for food. *See also* **maguey**. *Alternate forms:* mascal, mescale, mezcal, muscal, muscale. (2) California: 1833. An intoxicating drink prepared with the fermented juice or pulp of the agave plant. By extension, any intoxicating drink. *Also called* mescal liquor. (3) Southwest: 1887. Another name for the peyote plant. *See* **peyote**. (4) According to Blevins, this term also applies to a food prepared from mescal (1). The *DRAE* references *mezcal* as a variety of agave or a liquor obtained by fermenting and distilling the heads of the plant. Santamaría defines *mexcal* (or *mezcal*) as an alcoholic drink extracted by distilling the fleshy leaf or the head of some species of maguey. He notes that the species used for making the drink are *Agave mexicana*, *A. wixlinzeni*, *A. desipiens*. The drink is popular in central and northern Mexico as well as in New Mexico and Texas.

mescal bean:
(1) *DARE*: 1856. *See* **frijolillo**. (2) *DARE*: 1888. The dried tip of the peyote plant, according to *DARE*. *Compare* mescal button. (3) According to Watts, "the bean of the *Sophora secundiflora*, an evergreen bush with violet flowers."

mescal bud:
The young flowering stalk of the agave plant, as referenced by Blevins.

mescal button:
Southwest: 1887. The dried top of the *peyote* cactus. It induces hallucinations when ingested. By extension, this name is also

applied to the peyote cactus itself. *See* **peyote**. *Also known as* mescal head.

mescal ceremony:

A ceremony performed by Plains Indians that incorporates mescal liquor.

mescal rattle:

According to Blevins, a rattle made from a gourd used in a mescal ceremony.

mescal thread:

A thread from the agave plant.

Mescaleros:

(*mezcalero* [meskaléro] < *mezcal* or *mexcal* [see above] and suffix *-ero*, 'member of tribe,' in this case, 'mescal eaters'). Carlisle: 1927. A tribe of Apaches inhabiting the region east of the Rio Grande, so named because the baked mescal root was an important part of their diet. The *DRAE* defines *mezcalero* as an individual belonging to a tribe of Apache Indians located in Mexico.

mescalism:

Glossed by Blevins as "the practice of taking peyote (mescal) to gain self-knowledge."

Meskin, Mexkin: *See* **Mexican—Mex.**

mesquite:

(*mezquite* [meskíte], apocope of *mizquicuáhuitl* 'mesquite tree' < Nahuatl *mízquitl* 'tree that produces gum that can be used as dye' and *cuáhuitl* 'tree'). (1) *DARE*: 1805; Texas: 1834. A shrub or small tree of the genus *Prosopis*, especially *P. juliflora*. By extension, a thicket formed by these plants. *Alternate forms:* masketo, mesketis, meskit, mesquiet, mesquit, mesquito, mezquit, mezquite, moscheto, mosquito, musqueto, musquit, skeet. (2) Texas: 1898. Referenced by the *DARE* as "a horsemint." (3) Louisiana: 1913. A variety of *huisache*, including *Acacia farnesiana*. (4) *See* **mesquite grass**. The *DRAE* defines *mezquite* as an American rubber-producing tree of the *Mimosa* family, similar to an acacia. An extract obtained from the leaves can be used to cure ophthalmia. Santamaría describes the tree in more detail than the *DRAE*. He gives the genus and species *Prosopis juliflora* (Cf.

above) and indicates that it is a leguminous tree found in abundance in
Mexico. It may grow to a great height, but ordinarily does not exceed
seven to nine feet. Its branches are spread apart and don't provide a
very complete shade; its leaves are composed of an even number of
spiny leaflets; its fragrant white flowers grow in sprays or sprigs; and
it produces a beanlike fruit. The tree grows in high altitudes and arid
climates, especially in sandy ground near the edge of rivers. Its bark
exudes a pungent gum used by some residents of Mexico as a food
and as an adulterating agent for gum arabic when dissolved in sugar
water. The tree is also valued for its compact heavy wood, which can
be polished; its fruit and leaves, which are often used for forage; its
seeds, which are toasted and mixed with coffee. When ground into a
flourlike substance, the fruit makes a pleasant-tasting drink, and the
leaves when boiled are used as a home remedy to cure inflammation
of the eyes (the curative is known as *bálsamo de mezquite*).

honey mesquite:

A common variety of mesquite found in the Southwest. *Alternate term:* algarroba.

mesquital:

(*mesquital* [meskitál] < *mezquite* [see above] and suffix -*al* 'an
abundance of'). A grove of mesquite (1), or an area where it is the
prominent form of vegetation. The *DRAE* concurs.

mesquite bean:

California: 1846. The seed or seedpod of the mesquite, which
Blevins notes is prepared as a food by Indians and ground to form
the basis of an alcoholic drink.

mesquite grass:

Texas: 1823. Any of a number of grasses growing near mesquite.
They are used as forage for animals. The *DARE* gives a number of
plants often called mesquite grass, including **grama grass**, a velvet grass (including *Holcus lanatus*), buffalo grass (*Buchloe dactyloides*), one of two needlegrasses (*Stipa viridula* or *Aristida
purpurea*), a **galleta** (either curly mesquite or *Hilaria jamesii*), or
a muhly grass (including *Muhlenbergia porteri*). Alternate form:
mesquit grass.

mesquite meal:
A food made from the ground seed of the mesquite plant.

mesquite prairie:
According to Watts, a prairie comprised of mesquite grass.

mesquite root:
Glossed by Blevins as "a good fuel in a barren country."

mestaña, mesteño: *See* **mustang** (1).

metate:
(Sp. model spelled same [metáte] < Nahuatl *métlatl* 'stone for grinding corn'). Texas: 1834. A stone with a rectangular, concave surface upon which corn and other grains are ground. The *DRAE* defines it as a stone upon which corn and other grains are ground using a cylindrical stone instrument, similar to a mortar and pestle. It is used by rural women in Mexico and Guatemala; in Spain it is used to grind chocolate by hand. Santamaría concurs, adding that the *metate* generally is four-sided and somewhat cone-shaped and is supported by three feet that protrude from the bottom of the stone. *Compare* **molcajete** *and* **mortero**. *See also* **mano**.

Mexican:
(1) New York: 1912. Of inferior quality, shoddy or shabby; makeshift or stopgap; also illegal. The *DARE* notes that this meaning is derogatory, used chiefly in the West and Southwest. (2) *DARE*: 1968. Regarding clock time or scheduled events, belated, tardy, or unreliable. *Compare* **Navajo—Navajo time**. (3) *DARE* (from Texas to California): 1854. Spicy (said of foods). (4) Southwestern California: 1962. As the *DARE* notes, in several combinations, such as Mexican toothache, Mexican disease, and Mexican sickness, it refers to diarrhea. (5) A Mexican peso. *Also known as* adobe dollar, 'dobe dollar. (6) The typical bean used in Mexican dishes: pinto or kidney bean (*Phaseolus vulgaris*). The adjective *Mexican* is also used in various combinations, most of which denote plants and animals native to the border states and northern Mexico. Other adjectival constructions refer to aspects of southwestern culture, often reflecting the cowboy's sarcasm. Those that are especially pertinent to his era and profession are listed below.

Mex:

Glossed by Watts as "a common abbreviation of Mexican, used by Anglos as a noun and adjective." The poem "A Border Affair" written by Badger Clark and later set to music and retitled "Spanish Is the Lovin' Tongue" by Bill Simon, an Arizona cowboy, contains the line: "She was Mex and I was white." *Alternate forms:* Meskin, Mexkin.

Mex livin':

Carlisle: 1853. A table stocked with typical Mexican dishes.

Mexican bit:

A horse's bit that uses a ring in place of the standard "Anglo curb-chain and curb strap," according to Watts.

Mexican breakfast:

Referenced by Hendrickson as a jocular expression for "a cigarette and a glass of water."

Mexican buckskin:

Adams indicates that this term is used by northern cowboys for a longhorn driven north from Texas.

Mexican fireball:

According to Clark, "a short, roundish cactus with long, thin spines." He indicates that it is often hard to see and causes considerable pain when stepped on by horses and people. The *DARE* references the genus and species as *Ferocactus acanthodes var lecontei*.

Mexican iron:

Rawhide, so named because Mexicans use it for its strength.

Mexican packsaddle:

Another name for the **aparejo**.

Mexican peak:

A **sombrero**.

Mexican promotion:

A new title, without a raise in pay, as referenced by Hendrickson.

Mexican saddle:
Clark: 1840s. Correctly glossed by Watts as "a heavy saddle with a high cantle and bow and a flat, wide-based saddlehorn."

Mexican spur:
Clark: 1860s. A spur with an especially large rowel. While Mexicans favored this type of spur, some Anglo cowboys found it unnecessarily cruel to the horse.

Mexican standoff:
Originally, a gunfight with no clear winner; later, an expression for getting away alive from a serious situation. Hendrickson notes that it also came to refer to a pitching duel in baseball.

Mexican strawberries:
Beans.

Mexican sweat:
Texas: 1969. A card game in which each player receives seven cards placed face down. Players take turns turning cards over and placing bets to see who can beat the card turned face up. *Also known as* "red dog" *and* "don't peek."

Mexican town:
West: 1930. A barrio occupied primarily by Mexicans. *See also* **Sonora town**, **Chihuahua town**.

Mexicanized:
Carlisle: 1925. Glossed by Carlisle as "made in the Mexican manner."

Mexicano:
(same or *mejicano* [mexikáno] < *México* and suffix *-ano* 'of or pertaining to'). (1) A Mexican; Watts indicates that this term is common on ranges in the West. (2) Carlisle: 1931. According to Carlisle, "a black Mexican sweet cigarette or cigar." *See also* **cigarro**.

Mexicans don't count:
As Hendrickson notes, this was a derogatory expression used by gunmen in the Southwest, suggesting that they kept count of all

of the men whom they had killed, except the Indians and Mexicans. *Also* "Indians don't count."

mochila:

(Sp. model spelled same [motʃíla] < *mochil* 'messenger boy' [because a messenger often carries a *mochila* or knapsack] < Basque *mutil* or *motil* 'boy' or 'servant' < Latin *mutilis* 'mutilated,' 'blunt,' or 'cropped.' The term apparently referred to small boys who wore their hair short.) Oregon: 1856. A cloth or leather cover for a saddle, often with pockets, called **cantina***s*. Referenced in the *DRAE* as a sort of cover hanging from the saddletree on a type of saddle with short stirrups. Santamaría glosses it as a saddlebag or knapsack in the shape of a small chest or bag. *Alternate forms:* macheer, machere, machilla, mecheer, mochile, mochiler.

mocho:

(Sp. model spelled same [mótʃo], of uncertain origin). Bentley: 1824–1830. A cow with a drooping horn or a damaged ear or tail. Glossed in the *DRAE*, among other things, as an animal missing a horn. *See also* gotch.

moharrie: *See* **mujer.**

mohina:

(*mohíno* [moíno], term of uncertain origin, perhaps related to *moho* 'rust,' 'mold,' or 'mildew,' that originally compared an unhappy person to a rusty object or a plant covered with moss or mold. The principal meaning of *mohíno* in Spanish is 'sad' or 'gloomy.') Carlisle references this term as "animal-like," but no Spanish source gives a similar definition. The quote provided by Carlisle indicates that the term probably refers not to the nature of an animal, but to a color ("Buckskin, black, *mohina*, grey, r'arin' roan or buckin' bay . . ."). The *DRAE* indicates that this term may apply to a horse or cow with a black hide and face. Cobos gives a similar definition for *mojino*.

molcajete:

(Sp. model spelled same [molkaxéte] < Nahuatl *molcáxitl* or *mulcáxitl* < *molli* 'stew or mole' and *cáxitl* 'earthenware bowl'). A roundish, three-legged mortar used for grinding hot peppers and spices. The *DRAE* references it as a large stone or earthenware mortar with three short, strong feet, used for preparing salsas. Santamaría indicates that it is a small, three-legged mortar used by the lower classes to grind spices and *chiles* and to prepare salsas; it is even used occasionally as a serving dish for salsas. The instrument used with the *molcajete* for grinding is called a *tejolote. Compare* **metate, mortero, mano.**

Montana:
(*montaña* [mõŋtáɲa] < Vulgar Latin **montanea*, neuter plural form of adjective *montaneum* 'mountain'). Clark: 1860s. The forty-first state of the union; its name comes from the Spanish *montaña* 'mountain.' *Alternate form:* Montany.

> **Montana feathers:**
> Straw filling for a mattress.

> **Montana peak:**
> According to Hendrickson, "a cowboy hat with a conical top."

monte:
(Sp. model spelled same [mõŋte] < Latin *montem* 'mountain'). (1) California: 1851. An uncultivated piece of land, generally heavily thicketed with **chaparral** or **mesquite.** The *DRAE* references it as uncultivated land covered with trees, shrubs, or bushes. Santamaría glosses it as wild vegetation in general. (2) Clark: 1840s. Either a card game played with forty-five cards in which bets are made on the two cards dealt to each player or a con game in which the dealer lays down three cards and bets that a player cannot find a certain card, generally the queen of spades or an ace. The *DRAE* references *monte* as a game of chance and betting in which the dealer takes two cards from the bottom of the deck and two from the top and then returns all four cards to the deck and starts revealing cards until one that matches one of the original four in number is found to win a hand. *Monte* also refers to a popular card game also known as *banca.* The *DRAE* also references *monte* as a pile (or mountain) of cards left over after each player has had his share; the *OED* suggests that the card games were named after this pile of cards. (3) *Monte* is also used as a combining element in monte bank, monte banker, monte dealer, monte layout, monte sharp (a cheater), monte table, and monte thrower (a dealer in three-card monte).

La Montura de los Californios
(Early California Saddle)

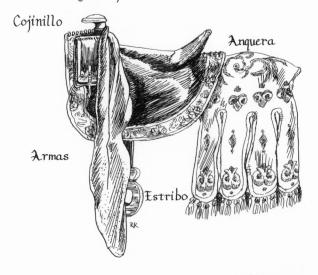

Cojinillo

Anquera

Armas

Estribo

RK

montura:

(Sp. model spelled same [mõ̯ntúra] < French *monture* 'mount'). A saddle or saddle equipment. The *DRAE* glosses it as a horse for riding (mount) or a term for saddle equipment.

Moqueño:

(Sp. model spelled same [mokéɲo] < *moqui* [an Indian tribe] and suffix *-eño* 'native to' or 'belonging to'). Carlisle: 1925. A member of the Moqui tribe native to Northeastern Arizona and Central Western New Mexico. Cobos glosses it as a Moqui Indian.

moro:

(Sp. model spelled same [móro] < Latin *maurus* 'inhabitant of Mauritania.' Corominas notes that the use of this term as a color for a horse alludes to the dark skin tone of the Moors.) A bluish-gray color for a horse. The *DRAE* indicates that it describes a black horse with a white mark (sometimes in the shape of a star) on the forehead and

La Montura del Vaquero
(Mexican Cowboy Saddle)

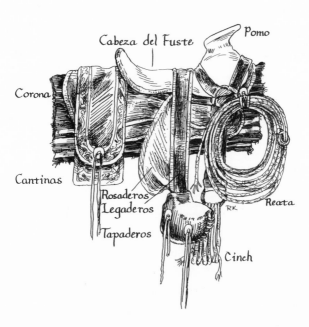

Cabeza del Fuste · Pomo · Corona · Cantinas · Rosaderos · Legaderos · Tapaderos · Cinch · Reata · RK

white marks on one or more legs. Santamaría notes that in Mexico it means bluish-white with black or dark-colored marks. Though generally a color for a horse, it may refer to other things as well.

morral:

(Sp. model spelled same [moŕál] < *morro* 'thick lips' or 'knoll or hillock,' of uncertain origin). (1) Western Texas: 1915. A grain-filled feedbag or nosebag, which is hung from the saddlehorn when the horse is not feeding. (2) By extension, any bag made of fiber or coarse cloth and hung from the saddle horn for carrying provisions. The *DRAE* references *morral* as a large sack or bag containing fodder which is hung from an animal's head so that the animal can eat when it is not in the stable. It is also a sack worn on the back by hunters, soldiers, and travelers to carry provisions or clothing. *Alternate forms:* marrell, morrall, morrel.

put on the morral:
　　To chow dowm, eat. Also "put on the nosebag," according to
Watts.

mortero:
　　(Sp. model spelled same [mortéro] < Latin *mortarium* 'mortar [bowl
for pounding solids]'). A mortar for grinding grains and seeds in the
form of a hole excavated into bedrock by Indians. A **mano** or *tejolote* is
the instrument used for grinding. The *DRAE* defines it as a cup-shaped
utensil made of wood, stone, or metal used for grinding spices, seeds,
chemicals, and other substances. *Compare* **metate, molcajete,** and
mano.

moscheto, mosquito: *See* **mesquite** (1).

mosey:
　　(apheresis of *vamos* [bámos], first person plural conjugation of *ir* 'to
go' < Latin *īre* with the English wordplay suffix -ey). A verb meaning
to leave, to escape, to decamp, or to sneak away. Like **vamoose,** this
term comes from the Spanish *vamos,* first person plural conjugation
of the verb *ir* 'to go'; hence, in Spanish, it means 'let's go.' Hendrickson's suggestion that the word comes from Moses or Mose and refers
to the "slouching manner of wandering Jewish peddlers in the West"
is implausible.

mozo:
　　(Sp. model spelled same [móso], of uncertain origin, perhaps
related to Basque *motz* 'blunt' or 'cropped,' originally referring to the
short haircut worn by small boys). Clark: 1830s. A young man, but
especially one serving as a domestic servant or assistant. Adams and
Hendrickson note that in the Southwest it generally refers to an assistant on a pack train. According to Clark, the term originally meant a
servant or assistant in general but more recently has come to mean a
"toady or overly obsequious employee." The *DRAE* gives several
definitions for *mozo,* among them a youth and a man who acts as a
servant in a household or who is a public servant with little authority.

moza:
　　A female servant. Spanish sources concur.

mugre:
　　(Sp. model spelled same [múɣre], back formation from *mugriento*
< *mugoriento* < dialectal *mugor* 'filth; mold; fermentation' < Latin

mūcorem 'mold, mildew'). Grease, dirt, or general uncleanliness. Bentley notes that it also applies to any disreputable person and is occasionally used derisively to refer to an Indian or Mexican. He also mentions that it is not widely used by those who are not proficient in the Spanish language. The *DRAE* references *mugre* as a noun meaning filth, grime, or dirt.

mujer:
   (Sp. model spelled same [muxér] < Latin *mulierem* 'woman'). Carlisle: 1845. Woman or wife. The *DRAE* concurs with both definitions. *Alternate form:* **moharrie**.

mulada:
   (Sp. model spelled same [muláða] < *mulo* < Latin *mūlum* 'mule' and the collective suffix *-ada*). Clark: 1840s. Correctly glossed by Watts as "a drove of mules." The *DRAE* concurs. Santamaría indicates that the term *mulaje* is used in Mexico with the same meaning.

mulero:
   (Sp. model spelled same [muléro] < *mulo* [see above] and the agentive suffix *-ero*, 'profession or trade'). A muleteer or muleskinner, a man who attends to or drives a team of mules. The *DRAE* glosses it as the man who cares for mules.

musqueto, musquit: *See* **mesquite** (1).

mustang:
   (Of uncertain origin. Probably a combination of *mesteño* [mestéɲo], *mestengo* [mestéŋgo], *mestenco* [mestéŋko], and *mostrenco* [mostréŋko]. See accompanying explanation). (1) Clark: 1800s. An untamed horse, or one that used to be tame, but has returned to the wild. The term originally referred to the horses brought to this continent by Spanish settlers, many of which escaped or were stolen by Indians and ended up running in wild herds in the West and Southwest. The origin of this term is disputed. One theory holds that *mustang* derives from *mesteño*, a Spanish term whose principal meaning is an animal (or thing) belonging to the Mesta, an association of owners of livestock (founded in 1273 by the Spanish government, according to Watts) that bred, fed, and sold their animals for their common good. A *mesteño* was an animal that had become separated from its owner and was considered to be the property of the entire Mesta. Although this

term shows a semantic similarity to the English word, it is difficult to justify the nasal and velar consonants in the derived form. Three more likely sources are *mestenco*, *mestengo*, and *mostrenco*, all of which mean 'having no known owner' (according to the *DRAE*, *mestengo* refers especially to animals). The first two terms probably derived from *mesteño*, and the third is itself an adaptation of *mestenco* (with influence from the verb *mostrar* 'to show,' since stray animals had to be presented to the Mesta). It is likely that the English *mustang* derived from one of these three terms or from a combination of the three. *Alternate forms:* mestang, mestaña, mestengo, mesteño. (2) Carlisle: 1929. As a verb, to hunt mustangs with the intention of snaring and domesticating them. (3) By extension from (1), a mustang is also a person who is uncouth or unaccustomed to "civilized" society.

mustang court:
Hendrickson references this term as synonymous with *kangaroo court*. In the Southwest this was one run by **vigilantes** rather than legal officials, especially in early Texas or in mining communities.

mustang cattle:
Wild black cattle that roamed freely over regions of Texas.

mustang clover:
California: 1925. A plant of the genus *Gilia* or the *Linanthus montanus*.

mustanger:
A man who hunted mustangs for gain or for sport. Interestingly, Santamaría references a similar term in Mexican Spanish, *mustanguero*, which he defines as a name given in northern Mexico and southern parts of the United States to hunters of wild horses on the open prairies. In this case, Spanish has reborrowed the English form and its accompanying meaning. *Alternate terms:* mustang hunter, mustang runner.

mustanging:
Hunting wild horses for trade or sport.

mustangler:
A man who herds mustangs. Watts indicates that this term is a blend of mustang and wrangler.

run mustang:
According to Watts, "to hunt wild horses from the saddle."

muy hombre:
(Sp. model spelled same [mwí] < Latin *multum* 'very, much' and [ómbre] < Latin *hōminem* 'man'). Carlisle: 1929. A good man. The *DRAE* confirms that this phrase is used in Spanish to refer to a strong or courageous man.

naja:

(*cernaja*? [sernáxa] < *cerneja* 'fetlock' < Latin *cerniculum* 'part of the hair'). Watts describes this as "a small decoration hanging from the headband of a bridle onto the horse's face, rather like an inverted horseshoe or crescent moon, reminding one of a similar decoration worn by the Moors." Spanish sources do not reference this term, but it may be an aphæresis of *cernaja*, which the *DRAE* defines as a sort of ornament with fringe or tassels placed on an ox's forehead to ward off flies.

Navajo:

(Sp. model spelled same [naβáxo], either < Spanish *nava* 'plain surrounded by mountains' of pre-Roman origin or < Tewa *naba* 'cultivated field' via Spanish). The largest American Indian group in the United States. They inhabit regions of Arizona, New Mexico, and southeastern Utah. Their language is from the Athapascan group, and their economy is based primarily on agriculture and raising sheep. They are also known for their artwork, including silversmithing, sand painting, and blanket weaving. *Alternate form:* Navaho.

Navajo rug:

Clark: 1940s. A rug woven by Navajo Indians, especially valued by tourists in the Southwest. A rug could have made its way into a cowboy's bedroll or into the **casa grande** on the ranch or **hacienda**.

Navajo silver:

Clark: 1940s. Silver jewelry, spoons, belt buckles, and other items designed and created by Navajo Indians.

Navajo

Navajo time:

Northeastern Arizona, southeastern Utah: 1978. The *DARE* glosses this as "a flexible system of time, a lack of punctuality." *Also called* Indian time. *Compare* **Mexican** (2).

Nevada:

(Sp. model spelled same [neβáδa] < *nevar* 'to snow' < Vulgar Latin *nivāre* plus the derivative suffix, *-ada*). Clark: 1859. The thirty-sixth state of the Union, named for the Sierra Nevada mountains to the west of the state.

New Mexico:

OED: 1834. The forty-seventh state of the Union. Originally called Nuevo México in Spanish.

New Mexican rain:

New Mexico: 1965. According to the *DARE*, dust clouds. *Also called* an Arizona cloudburst.

nopal:

(Sp. model spelled same [nopál] < Nahuatl *nopalli* < *nochtli* 'prickly pear' and *palli* 'flattened object'). Colorado: 1823. A prickly pear cactus; also the flat section or leaf (*penca*) of such a cactus. Santamaría glosses it as the common name of several cacti that produce a prickly pear, especially *Opuntia cactus* and *O. hernandezii*, a plant that grows to about ten feet in height and has flattened stalks composed of a series of fleshy, oval-shaped sections covered with spines. The cactus also produces yellow flowers with many petals and spiny, edible fruits that are green when unripe and turn yellow or cherry-colored when they mature.

noria:

(Sp. model spelled same [nórja] < earlier form *nora* or *annora* < Arabic *nāûra* 'chain pump'). Referenced by Bentley as a "well, spring, or water hole." He notes that it may also refer to a machine that raises water from a well or cistern. Santamaría glosses it as a provincialism used in northern Mexico for a well or cistern. The *DRAE* defines it as a machine composed of two large wheels, a horizontal wheel that is moved by a lever pulled by a horse or mule, and a vertical wheel that is engaged in the first and moves a thick rope with buckets to draw water up from a well. The Royal Academy confirms that the term may refer to the well from which water is extracted by the machine described above.

norte:

(Sp. model spelled same [nórte] < Anglo Saxon *north*, probably via French *nord*). A weather phenomenon affecting the Gulf of Mexico and nearby regions of Mexico and Texas. It consists of strong cold winds that blow from the north. Santamaría describes it as a wind that blows from the north, generally from October to December, but sometimes also in January or February, in tropical zones of Mexico.

Islas glosses it as a hurricanelike wind that blows from the north, and Cobos translates it simply as a "north wind." *Also called* a norther.

no sabe: *See* **savvy.**

novia:

(Sp. model spelled same [nóβja] < Vulgar Latin *noviam* 'newly-wed woman' or 'woman being married'). Bentley: 1929. A sweetheart or girlfriend. Bentley suggests that in Spanish this term is confined to a bride or a girl about to be married. However, the *DRAE* gives a broader definition, indicating that it may mean someone who engages in romantic relations with the expectation of someday being married. Simon and Schuster's International Dictionary gives 'girlfriend' and 'sweetheart' as two of the meanings of this term. *See also* dulce.

Nuevo Mexico:

(Sp. model spelled same [nwéβo] 'new' < Latin *novus* and [méxiko] 'Mexico,' of uncertain origin; Cobos gives the following etymology: Nahuatl *Mexico* 'where the god *Mexictli* is' < *Mexictli* 'the god of the center of the maguey plant' < *metl* 'maguey' and *xictli* 'navel or center' plus the locative particle *co*). Carlisle: 1928. The Spanish name for New Mexico, also sometimes used by English speakers in the Southwest. *Alternate form:* Nuevo Mejico.

odale: *See* **andale.**

ojo:

(Sp. model spelled same [óxo] < Latin *oculum* 'eye'). In the Southwest, a spring (of water). The *DRAE* concurs. Santamaría and Cobos reference *ojo de agua* as a spring.

ojo caliente:

(Sp. model spelled same [óxo] [see above] and [caljéŋte] < Latin *calentem* 'hot'). Carlisle: 1888. A hot spring. Cobos concurs.

oreanas: *See* **orejanos.**

Oregon:

(*oregón* [oreɣón] < *orejón?* [orexón] < Latin *auriculam* 'little ear' and the Spanish augmentative *-ón*). The thirty-third state admitted to the Union in 1850. Hendrickson's contention that the model for *Oregon* may be the "Spanish *oregones*, meaning 'big-eared men' and referring to Indians who lived there" is unlikely, since the form could only result from a scribal error ({g} for {j})in Spanish and a spelling pronunciation in English. More likely sources are the other possibilities he points out: (1) "the Algonquian *Wauregan* (beautiful water) for the Colorado River" or (2) "an unclear Indian name possibly meaning 'place of the beaver' that was misspelled on an early French map." Thus *Oregon* is probably not a Hispanicism.

orejanos:

(Sp. model spelled same [orexáno] < older form *orellano* 'lateral; separated; set to one side' < *orilla* 'edge, border,' diminutive of Latin *ōram* 'edge; shore.' Corominas indicates that this term does not come from *oreja*, as is commonly believed. It originally referred to wild animals or those that kept to remote or solitary places. Later the term was influenced by *oreja*, since animals that were not *orellanos* were earmarked). California, Oregon, Nevada: 1924. Wild cattle, or cattle that have not been earbranded. Also any unbranded cow, bull, calf, or (rarely) horse. The *DRAE* glosses *orejano* as an animal that does not have a mark or brand on its ear or any other part of its body. Islas concurs. *Alternate forms:* oreanas, orejanas. *Also known as* black cattle, cimarrones, longears, mesteñas, mustang cattle, mustangs, Spanish cattle, slick-ears, wild cattle.

otero:
(Sp. model spelled same [otéro] < *oto*, which was an earlier form of *alto* 'tall' < Latin *altum* 'tall'). Blevins indicates that this term is "cowboy talk for a big steer." The *DRAE* glosses it as an isolated hill that is the dominant feature of a plain. Spanish sources do not reference it as an animal, but perhaps it is a semantic extension referring to the dominant animal of the herd.

otie: *See* **coyote.**

overo:
(Sp. model spelled same [oβéro], from an earlier form *hobero*, of uncertain origin; it is possibly from Vulgar Latin *falvus* 'peach-colored,' but that does not explain the term's ending). Adams glosses this term as a borrowing from Argentine Spanish that refers to a **pinto** horse with white spots originating on the underside and extending upward. Such a horse is also characterized by multiple smaller dark spots. The *DRAE* glosses it as a peach-colored animal, especially a horse. In the Americas, it refers to a pinto or piebald horse. Santamaría references it as a pinto, or a horse or cow that is white with reddish-brown or black spots. He notes that the meaning of 'peach-colored horse,' as referenced in the *DRAE*, is not used in the Americas. Islas describes *overo* or *overo colorado* as a pale or light-colored horse with a white face and legs.

padrino:

(Sp. model spelled same [paðríno] < Vulgar Latin *patrīnum* 'god-father'). Carlisle: 1912. A rider who accompanies a bronco buster during the breaking of a difficult horse to aid him if the need arises. Not referenced in Spanish sources. *See also* **madrina.**

paint:

(possibly a calque from Spanish *pinto* [see below]). *OED:* 1848. A spotted or "calico" horse. *See also* **pinto.**

palau: *See* **pelado.**

palaver:

(*palabra?* [paláβra] < earlier form *parabla* 'word' < Latin *parabolam* 'comparison; similarity'). (1) *OED:* 1735. A discussion or conference, often one in which a great deal is said, but very little is accomplished; inconsequential chatter. (2) *OED:* 1733. As a verb, it means to talk incessantly or to talk flatteringly. Although there are very early attestations for this term in English, Hendrickson indicates that it was commonly used in the Southwest during the heyday of the cowboy. It should be noted that this term may have come from Spanish *palabra* or Portuguese *palavra* (both terms mean 'word'), or it may have derived from different sources, depending on the meaning and time frame in which the term was used.

palo:

(Sp. model spelled same [pálo] < Latin *palum* 'post'). This Spanish term for 'mast,' 'tree,' or 'stick' is extremely common in the Southwest, especially as a combining element in plant names.

palo alto:

(Sp. model spelled same [pálo] [see above] and [álto] < Latin *altum* 'tall'). According to Smith, this was the name used by Spanish explorers for various tall trees native to the Southwest, especially the redwoods of California. The city of Palo Alto, California, takes its name from these trees.

Palo Alto hat:

(Sp. model spelled same [pálo] [see above] and [álto] [see above]). Watts describes this as a "wide-brimmed 'slouch' hat" and indicates that it was the forerunner of the Stetson hat.

palo hierro:

(Sp. model spelled same [pálo] [see above] and [ǰéřo] < Latin *ferrum* 'iron'). *OED:* 1894. Ironwood (*Olneya tesota*), a hardwood tree native to arid regions. The *OED* indicates that it produces racemes of white flowers. Santamaría references *palo (de) hierro* or *palo (de) fierro* as the generic name of various trees and bushes with extremely strong wood, especially the leguminous *O. tesota* of northwestern Mexico. *Also known as* tésota, uña de gato, cat's claw. The Indians of Sonora, Mexico, and Arizona toast the seed of this plant and grind them to make a type of *pinole*. The name *palo de hierro* (as well as its variations) also applies to other leguminous plants, including the resin-producing *Mesua ferrea*, whose bark is used as a pectoral and as a home remedy for snake bites.

palo verde:

(Sp. model spelled same [pálo] [see above] and [βérðe] < Latin *viridis* 'green'). Carlisle: 1901. A tree with bright yellow flowers (*Cercidium microphyllus*) native to arid regions of the Southwest, especially Arizona and California. Referenced by Santamaría as the *chumari* plant of Sinaloa, Mexico, which is similar to the *jaboncillo* and is sometimes called by that name. It may also refer to a leguminous plant (*Parkinsonia aculeata*) or to the *Cercidium peninsulare*, native to Baja California. A rosaceous plant called *guayule* or *palo prieto* may also be called by this name. In the American Southwest it is *also known as* retama, lluvia de oro 'rain of gold'. Along with **chaparral**, **mesquite**, cacti, and other typical plants, the *palo verde* is often featured in desert backdrops in western films.

palomilla:

(Sp. model spelled same [palomíʝa], diminutive of *paloma* 'dove' <
Latin *palumbem* 'ringdove' or 'woodpigeon,' via Vulgar Latin *palum-
bam*). Watts defines this as a "white or cream-colored horse with a
white mane and tail." He indicates that in the nineteenth century it was
sometimes confused with the palomino and paint horses. The *DRAE*
references it as a very white horse, similar in color to a dove.

palomino:

(Sp. model spelled same [palomíno] < *paloma* 'dove'[see above]
plus the diminutive -*ino*). A horse of a golden or grayish-yellow color,
according to Watts. This term may be used as an adjective or a noun.
Islas is the only Spanish source that references this term, and he
defines it as a term used in northern Mexico for a horse of a light bay
color with a marble-colored mane and tail. Islas and Santamaría gloss
palomo as a dull milklike color for a horse. Cobos defines the same
term as "beige or cream-colored." The *DRAE* references a horse of a
similar color known as *isabelino*. The Royal Academy indicates that
this describes a horse of a pearl color, or a color between white and
yellow. *Alternate terms:* **California sorrel**, Isabella.

pansaje:

(*panzada?* [pansáða] < *panza* 'stomach, belly' < Latin *panticem*
and the suffix -*ada* 'abundance or excess'). Referenced by Watts and
Blevins as a barbecue or social meal eaten in the open air. Blevins
indicates that women were not invited to such gatherings until after
the turn of the twentieth century. This term is not referenced in Spanish
sources, but it may be related to *panzada*, which the *DRAE* defines as a
bellyfull, fill or big feed.

parada:

(Sp. model spelled same [paráða] < *parar* < Latin *parāre* 'to prepare; to make ready; to put into place'). Carlisle: 1923. Glossed by
Watts as "a main herd of cattle." Adams adds that the term is used
principally in California, Oregon, and Nevada. He also notes that it
sometimes refers to a "herd of broken horses." The *DRAE* glosses it
as a place where cattle gather. The term *parade*, which has the same
meaning in the Southwest, probably derives from this Spanish term.

parada grounds:
The location where a herd of cattle are gathered for various purposes.

partida:
(Sp. model spelled same [partíða] < *partir* < Latin *partīre* 'to divide; depart'). Bentley: 1929. (1) A group of cattle. (2) A party of men, often a band of outlaws. Watts defines this as a term meaning "a small bunch," which can be applied to men or cattle. Blevins, on the other hand, indicates that the term refers to a large grouping. The *DRAE* glosses it as a gathering of people for a certain task. Santamaría references it as a herd of livestock, generally cattle, gathered for any purpose, but especially for a cattle drive. Cobos indicates that it refers to a flock of sheep, generally around one thousand head.

pastura:
(Sp. model spelled same [pastúra] < Late Latin *pastūram* 'action of grazing'). Carlisle: 1888. Correctly glossed by Carlisle as "pasture or grazing ground." The *DRAE* references it as grass where animals graze, or the portion of food alotted as one meal for an ox.

patron:
(*patrón* [patrón] < Latin *patrōnum* 'patron; defender'). (1) Bentley: 1859. The owner of a ranch or large estate, similar to an **hacendado**. Also, by extension, a captain or boss. (2) A patron saint. The *DRAE* gives several definitions for *patrón*, among them a master or owner, or an employer or boss. Simon and Schuster's International Dictionary confirms that the term also refers to a Catholic patron saint.

peal:
Sp. model spelled same [peál] or *pial* [pjál] < *pie* < Latin *pedem*). (1) A stocking; also a foot, according to Adams. The *DRAE* glosses it as the part of a stocking that covers the foot. (2) Adams also glosses this term as "a worthless person." The Royal Academy confirms this usage, stating that it may refer to a useless, dull, or contemptible person. (3) A rope. The *DRAE* and Santamaría concur with this definition. The *DM* references it as a rope or cord made of strong twisted fiber used to snare animals by the feet. From southeastern Mexico to South America, it refers to a twisted strip of rawhide cured with wax. (4) Carlisle: 1929. As a verb, to throw an animal by catching its forefeet

with a rope. The *DRAE* lists two terms with this definition, *pealar* and *apealar*. Santamaría and Islas note that *pialar* and *apialar* are also common in Mexico. *Alternate form:* piale.

pelado:

(Sp. model spelled same [peláðo] 'bald; poor,' perfective participle of *pelar* 'to pull out hair' < Latin *pilāre*). Clark: 1840s. Among Anglos, a dishonest, unemployed, or contemptible Mexican. Referenced in the *DRAE* as a poor person or (in Mexico) a person belonging to the poorest and most uncultured classes, a boor. Santamaría also glosses it primarily as a poor person, but also a popular figure from the lower classes. He is a ragged, wretched, and uncultured person, but generally good-natured. It may also refer figuratively to an ill-mannered person who uses obscene language. Cobos indicates that in New Mexico and southern Colorado it means "broke or penniless." *Alternate forms:* palau, pelayo.

pendejo:

(Sp. model spelled same [peŋdéxo] < Vulgar Latin *pectiniculum* 'pubic hair,' diminutive of *pectenem* 'pubes'). Hendrickson cites another source that glosses this term as "asshole." The *DRAE* defines it as a weak, cowardly man or a stupid, foolish man. It also refers figuratively to a person who lives a licentious lifestyle, a slattern. Santamaría concurs with the first two of these definitions and notes that in Mexico this term is derogatory and obscene, considered improper among well-mannered people.

petalta:

(Sp. model spelled same? [petáḷta], etymology not found). A herd of cattle gathered so that some can be cut out. Spanish sources do not reference this term.

petate:

(Sp. model spelled same [petáte] < Nahuatl *petatl* 'straw mat'). Bentley: 1847. A mat made from palm leaves used to protect saddle-packs from the rain. Bentley notes that humbler Mexicans use these mats for floor coverings. This term also refers to a bag made from the same material, used for rice, coffee, and other commodities. Santamaría glosses *petate* as a borrowing from the Aztec language for a mat woven from palm-leaf strips. He notes that such mats are used throughout the continent, generally for the purpose of sleeping on them. Islas concurs, and adds that these mats can also be made from reeds or bulrushes. Perhaps a cowpoke or two, injured or lost, found shelter in a **jacal** and slept on a *petate*.

peyote:

(Sp. model spelled same [pejóte] < Nahuatl *péyotl* or *péyutl* 'cocoon of the silkworm'). A spineless cactus with intoxicating properties (*Lophophora williamsii*) that Indians use to make a hallucinatory drug. Santamaría references it as a generic name for various cacti, including *Ariocarpus retusu, Anhalonium prismaticum, A. elongatum, Mamillaria ariolosa, M. elongata, M. furfuracea*, and *M. prismatica*. However, he indicates that it refers properly to the *Lophophora*, a spineless species of *biznaga* that grows to a height of four to six inches, though as little as one-half inch may be visible above the soil, and for this reason it is sometimes called a root rather than a cactus. The plant contains a narcotic substance often studied for its physical and chemical properties. The Aztecs used it as a tonic, spreading it on their legs so that they could withstand long journeys. They also said that anyone who ingested the substance would see visions and be able to predict the future. Santamaría quotes Sahagún, who states that the hallucinatory effects of the peyote drug lasted for two or three days, during which time a person who had taken it had the courage to fight without fear, thirst, or hunger. He notes that it was commonly taken by Chichimeca Indians. *See also* **mescal**.

peyote cult:

Clark: 1930. A church in the Southwest (Clark indicates it is a "branch of the American Indian Church") whose members ingest peyote as part of religious ceremonies. Meetings are held in secret, since the use of peyote was made illegal in the 1930s.

piale: *See* **peal.**

pinto:

(Sp. model spelled same [pínto] < *pintar* 'to paint' < Vulgar Latin **pinctāre* < **pinctum*, perfective participle of the Latin *pingere* 'to paint; draw'). (1) Hendrickson: 1860. A spotted horse. *Also called* paint. (2) Clark: 1910s. A spotted variety of kidney bean. The *DRAE* glosses *pinto* as an adjective that describes animals and things of diverse colors. Santamaría indicates that it generally refers to things that are black and white. He also references it as a certain kind of bean with yellow, red, and black spots. Such beans are common in northern Mexico.

piñon:

(*piñón* [pi.ɲón] 'pine nut' < *piña* 'pine cone' < Latin *pīneam* plus the augmentative *-on*). Any of various dwarf pines that produce edible nuts. Watts gives *Pinus edulis, P. monophylla,* and *P. parryana* as examples and notes that Indians made the nuts of these trees part of their diets. The term also refers to the nuts of these trees. The *DRAE* glosses *piñón* as the seed of the pine tree and as a shrub of the euphorbiacous family, which grows in warm regions of the Americas to a height of about six and one-half to sixteen feet. It has heart-shaped leaves, petiolate and divided into lobules. It produces flowers on stalks and fleshy fruit with oily seeds, which are used medicinally as a purgative and commercially for their oil. The roots of the plant are made into a violet-colored dye. Santamaría references it as the purgative fruit of various species of the *Jathophas* species, especially *J. curcas, J. multifida,* and *Curcas purgans.* The name also refers to the plant itself, which produces a drupe or small nut, about three-quarters of an inch long, with strong oily, emetic, and poisonous properties. Cobos references *piñon* as the nut pine and its edible seed. It is common in the (Old) West. *Alternate forms:* pinion, pinyon.

piñoneros:

(Sp. model spelled same [pi.ɲonéros] < *piñón* [see above] and suffix *-ero*, 'profession or trade'; here, 'gatherer of *piñones*'). Carlisle: 1931. Carlisle glosses this term as "one who gathers piñon nuts." Cobos concurs, and adds that it may also refer to a seller of piñon nuts.

piola:

(Sp. model spelled same [pjóla] < Western Leonese *piola* 'hemp; twine; rope' < *apea* 'rope for tying horses' < Vulgar Latin *pedem* 'foot'). A rope, similar to a **reata**, except thinner. The *DRAE* glosses it as a thin rope or cord.

pistola:

(Sp. model spelled same [pistóla] < German *pistole* 'pistol'). Carlisle: 1925. A pistol. The *DRAE* glosses it as a short, generally semiautomatic firearm that one aims and shoots with one hand.

pistolero:

(Sp. model spelled same [pistoléro] < *pistola* [see above] and suffix *-ero*, 'profession or trade'). *OED:* 1937. A gunman. The *DRAE* references it as a person who uses a pistol to assault, rob, or commit some crime. Santamaría gives a similar definition. He glosses *pistolero* as an illegally armed person who, with a pistol or revolver, participates in criminal activities, including homicide, generally in exchange for payment from some third party. Certainly the Old West had its share of *pistoleros*, but they were not as prevalent as Hollywood or pulp fiction would have one believe.

pita:

(Sp. model spelled same [píta], of uncertain origin, probably from the Caribbean). (1) Clark: 1760s. A fiber obtained from the agave or **maguey** plant or from another similar plant. (2) A bag, box, rope, or net made from pita fiber. The *DRAE* glosses *pita* as a native Mexican perennial plant of the Amaryllidaceous family. Growing in a triangular pyramid, its light-green, fleshy, spiny leaves are about six to eight inches wide at the base and up to four-and-one-half feet long. It produces yellow flowers in bunches on a central stalk that does not develop until the plant is twenty or thirty years old. On reaching maturity, the stalk develops very quickly, growing to a height of twenty to twenty-three feet in a matter of days. The plant is very useful for making living fences in dry, hot regions. Although it originated in Mexico, it now grows naturally on the coasts of the Mediterranean. Its leaves produce a strong fiber and some varieties contain a sugary liquid that can be extracted to make **pulque**. The term *pita* is also used in Spanish to refer to the thread produced by the plant. Santamaría concurs with the definitions provided by the *DRAE* and adds that the most common genera to bear the name *pita* are *Fourcraea* and *Agave*.

pitahaya:

(Sp. model spelled same [pitáĵa], of Caribbean origin). Carlisle: 1848. A generic name for various organ-pipe cacti, especially the

Lemaireocereus thurberi (Watts notes that the Mexicans call this plant *pitahaya dulce*) and the *Carnegia gigantea* or *saguaro*, often depicted in illustrations of the Old West and cowboying. Santamaría glosses it as the common name given to several cacti of the genera *Cereus*, *Pachycereus*, *Lamaireocereus*, and others, as well as to the fruit produced by these plants. The cacti are native to tropical regions of the Americas and, similar to the **nopal** or "prickly pear cactus," grow in prolonged stalks without leaves. Most have three wings and ribs, and the plants are often gigantesque and herbaceous, and are covered with small acicular spines along the ridges of the plant. The spines may be navel-shaped or in small axillary bundles. The flowers of the plant are large and extremely showy. They may be salmon-colored, yellow, or white and generally open only at night and exude a fragrant aroma. They grow on the ends of the stalks, frequently in a tubulated calyx with a corolla formed of wide hanging petals.

población:
(Sp. model spelled same [poβlasjón] 'population' < *poblar* 'to settle; populate' < *pueblo* 'town' < Latin *populum* 'people; citizenry' plus the derivative suffix *-ción*). Hoy references this term as a population, town, or settled area. He notes that *población* appears on signs indicating a nearby urban area, and Spanish sources concur that it refers to a city, town, or village. Cobos agrees and adds that in colonial New Mexico it meant "a group of ranches."

poblado:
(Sp. model spelled same [poβláðo] 'population' < *poblar* [see above] perfective participle of the same). Referenced by Hoy as an "urban settlement." Spanish sources concur. *Also called* **pueblo, población**.

poblano:
(Sp. model spelled same [poβláno]). A large-brimmed, low-crowned hat worn by cowboys since the eighteenth century, according to Blevins. Spanish sources reference this term as an adjective meaning 'rustic' or 'rural,' but not as a type of hat.

poco:
(Sp. model spelled same [póko] < Latin *paucum* 'small in number'). Clark: 1840s. A modifier meaning 'a little bit' or 'very little.' It is used with a variety of (usually Spanish) terms, as in *poco dinero* 'little

money,' *poco español* 'little Spanish,' etc. The *DRAE* references this term as a noun meaning a scarce quantity of something, an adjective meaning scarce, limited, or short in quantity or quality, and an adverb meaning to a small degree or in reduced quantity.

poco a poco:
(Sp. model spelled same [póko] [see above] plus Spanish *a* 'by'). Correctly glossed by Blevins as "little by little." Spanish sources concur.

poco frio:
(*poco* [póko] and *frío* [frío] 'cold' < Latin *frīgidus*). Somewhat cold.

poco malo:
(Sp. model spelled same [póko] and [málo] 'bad; ill' < Latin *malum*). "A little sick," according to Blevins. This is an Anglo formation, not referenced in Spanish sources nor used by Spanish speakers.

poco pronto:
([póko] and [prónto] 'quick' < Latin *prōmptum*). Carlisle: 1922. Carlisle references this term as "pretty soon," and Blevins glosses it as "right now." This is an Anglo formation, not referenced in Spanish sources nor used by Spanish speakers.

poco tiempo:
(Sp. model spelled same [póko] and [tjémpo] 'time' < Latin *tempus*). Carlisle: 1902. This term means "pretty soon," as indicated by Charles Lummis in his novel *The Land of Poco Tiempo*: "here is the land of *poco tiempo*, the home of pretty soon." This is an Anglo formation, not referenced in Spanish sources nor used by Spanish speakers.

poquito:
(Sp. model spelled same [pokíto], diminutive of *poco* [see above]). New Mexico: 1931. A very little bit.

pomo:
(Sp. model spelled same [pómo] < Latin *pōmum* 'edible fruit'). The saddlehorn on a Mexican saddle. *Also known as* apple, **manzana**. The *DRAE* glosses it as a round handle on a door, box, or other item.

poncho:

(Sp. model spelled same [poṇʧo], of uncertain origin, perhaps from the Spanish adjective *poncho*, a variant of *pocho* 'discolored'). A cloak consisting of a blanket (or more recently a square piece of oiled cloth, rubber, or nylon) with a hole in the middle for the head to fit through. The *DRAE* describes it as a square or rectangular blanket made from sheep wool, alpaca, vicuña, or any other woven material, with an opening in the center for the head. The garment covers the shoulders and generally hangs to the waist or lower. *Alternate form:* ponchar.

por amigo:

(Sp. model spelled same [poramíɣo] < Spanish preposition *por* 'because, for' plus *amigo* [amíɣo] < Latin *amīcum* 'friend'). For friendship; because you're my friend. Hendrickson cites Dobie: "*Por amigo*, I tell you how to get it. Dig here and you will find a burroload of gold money" (*Coronado's Children*).

potro:

(Sp. model spelled same [pótro] < earlier form *poltro* < Vulgar Latin **pullitrem* 'young horse'). Bentley: 1929. Watts notes that this term has various meanings in the Southwest. It is primarily a colt or a young unbroken stallion. However, it may also refer to any wild horse. The *DRAE* glosses it as a horse from the time it is born until it loses its milk teeth (about four and a half years of age). Santamaría indicates that it also refers to any uncastrated, skittish, and unruly horse from the time it is born until it is broken. He also defines it as a general term for any unbroken horse. *Alternate form:* potrillo.

potrero:

(Sp. model spelled same [potréro] < *potro* [see above] and instrumental/agentive suffix *-ero*). (1) *OED:* 1848. A pasture for horses or cattle, it may be fenced or unfenced. Referenced in the *DRAE* as a site dedicated to the raising and grazing of horses. Santamaría glosses it as a piece of good pasture land that is marked with stakes and used for the grazing and fattening of livestock. (2) A herder of *potros*. The *DRAE* glosses it as a person who cares for *potros* when they are in the pasture. (3) Clark: 1840s. A narrow ridge between two canyons. (4) Southwest: 1872. A narrow plateau or **mesa** with steep sides. Cobos references it as "a gap or narrow ridge between cliffs or a finger of lava rock."

pozo:

(Sp. model spelled same [póso] < Latin *puteum* 'hole; well'). Clark: 1850s. A spring; a well. Clark indicates that it refers to a shallow spring, about two feet deep and fifteen to twenty feet in diameter. The *DRAE* defines it as a well, generally one that is surrounded by a stone or brick structure. Another in a series of terms that refers to that essential commodity in the desert Southwest: water!

presidente:

(Sp. model spelled same [presideṇte] < *presidir* 'to preside' < Latin *praesidēre* 'to be seated at the front' or 'to protect'). Bentley: 1863. In the Southwest, the mayor or other leader of a town or the owner of a ranch. The *DRAE* gives several definitions, including the leader of a government, council, tribunal, junta, society, or other unit. No Spanish source references *presidente* as the owner of a ranch, however.

pronto:

(Sp. model spelled same [próṇto] < Latin *prōmptum* 'prompt; available'). *OED:* 1850. General Spanish term for 'quickly, soon.' English usage of this term probably originated in the American Southwest, but is now extremely widespread and recognized throughout the United States.

prontito:

(Sp. model spelled same [proṇtíto] < *pronto* [see above] and diminutive suffix *-ito*). Arizona: 1931. Right away, in a hurry.

pueblo:

(Sp. model spelled same [pwéβlo] < Latin *populum* 'people; citizenry'). *OED:* 1818. A Mexican town or an Indian village in which the buildings are composed of **adobe**, brick, or stone. Referenced in the *DRAE* as a town, village, or a small community.

pre-pueblo:

Carlisle: 1930. Carlisle references this term as referring to a time period prior to pueblo life, or the time when Indians resided in pueblos.

puebleno:

(*puebleño* [pweβléɲo] < *pueblo* [see above] and the Spanish suffix -*eño* 'native of'). Carlisle: 1931. Carlisle references this as an adjective meaning "of the village." The most common term for this in Spanish is *poblano*, but Santamaría and Sobarzo reference a variant form *puebleño*, which can be either a noun referring to the inhabitant of a pueblo or an adjective meaning rustic, coarse, wild, or unpolished.

pulque:

(Sp. model spelled same [púlke], apocopated form of Nahuatl *poliuhqui-otli* 'putrefied wine,' so named because of the strong smell of the drink and because of the process of allowing it to 'putrefy' or ferment in leather containers). Clark: 1830s. An intoxicating drink made from fermented agave sap. The *DRAE* describes it as a thick white drink from the Mexican highlands obtained by fermenting the juice extracted from the **maguey** plant with an *acocote* (a long calabash with perforations at both ends). Santamaría references it as a thick white, spiritous, and intoxicating drink with an unpleasant taste and nauseating properties. The drink is popular among the poorer classes on the Central Plateau and, along with chiles and tortillas, forms a principal source of nutrition.

pulqueria:

(*pulquería* [pulkería] < *pulque* [see above] plus the collective suffix -*ría*). Bentley: 1847. A store where pulque is sold. Spanish sources concur.

punche:

(Sp. model spelled same [pún̯ʧe], of uncertain origin, possibly from an American Indian language). Carlisle: 1848. Referenced by Carlisle as a light, mild tobacco used and traded by Indians in the southwestern United States. Cobos indicates that it may refer to tobacco in general or to a "low-class, homegrown tobacco" cultivated in New Mexico. He notes that it is quite potent and is sometimes called *punche mexicano*.

pungle:

(*póngalo* [póŋgalo] < imperative of the Spanish *poner* < Latin *pōnere* 'to place,' plus the masculine direct object pronoun). Hendrickson glosses this as "an old term for pay money." He indicates that it comes from the Spanish *póngalo*, the imperative form of *poner*, 'to put or place.' The *DRAE* gives several definitions for *poner*, among them to bet money, especially in a card game.

puya:

(Sp. model spelled same [pújₐ], variant of *púa* < **pūga*, of uncertain origin, perhaps from an Italian dialect or from pre-Celtic Indo-European, and related to *pungere* 'to prick' and *pūgio* 'dagger'). Carlisle: 1913. Carlisle glosses this term as a thorn. The *DRAE* defines *púa* as a thorn and *puya* as a steel-plated point at the end of a rod or goad-stick that cowboys and picadors (in bullfights) use to goad or punish animals. Islas indicates that *puya* and *púa* are synonyms in Mexico and refer to a long sharp thorn found at the end of a **maguey** leaf.

quebrada:

(Sp. model spelled same [keβráða], perfective participle of *quebrar* 'to break'< Latin *crēpāre* 'rattle, crackle'). Carlisle: 1916. A ravine or barranca. The *DRAE* gives several definitions for this term, among them a narrow pass between mountains, a cleft in a mountain, or (in the Americas) a stream or rivulet that runs through a fissure in the land.

querencia:

(Sp. model spelled same [kerénsja] < *querer* < Latin *quaerere* 'to seek; inquire; request'). The place where a person (or animal) was born. Also a favorite spot or 'haunt.' Watts, quoting Dobie, says that Texan cowboys use the term to refer to a longhorn's birthplace or a place the cow persistently returns to. The *OED* notes that in bullfighting it refers to the place in the ring where a bull takes his stand, or his "stamping ground." The *DRAE* indicates that it refers to the inclination or tendency of a person or animal to return to the place where s/he was raised or has become accustomed to. It may also refer to the place itself. Santamaría quotes Valle, who reports that this term refers (in Nicaragua) to the native territory of an animal, meaning the place where it was raised, where it has become accustomed to graze, and whose pathways and landmarks it knows and remembers instinctively. By extension, it is also used for the place a person calls home and where his or her loved ones reside.

quidow: *See* **cuidado.**

quirt:

(*cuarta* [kwárta] 'fourth; one-fourth' < *cuarto* 'quarters, room' < Latin *quartum* 'quarter'). Bentley: 1846. (1) A riding whip with a short, often weighted, handle used to discipline an unruly horse or to encourage a slow one. (2) As a verb, to hit or whip with a *quirt*. The *DRAE* glosses *cuarta* as a short riding whip. Santamaría concurs, adding that it is made entirely of a type of leather called *peal*. At one end it has a handle or ring made of the same type of leather the cowboy puts over his wrist, and at the other end is a thin strap used as a whip. *Alternate form:* quisto.

quisto: *See* **quirt.**

raiz diabolica:

(*raíz* [r̄aís] 'root' < Latin *radicem* 'root' and *diabólica* [djaβólika] 'devilish' < Latin *diabolicam*). The drug **peyote**, found in **mescal buttons**. Spanish sources do not reference this term.

ramada: *See* **enramada.**

ranch:

(*rancho* [r̄án̪ʧo] < *rancharse* or *ranchearse* 'to lodge; to quarter [soldiers]' < French *se ranger* 'to establish one's self in a a place' < *rang* 'row, line'). (1) Clark: 1800s. Originally, a cattle-breeding establishment in the West. It was generally a large operation. According to Watts, the meaning of this term was later broadened to include an establishment of any kind along a trail, including trading posts, stagecoach stations, restaurants, and even brothels. *Alternate form:* rancho. (2) The main building on a cattle-raising ranch, or the main building and smaller buildings adjacent to it or surrounding it. (3) According to Hendrickson, "a dude ranch." (4) As a verb, to breed and raise cattle or other livestock. The *DRAE* gives several definitions for rancho; most refer to establishments much smaller and more limited in function than the American ranch. The Royal Academy indicates, however, that in the Americas a *rancho* may be a farm or grange where horses and other quadrupeds are raised. Santamaría defines *rancho* as a small, modest, or humble farm. It appears that the western meaning of an extensive cattle-breeding operation was adopted after the word was borrowed into English.

home ranch:

Carlisle: 1930. One's own cattle brand.

ranch brand:
Hendrickson: 1874. As opposed to a 'road brand,' which is applied once an animal has started on the trail, a ranch brand is one placed on an animal while it is young, at the home ranch.

ranch egg:
"A fresh egg," according to Hendrickson.

rancher:
OED: 1836. The owner and operator of a ranch (1). *See also* **ranchero** below.

ranchera:
The wife of a rancher. Blevins notes that this term is obscure.

rancheral:
Bentley: 1847. An adjective meaning of or pertaining to a ranch.

ranchero:
(Sp. model spelled same [r̄aṇʧéro] < *rancho* [see above] and the agentive suffix *-ero* 'profession or trade'). *OED:* 1826. A term used in the Southwest and California for a rancher or cattleman. It also occasionally meant a cowboy. The *DRAE* references it as the operator of a rancho.

ranchette:
OED: 1956. A small ranch, one covering only a few acres of land.

ranch hand:
An employee of a ranch.

ranch house:
Carlisle: 1922. The main building on a ranch.

ranching:
Bentley: 1912. The raising of livestock. *See* **ranch** (4).

ranchito:
(Sp. model spelled same [r̄aṇʧíto], diminutive of *rancho* [see above]). *OED:* 1850. A small ranch. *See also* **ranchette** above.

ranch-jumping:
Carlisle: 1803–1899. Carlisle glosses this term as the process of purchasing a piece of unoccupied land at a low price, securing the water rights, and then reselling the land at a much higher price.

rancho:

(Sp. model spelled same [r̄ánˌʧo]). Texas: 1841. Another name for a ranch (1), especially one owned and operated by Hispanics.

ranchman:

Carlisle: 1922. Usually the owner of a ranch, but also the boss of the cowboys or a cowboy employed by the ranch. In this last sense, *ranch hand* is also used.

road ranch:

Referenced by Blevins as a way station for travelers.

rancheria:

(*ranchería* [r̄anˌʧería] < *rancho* [see above] and the collective suffix *-ería*). Bentley: 1844. Generally, an Indian encampment (usually Apache). Watts notes that it occasionally referred to a ranch's headquarters, and Bentley indicates that it applied to a group of **rancheros** with their families, shelters, and supplies. According to Bentley, this term is not common in English "except in historical writings." The *DRAE* glosses it as a group of ranchos or huts. Cobos references it as "a group of ranches or an Indian settlement." *Alternate forms:* rancheree, rancherie.

reata:

(Sp. model spelled same [r̄eáta] < *reatar* 'to retie' < *atar* 'to tie' < Latin *aptāre* 'to adapt; to subject'). Bentley: 1838. A rope, made of braided rawhide or leather, according to Blevins (who cites Mora). Watts notes it occasionally referred to a grass rope. Some sources list it as a synonym for *lariat*, but Clark indicates that the reata is much shorter than the lariat and is used for many purposes, but not for catching cattle. However, neither Watts nor Blevins agrees with Clark. They observe that reatas are made from four to eight strands of leather or rawhide (four being the most suitable for everyday work) and generally measure forty to sixty feet in length, with a diameter three-eighths inch being the most common. These are and were used for roping cattle and other chores. Referenced in the *DRAE* as a cord, strap, or rope used for tying, or a rope used especially for tying horses or mules in single file. Santamaría glosses it as a rope in general, but especially a rope of twisted fiber, used by *charros* in their profession. *Alternate forms:* riata, rieta, rietta. *See also* lariat, lasso. *Also called* a string.

Rebozo

reata larga:
(Sp. model spelled same [r̄eáta] [see above] and [lárγa] 'long' < Latin *largam*). A long reata, usually more than one hundred feet long. Blevins, citing Mora, notes that skilled cowboys could rope cattle some sixty feet away with the *reata larga*.

reatero:
(Sp. model spelled same [r̄eatéro] < *reata* [see above] and suffix *-ero*, 'profession or trade'; here, 'maker of reatas'). A manufacturer of reatas.

un buen reata:
(Sp. model spelled same [un] 'a' and [bwén] 'good' and [r̄eáta] 'rope'). Carlisle: 1929. An all-around good cowboy.

rebozo:
(Sp. model spelled same [r̄eβóso] < *bozo* 'down [on the upper lip],' of uncertain origin, perhaps from Romance **bucciu* < Latin *buc-*

cam 'cheek'). Carlisle: 1836. A shawl worn by Mexican and Indian women. It can be used to cover the head and shoulders or as a carrying instrument. Watts indicates that this term is used in the Southwest, especially western Texas and California. The *DRAE* references it simply as a woman's *mantilla* or veil. Santamaría defines it as a large square shawl used by middle-class and poor women to cover their shoulders. It is seen most often in the interior of Mexico. *See also* **serape**. *Alternate forms:* rabozo, rebosa, reboso, robezo.

remuda:
   (Sp. model spelled same [r̄emúða] < *remudar* < *mudar* < Latin *mūtāre* 'to change'). Clark: 1840s. A herd of domesticated horses on a ranch or trail drive under the charge of a *remudero* or wrangler. At the beginning of each shift, cowboys would choose their mount from this herd. Horses in this type of herd are said to be in *remuda*. Watts indicates that since the turn of the century this term has been used on occasion to allude to a cowboy's personal string or even a single horse. Spanish sources provide similar definitions, but none exactly like the southwestern meaning. The *DRAE* glosses *remuda* as a change, such as a change of clothing. Santamaría defines it as a relay or draft horse, or a horse or mule that relieves another animal that has become tired from working. *Alternate form:* remouda.

remudadero:
   (Sp. model spelled same [r̄emuðaðéro] < *remudado*, perfective participle of *remudar* and suffix *-ero*). The corral in which a remuda is kept. Not referenced in Spanish sources.

remudera:
   (Sp. model spelled same [r̄emuðéra] < *remuda* and the agentive suffix -era). Bentley: 1929. A bell-mare, the lead mare in a herd of domesticated horses.

remudero:
   (Sp. model spelled same [r̄emuðéro] < *remuda* and suffix *-ero*, 'profession or trade'). A wrangler, the hand in charge of caring for the remuda. This is considered a position appropriate for a young or inexperienced hand.

renegade:
   (*renegado* [r̄eneɣáðo], perfective participle of Spanish *renegar* < *negar* < Latin *negāre* 'to deny' plus the intensifying prefix '*re-*'). (1)

An outlaw. (2) A wild cow or horse. The *DRAE* gives several definitions, among them a rough or indecent person. Cobos indicates that *renegado* is "said of one who curses as a matter of habit."

renegade rider:
A cowboy hired by a rancher to travel to surrounding ranches and pick up any stray cattle with his employer's brand.

retranca:
(Sp. model spelled same [r̄etráŋka], origin not found). The leather strap that holds the **aparejo** on the back of a horse or mule. Cobos is the only Spanish source that references this term; he glosses it as "a barnyard gate or originally a brake for a wagon."

rio:
(*río* [r̄ío] < Latin *rīvum* 'stream; canal'). Carlisle: 1859. The General Spanish term for river, commonly used in placenames. Clark comments that the term frequently appears in redundant constructions, such as the Rio Grande River.

rodeo:
(Sp. model spelled same [r̄oðéo] < *rodear* 'to surround; to encircle' < *rueda* < Latin *rotam* 'wheel'). *OED:* 1834. Originally, this term referred to a "round-up" or driving together of cattle with the purpose of inspecting, counting, separating, or branding them. Later, it came to have the meaning it does today, namely a contest in which competitors demonstrate their skill in riding, roping, and throwing cattle. The *DRAE* gives several related meanings for the term *rodeo*, including a place where cattle are gathered to rest or spend the night, or to be counted or sold. *Rodeo* also describes the process of gathering cattle for these purposes. The *DRAE* also notes that in some Latin American countries, the term also refers to a contest in which competitors ride wild horses and steers bareback and demonstrate their skill in throwing lassos.

rodeo arena:
The arena where rodeo competitions are held. *Also called* rodeo ground.

rodeo chaps:
According to Blevins, extra heavy chaps used in rodeo competitions. Sometimes they are painted with resin to make them grip the legs better and to protect the rider against chutes and fences.

rodeo clown:
An accomplished horseman dressed as a clown who diverts the attention of the horses and bulls (while at the same time amusing the crowd) so that a fallen rider can escape. *Also known as* a bullfighter.

rodeo cool:
Beer that is not cold, but considered cool enough to drink when one is especially thirsty, such as at a rodeo.

rodeo cowboy:
A cowboy who is skilled in rodeo events, but is not necessarily comfortable on the range.

rodeoing:
Hendrickson: 1982. Participating in a rodeo as a competitor.

romal:
(*ramal* [r̄amál] < *ramo* 'bunch, cluster' < Latin *ramum* 'branch'). A braided whip or quirt made from the ends of reins. Blevins indicates that these whips were about three feet long and were commonly used by Californios. The *DRAE* gives several descriptive entries, including a halter attached to an animal's cavesson. Cobos glosses it as a rope or a leash attached to a horse's reins.

rosaderos:
(rozadera [r̄osaδéra] < perfect participle of *rozar* 'to scrape or scratch' < Vulgar Latin **ruptiāre* (a back-formation of the perfect participle *ruptum* 'broken' and *-era* 'utensil or tool'). (1) Carlisle: 1922. The leather fenders of a saddle; they are located under the stirrup-leathers and are about the same length. *Also known as* **sudaderos**. (2) The term also refers to bedrolls, according to Watts. Islas is the only Spanish source to reference this term, but he does not concur. He states that it may refer to a protective piece of leather tied on the right leg and fastened at the waist to keep the **reata** (rope) from rubbing or chafing. Alternately, it refers to a piece of leather attached to the loop of the rope itself for a similar purpose.

sabe, saber: *See* **savvy.**

sabinas:

(*sabino* [saβíno] < *sabina* < Latin *sabīnam* 'savin'). Adams indicates that this term describes cattle with hides that are speckled with red and white. *See also* **sabino.** *Alternate forms:* savino.

sabino:

(Sp. model spelled same [saβíno] < *sabina* < Latin *sabīnam* 'savin'). Referenced by Adams as a horse that is light reddish or roan-colored and has a white belly. The *DRAE* glosses it as light red or pinkish. Santamaría and Islas define it as a horse (generally a sorrel- or chestnut-colored horse) with mixed dark and white hair on its body and a white face, belly, and legs. Cobos indicates that it refers to a pinto horse.

sacaton:

(*zacatón* [sakatón], augmentative of *zacate* 'hay; fodder' < Nahuatl *zacatl*). Bentley: 1863. A southwestern plant (*Sporobolus wrightii*) sometimes used as forage. The *OED* indicates that the term refers to various species of the genera *Sporobolus* and *Epicampes*. Santamaría glosses it as the common name of various wild grasses, including *Muelembergia disticophylla* and *S. wrightii*, used for making an industrial fiber. It generally grows in long, rigid rootstalks with leaves. In southeastern Mexico it is the primary vegetation on the plains or savannahs, where it grows as a shrub or in isolated groups of trees. *Also called* pajón (Mexico), bear grass (USA), it is commonly used as forage for cattle. *Alternate forms:* sacate, sacatone, zacaton.

Islas and the *DRAE* both note that fiber from the plant's roots is used for brooms and brushes. Cobos references *zacatón* as "bunch grass or porcupine grass."

saguaro:

(Sp. model spelled same [saɣwáro] or *sahuaro* [sawáro] < Cahita *sahuo*). *OED:* 1856. The famous giant cactus of the Southwest *(Carnegiea gigantea)*, growing up to sixty feet in height, according to Blevins, and linked forever in the popular mind with cowboying. Many western movies shot in places like Old Tucson made ample use of this impressive plant in scenes depicting trail rides and desert locales. Islas and Santamaría both reference this term as a giant cactus native to northwestern Mexico and the southwestern United States. It also refers to the fruit of the cactus. *Alternate forms:* sagarro, sahuaro, suaro, suhuaro, suwarro.

salado:

(*asoleado* [asoleáðo] perfective participle of *asolear* 'expose an animal to sunstroke' < *sol* < Latin *sōlem* 'sun'). Carlisle: 1929. Wind-broken or fatigued, said of a horse. The *DRAE* gives a number of definitions, among them: overheated from excessive sun exposure or afflicted with a condition that causes animals to suffer suffocation and violent palpitations. Santamaría references *asoleado* as fatigued or exhausted, referring to humans or animals. *Alternate forms:* sallowed, salowed, solado.

salina:

(salina [salína] < Latin *salīna* 'salt-mine'). Watts: 1840s. According to Watts, a salt bed or a salt lick for animals. Referenced in the *DRAE* as a salt mine or a place where salt accumulates after saltwater has evaporated. Also used as a toponym in the West, such as in Salina, Utah, or Salinas, California.

sallowed: *See* **salado.**

saltillo blanket:

[Sp. model spelled same [saltíǰo], place name). A blanket that was commonly used in Texas as a **poncho.** It was originally made in Saltillo (Coahuila, Mexico).

sancho:
(Sp. model spelled same [sán̩ʧo], proper name). An orphaned calf. *See also* **dogie, leppy**. Santamaría defines it as any animal cared for by a mother that is not its own; he notes that in Mexico the diminutive *sanchito* is more common. Islas references it as a domestic animal raised by someone other than its mother and, as a result, generally accustomed to humans so it is docile and tame.

sangre regular:
(Sp. model spelled same [sáŋgre] 'blood' < Latin *sanguinem* and [reɣulár] 'ordinary' < Latin *regularem*). Carlisle: 1850. Glossed by Carlisle as "good stock; breeding." Not referenced in Spanish sources, but the phrase means 'ordinary blood.'

Santa Fe:
(Sp. model spelled same [sáŋta] < Latin *sanctus* 'sacred' and [fe] < Latin *fidem* 'faith'). Carlisle: 1888. The capital city of New Mexico, used as a combining element in terms relating to the history of the region.

Santa Fe expedition:
Referenced by Clark as "a military-commercial expedition by the Republic of Texas to claim the eastern part of New Mexico in 1841."

Santa Fe tea:
A tea made from the leaves of a plant native to the Santa Fe region (*Alstonia thaeformis*), according to Blevins.

Santa Fe town:
A settlement along the Santa Fe Trail.

Santa Fe trader:
A person who traded on the Santa Fe Trail.

Santa Fe Trail:
A trade route running from St. Louis to Santa Fe. *Also called* Santa Fe Road.

Santa Fe wagon:
A wagon used on the Santa Fe Trail.

sarape:

(Sp. model spelled same [sarápe], origin not found). Watts glosses this as a band of silk or wool, generally about twelve inches wide and sometimes fringed on the ends. It is worn like a belt, wrapped several times around the waist. Watts includes *serape* as an alternate form, but he indicates that *serape* also has separate meanings (*see* **serape**). This item of clothing is commonly seen in illustrations depicting the early vaqueros. The *DRAE* and Santamaría give similar meanings for the term. Both gloss *sarape* as a wool blanket or cotton quilt with a hole in the center for a person's head. Generally brightly colored, it is worn as a protection against the cold or used as a blanket. In Mexico, *zarape* is also an acceptable spelling.

savanero:

(*sabanero* [saβanéro] < *sabana*, of Taino origin plus the suffix -*ero*, in this case, 'pertaining to' or 'from'). Watts: 1850–1900. A herder of animals or a packer or muleteer. Watts indicates that savanero was used originally as a loose term for a plainsman. In Spanish sources, it denotes a person who lives on a plain or one who herds or cares for a herd of livestock on a plain.

savvy:

(*sabe* [sáβe], third person singular conjugation of *saber* < Latin *sapere* 'to have intelligence; to understand'). (1) Bentley: 1909. As a verb, to know or understand. Also used interrogatively, meaning 'do you understand?' (2) Carlisle: 1887. As a noun, an understanding or thorough knowledge of something; also practical knowledge. In this sense, it could refer to humans or animals. For example, a horse could be said to have a great deal of "cow savvy." (3) As an adjective, shrewd, clever or quick-witted, as in Blevin's example: "a beaver is a *sabe* critter." *Alternate forms:* sabbey, sabe, saber, savez, savy.

no sabe:

(Sp. model spelled same [nó] and [sáβe], third person singular conjugation of *saber*). Not to understand. *Alternate form:* no savvy.

cow savvy:

An understanding of cattle or of herding techniques or the ranching business, said of humans or horses.

sabes?:

(*¿sabes?* [sáβes], second person singular conjugation of *saber*). Carlisle: 1921. Do you understand?

schapps, schaps: *See* **chaps.**

seago:

(*soga* [sóγa] < Late Latin *sōcam* 'rope,' possibly of pre-Roman origin). A rope, especially a rope of loosely twisted hemp used for roping animals. Santamaría glosses it as a term used in Tabasco, Mexico, for a rope made from rawhide that is tanned and rubbed with wax and then twisted into a perfectly cylindrical shape. It is generally used for roping cattle and in other cowboy operations. This type of rope often exceeds eighty feet in length. The term is also used along the southern coast of Mexico to refer to a rope made from three braided strands.

segarrito: *See* **cigarro—cigarito.**

segundo:

(Sp. model spelled same [seγúŋdo] 'second' < Latin *secundum*). Carlisle: 1903. The second in command in any endeavor, but especially on a trail drive. *Also called* a strawboss. Spanish sources reference it as a person who is second in command.

serape:

(*sarape* [sarápe], origin not found). *OED:* 1834. Watts references this as a blanket used as a cloak or as an ornamental garment worn folded over one shoulder. Clark notes that in English it no longer means a wrap for men (*see* **sarape**) and often refers instead to a shawl worn by women (*see also* **rebozo**). Spanish sources gloss *sarape* as a brightly colored wool or cotton blanket with a hole in the center for a person's head.

skeet: *See* **mesquite** (1).

sierra:

(Sp. model spelled same [sjéřa] < Latin *serram* 'saw'). New Mexico and Texas: 1850. A mountain range; used frequently in the names of mountain ranges in the West, as in Sierra Madre, Sierra Nevada, High Sierra, etc. The *DRAE* concurs.

Serape

Cuarta

Calzoneras

RK

silla:

(Sp. model spelled same [síǰa] < Latin *sellam* 'chair'). In the Southwest, a saddle. The *DRAE* references it as a riding saddle consisting of a wooden saddletree and a leather cover filled with horsehair or goat's hair.

sillero:

(Sp. model spelled same [siǰéro] < *silla* [see above] and *-ero* 'occupation or profession'). Smith references this term as a saddlemaker. He does not indicate whether the term was or is commonly used by English speakers. Santamaría references it as a *guadarnés*, which can mean either 'harness room' or 'harness keeper.'

sisal:

(same [sisál], origin not found). A rope made from the fiber of the agave plant. Blevins indicates that it has been replaced in recent times by the popular Manila hemp rope. Spanish sources reference it as a resistent fiber obtained from various species of agave. They do not reference it as a type of rope. The English meaning is an example of metonymy.

sobre paso:

(*sobrepaso* [soβrepáso] < *sobre* < Latin *super* 'on or above' and *paso* 'step' < Latin *passum*). Correctly referenced by Adams as "a gait of a horse, a slow Spanish trot." Santamaría glosses *sobrepaso* as a horse's gait characterized by the simultaneous movement of the front and hind legs on the same side of the animal. It also refers to any quick, lengthened, comfortable gait. Islas defines it as a horse's gait that is something between a walk and a trot.

sobrecincha:

(Sp. model spelled same [soβresín.ʧa] < *sobre* < Latin *super* 'on or above' and *cincha* 'cinch' < Latin *cingulam*). Blevins quotes Smith, who indicates that this term is synonymous with *cinch* (*also known as* surcingle *or* girth) in the Southwest, and refers to the strap that passes under the belly of an animal to hold a pack or a saddle in place. The *DRAE* glosses it as the strap that runs under a horse's belly and over the saddle to hold the blanket, horsecloth, or caparison in place.

sobrenjalma:

(Sp. model spelled same [soβreŋxálma] < *sobre* 'on or above' < Latin *super* and *enjalma* [or *jalma*] 'light packsaddle'< Vulgar Latin *salma* < Latin *sagmam*). Carlisle: 1876. A covering for a packsaddle, made of wool or other materials. Spanish sources concur; Islas indicates that thick hemp is often used for this type of saddle covering.

sombrero:

(Sp. model spelled same [sombréro] < *sombra* 'shade' < Latin *sub* 'under' *umbra* 'shade' plus the instrumental suffix *-ero*). Bentley: 1836. This Spanish term for a hat refers more specifically in the Southwest (and more recently in other regions) to a Mexican-style man's hat with a broad brim.

Sonora:

(Sp. model spelled same [sonóra], place name). A winter rain originating in the south, near the Mexican state of Sonora. Spanish sources do not reference it.

Sonoran:

Relating to the Sonoran Desert or the Mexican state of Sonora. It is used in various combinations to refer to plants native only to that region.

Sonoro reds:

Adams indicates that the cowboys gave this nickname to the "red Mexican cattle."

Sonora town:

In the Southwest, the section of town inhabited by Mexicans. *See also* **Mexican town**.

Spanish:

The English adjective is used in a number of combinations to refer to things of Spanish or Mexican origin or associated with Spanish or Mexican culture. Those pertinent to cowboying and ranching are listed below.

Spanish bit:

A large, sharp bit, which can be harmful to a horse in the hands of an unskilled rider. *Also called* Spanish spade bit.

Spanish cattle:

Wild black cattle, generally of Mexican origin.

Spanish fever:

Splenic fever, an affliction that affects cattle. *Alternate terms:* **Texas fever**, Texas fever tick, Texas tick.

Spanish horse:

A horse descended from those brought by the Spanish explorers. It could be either a horse with solid, fine breeding (generally a bay or sorrel), or a mustang.

Spanish kidneys:

Hendrickson glosses this as a euphemism for a bull's testicles.

Spanish needle grass:

Prairie porcupine grass (*Stipa spartia*), not often used as forage because it is sharp and causes discomfort to the cattle. *Alternate term:* Spanish needle.

Spanish rig:

A saddle with a single cinch located at the front of the horse, usually directly beneath the saddlehorn.

Spanish River:

Another name for the Green River.

Spanish supper:

Carlisle: 1929. According to Watts, the tightening of the belt in the place of eating a meal.

Spanish Trail:

Any of a number of trade routes in the early days of the Southwest. Clark indicates that the term applied especially to two main roads, one leading from Santa Fe, New Mexico, to Los Angeles, California, and the other going from Salt Lake City, Utah, to San Bernadino, California, via Cedar City (Utah) and Las Vegas (Nevada). "Old Spanish Trail" that winds through Tucson and the surrounding area is part of the Santa Fe—Los Angeles route. Such trails would have been known to cowboys, rustlers, and renegades in the Old West.

Spanish trot:

An easy swinging horse's gait.

stampede:

(*estampida* [estampíða] < *estampía* 'tumultuous race; abrupt departure' < *estampar*, of Germanic origin, probably from French *estamper* 'to crush; to mash'). (1) *OED:* 1826. As a noun, the mass bolting of frenzied cattle. Also, more generally, the sudden bolting of any herd of animals, or even of humans, as in a gold stampede or land stampede. *Alternate form:* stompede. (2) Calgary, Alberta: 1912. By extension from (1), a southwestern celebration consisting of a **rodeo** and other contests and exhibitions. (3) *OED:* 1823. As an intransitive verb, to take flight suddenly (generally said of a herd of cattle or other animals). (4) *OED:* 1848. As a transitive verb, to cause a stampede (1), usually said of humans. This was a technique used by Indians and others to steal cattle. The Royal Academy defines *estampida* primarily as a sharp, loud noise, such as one made by the firing of a cannon. It also refers to the precipitous flight of a human or animal, or of a group of either of these. Spanish sources do not reference the term as a verb; usages (3) and (4) are extensions of (1).

stampeder:
(1) *OED:* 1862. A horse, cow, or steer that is easily alarmed and bolts suddenly; also an animal that frequently causes a herd of cattle to stampede. (2) California?: 1862. The *OED* indicates that this term also refers to a person who participates in a sudden, spontaneous, irrational movement of people, such as a gold rush.

stampede to the wild bunch:
To break the law or join a gang of outlaws.

stockamore: *See* **hackamore.**

suaro, suhuaro, suwarro: *See* **saguaro.**

sudadero:
(Sp. model spelled same [suðaðéro] < *sudar* 'to sweat' < Latin *sūdāre* plus the instrumental suffix *-ero*). "The lining of a saddle-skirt," according to Watts. Also a synonym for **rosadero**s. The *DRAE* glosses it as a small blanket placed under a saddle. Santamaría defines it as a term used by *charros* and peasants for a blanket placed on an animal's back and under the saddle to absorb the animal's sweat.

tablas del fuste:

(Sp. model spelled same [táβlaʂðelfúste] *tabla* < Latin *tabulam* 'board; plank' and *del* 'of the' and *fuste* < Latin *fūstem* 'club; stick'). Watts references this as the bars or slats on a saddletree. Spanish sources do not reference this exact combination of terms, but the *DRAE* defines *tabla* as a thin, flat piece of wood and Santamaría references *fuste* as the framework for a saddle.

tablita:

(Sp. model spelled same [taβlíta], diminutive of *tabla* < Latin *tabulam* [see above]). Southwest: 1930. A ceremonial Pueblo headdress. Carlisle's source indicates that it consisted of a thin board decorated with various symbols such as a sun, moon, or clouds. Cobos describes it as a thin brightly-colored wooden headdress used by Indian women during religious festivals in Santo Domingo, New Mexico. One of his citations also mentions the use of sun, moon, and clouds as common decorations.

tank:

(*tanque* [táŋke] 'tank' < Portuguese *tanque* < *tancar*, from a Western Iberian dialect). Carlisle: 1873. A pond or a reservoir for collecting and storing rainwater, often one dug out of the earth. This southwestern usage of the term probably comes from the Spanish *tanque*, which Santamaría indicates is a synonym for *estanque* 'tank or water deposit.'

tapadero:

(*tapadera* [tapaðéra] < *tapar* 'to cover' < *tapa*, probably from Gothic **tappa* 'plug; wooden peg; tap, spout' plus the instrumental suffix *-era*). Clark: 1840s. A piece of leather attached to the front of a stirrup in order to shield a cowboy's feet from the brush. In English, the term is generally used in the plural and is often shortened to "taps." Santamaría references *tapadera* as a term used in Tabasco, Mexico, for a shield placed in front of the stirrups of a saddle and formed in a conical shape in order to accommodate the toe of the rider's boot. Cobos indicates that the term is also used in New Mexico and southern Colorado. *Alternate form:* tapadera.

tapajos:
    (*tapaojos* [tápaexos] < *tapar* 'to cover' < *tapa*, probably from Gothic **tappa* 'plug; wooden peg; tap, spout' and *ojos* 'eyes' < Latin *oculum* 'eye'). Bentley: 1847. Blinders for a horse or mule. The *DRAE* references *tapaojos* as a term used in Colombia and Venezuela for a frontal on a halter or headstall that covers the eyes of a mule or horse. Santamaría concurs and adds that *tapojo* is also used colloquially. *Alternate forms:* tapa ojos, tapaojos.

tarrabee:
    (tarabilla [taraβíʝa], of disputed etymology. It may derive from *traba* 'tie, bond, or fastener' < Latin *trabam* 'beam or log' plus the diminutive *-illa*). Glossed by Adams and Blevins as a wooden hand tool for spinning thread in the making of cinches or girths. Santamaría concurs, noting that the instrument is used to twist horsehair or other fibers for halters and reins as well as cinches.

tasajo:
    (Sp. model spelled same [tasáxo], of uncertain origin). Carlisle: 1902. Buffalo or other meat cut into strips and preserved by drying it in the sun. *See also* **jerky.** The *DRAE* references it as a piece of dried meat cured with salt and smoke to preserve it. (The same or a similar process is also applied to fish or fruit.) Santamaría concurs and adds that such meat is a regional dish of Mexico. Cobos references it as sundried strips of melon, pumpkin, and other foods. *Alternate forms:* tassajo, tassejo.

tasajero:
    (Sp. model spelled same [tasaxéro] < **tasajo* [see above] plus the agentive or locative suffix *-ero*). According to Watts, this referred to a building in which *tasajo* was produced. Santamaría references it as a dealer or manufacturer of *tasajo*.

teguas:

(Sp. model spelled same [téɣwas] < Nahuatl *tehuan* 'that which accompanies others'). Bentley: 1889. Originally, lightweight rawhide ankle-length moccasins that lace in the front. Santamaría indicates that this term may be spelled various ways in Mexico (*teguas*, *tejas*, *tejuanas*, *texas*), and refers to a nation of Indians that inhabit Baja California and New Mexico (in English, Tewa). The term was subsequently generalized to other footwear, such as **huarache** sandals used by the Indians. The sandals are now worn by others besides the Tewa Indians and the term is known throughout northwestern Mexico. Sobarzo indicates that the sandals were worn by the Apaches. He suggests that the name comes from a Sonoran Indian language, possibly from the Cahita word *begua* 'leather; calfskin.' Islas notes that the sandals are worn principally by peasants, especially those in Chihuahua, Mexico.

Tejano:

(Sp. model spelled same [texáno] < *Tejas* or *Texas* (see below) and the Spanish suffix *-ano* 'pertaining to or originating from'). Carlisle: 1844. Originally a Texan of Mexican descent; however, in the second half of the nineteenth century it came to mean any Texan, but generally one of Anglo descent. Santamaría concurs that it means 'from Texas.' Cobos indicates that in New Mexico and Southern Colorado Spanish, it is used to refer to a white stranger in an uncomplimentary fashion, whether he is from Texas or from some place farther east. **Gringo** is an equivalent term. More recently, it has again been applied with its original meaning, as in *Tejano* (Tex-Mex) music. In northern Mexico the term can also refer to a cowboy hat and is used to distinguish it from the traditional **sombrero** that the *charro* or **vaquero** wore.

Tejas: *See* **Texas.**

temescal:

(*temascal* or *temazcal* [temaskál] < Nahuatl *tema* 'to bathe' and *calli* 'house'). A hot spring or sweat house, usually one made of adobe. Santamaría references it as a sweat bath used by Indians in rural central Mexico and Guatemala. It consists of a closed room filled with steam. *See also* **estufa.**

ten-gallon hat:

(*galón* 'type of ribbon' < French *galon* < Old French *galonner* 'to adorn the head with ribbons'). According to Watts, the typical western hat, with a high crown and a wide brim. It is not named for its capacity, but for the braided decorations or *galones* that adorn it. The number 'ten' was added later by English speakers who mistook the meaning of the Spanish word. The *DRAE* references *galón* as a thin, strong, braided decoration used on clothing and other items. Islas references *galoneado* as a hat decorated with *galones* and worn by a *charro*.

tequila:
(Sp. model spelled same [tekíla], name of a city in the Mexican state of Jalisco where the drink is produced < Nahuatl *tequillan* 'place where tributes are paid' or 'place of the workers' < *téquitl* 'tribute' or *tequíotl* 'work' and *tlan*, indicating abundance). A potent alcoholic drink made from the **maguey** plant. Santamaría describes it as the popular mezcal liquor whose production constitutes an important industry in the states of Jalisco and Guanajuato, Mexico. Its name comes from a city in the state of Jalisco, probably because the drink originated there. It is extracted from any of a number of agaves, but especially the *Agave tequilana*, which is *also called* the *mezcal de Tequila*, the *mezcal azul*, or the *zapalote*. The *DRAE* also references the drink as similar to gin.

teshuino: *See* **tiswin.**

Texas:
(Sp. model spelled same [téxas] < Caddo Indian *teyshas* 'allies or friends' appropriated by the Spanish in the 1540s who mistakenly took it to be a tribal name.) (1) A term written in lowercase referring to the canopy of a covered wagon adjusted and reinforced to with-stand wet weather. (2) Name of the second largest state in the Union, admitted in 1845 (as the twenty-eighth), which is intimately associ-ated with cowboying. As such it is combined to form compounds relating to fauna and flora native to or introduced to Texas. Animals include: Texas cow, Texas cattle or Texas herd, Texas longhorn, Texas pony, Texas armadillo, and Texas fever tick. Some typical plants include: Texas bluebonnet, Texas bluegrass, and Texas (white) oak. *Alternate form:* Tejas.

Texan:
Of or pertaining to Texas; with particular reference to the inhabitants of the state or to cattle originating from Texas, such as the longhorn breed.

Texas brag:

Referring to the staunch belief that things are bigger and better in Texas and that anything of any worth was invented or discovered there.

Texas butter:

A gravy substitute made from melted animal fat and thickened with flour.

Texas cakewalk:

A slang term for a "necktie party," that is, a hanging.

Texas fandango:

The **fandango** Texas-style.

Texas fever:

(1) According to Watts, "splenic fever in cattle." (2) The almost uncontrollable urge to relocate to or visit Texas. *See also* **Spanish— Spanish fever**.

Texas gate:

A particular type of gate that was common in the West after barbed wire was introduced.

Texas Rangers:

First organized in 1823, this group of lawmen was feared by the Mexicans in Texas because of the Rangers' cruel and inhumane treatment of them and others. See, for example, Américo Paredes's *With a Pistol in His Hand* or the movie version starring Edward James Olmos (*The Ballad of Gregorio Cortez*).

Texas rig:

Unlike the single, center-fire rig favored by some cowboys, the Texas version features double-rigging or a saddle with two cinches.

Texas saddle:

Fashioned after the Mexican pattern, these saddles tend to be large and heavy.

Texas skirt:

Part of the usual equipment that made up the Texas rig, this type of saddle skirt was square.

Texas tie:
Tying hard-and-fast, that is, attaching one end of the rope to the saddlehorn rather than dallying. Many who preferred this method were Texans.

Texas tree:
The type of saddletree on a Texas rig.

Texas turkey:
Not a turkey at all, but rather a jocular term for the armadillo.

Texian:
An earlier form replaced by Texan.

Texican:
Probably resulting from a blend of *Texan* and *Mexican*, this term was also replaced by *Tejano* or Texan.

Texas fever tick: *See* **Spanish—Spanish fever.**

Texas winged chaps: *See* **chaps.**

theodore: *See* **fiador.**

tilma:
(Sp. model spelled same [tílma], apocopated form of Nahuatl *tilmatli* 'thin cloak or blanket'). Carlisle: 1844. An inexpensive, shapeless garment, or a blanketlike cloak tied around the neck with a knot. The *OED* indicates that it was worn by Indians, and Watts says it was used by the poor. Santamaría references it as a cotton or wool blanket worn by poor peasants. It is worn like a cloak or mantle, and has a hole in the center for the head to fit through. The *DRAE* indicates that it is secured by a knot at the shoulder. Cobos references it as a kind of **poncho**.

tinaja:
(Sp. model spelled same [tináxa] < *tina* 'tub; vat' < Latin *tinaculam* diminutive form of the Latin *tīnam* 'long-necked wine bottle with a cork'). (1) Carlisle: 1844. A large stoneware vessel used for storing water. The *DRAE* concurs, noting additionally that the vessel which is fired can be either glazed or unglazed and is wider in the middle than it is at the base or the mouth. It is placed on a stand, hung from a ring,

or embedded in the ground for the purpose of storing water, oil, or other liquids. (2) Bentley: 1919. A water hole in arid regions of the Southwest, either manmade or naturally occurring. Cobos references *tinaja* as a naturally occurring rock **tank** that collects water.

tiswin:

(*tesgüino* [teṣɣwíno], from Tarahumara *tecuín* [tekwín] < Nahuatl *tecuino* 'to beat fast [referring to the heart]' or 'to be hot'). A mildly intoxicating drink brewed by the Apaches for religious ceremonies. Santamaría indicates that *tesgüino* is used in religious celebrations by the Tarahumara Indians who obtain it by fermenting liquid extracted from kernels of corn. *Tecuín* is another acceptable spelling, which Santamaría says preceded *tesgüino*. Cobos references *tesgüín* or *tisgüín* as "homemade corn liquor"; the *OED* also notes that it can be made from wheat or mesquite beans. *Alternate forms:* teshuino, tizwin.

tobiano:

(Sp. model spelled same [toβjáno], origin not found). A pinto horse with smooth, regular markings and a white color that starts at the back and rump of the animal and extends downward. *See also* **overo**. The *DRAE* glosses *tobiano* as an adjective used in Argentina to describe a golden-colored horse with large white spots on its hide. *Also known as* piebald.

tobosa: *See* **galleta** (1).

tonto:

(Sp. model spelled same [tóŋto], probably of expressive creation). Carlisle: 1846–47. (1) This Spanish word meaning 'fool' was applied by the Spanish to a number of Indian tribes, such as the Tonto Apaches. Sobarzo references *tonto* as a member of the *Vinni-ettinen-ne* Apache tribe, *also called* a **coyotero**. (2) Hendrickson notes that the term also referred to Indians who were disparaged by their fellow tribe members because they no longer followed the traditions of their people. It was in this sense that the term was applied to the Lone Ranger's sidekick.

tordo:

(Sp. model spelled same [tórðo], also *tordillo* [torðíʝo] < Latin *turdum* 'thrush,' plus the diminutivo suffix -*illo*). Dapple-gray, as a horse color. The *DRAE* and Corominas define the term as hair or coat the color of the thrush's plumage as applied to horses and mules. The Royal Academy also notes the color derives from a mixture of black and white hairs. Santamaría references seven types of *tordillo* and Islas adds another as horse coloring in Mexico.

tornillo:

(Sp. model spelled same [torníǰo], diminutive of *torno* 'turn; wheel; lathe' < Latin *tornum*). Clark: 1840s. This term with the general meaning of 'screw' has specific reference to the screw-pod mesquite (*Prosopis pubescens*) of Texas, New Mexico, and California. Also the bean of the plant, used as forage for cattle and horses. Santamaría also references the term with the same species and genus, noting that it grows on the shores of rivers along the northern border of Mexico. Cobos glosses it only as a "screw bean."

toro:

(Sp. model spelled same [tóro] < Latin *taurum* 'bull'). (1) Carlisle: 1876. The General Spanish term for bull. Watts indicates that it was not used frequently by English speakers. Blevins notes that it was used euphemistically in the nineteenth century because it was not considered appropriate to say "bull" in the presence of ladies. (2) This term was also used occasionally for jerked buffalo meat, according to Blevins.

trigueño:

(Sp. model spelled same [triɣéɲo] < *trigo* 'wheat' < Latin *trīticum* and *-eño* 'similar to'). A horse of a dark-brown color. The *DRAE* glosses it as wheat-colored, or something between brunette and blond.

tule:

(Sp. model spelled same [túle] < Nahuatl *tollin* or *tullin*, 'cattail or sedge'). Bentley: 1836. Either of two species of bulrushes of the genus *Scripus*, used to thatch primitive huts. Santamaría glosses it as a reed or bulrush whose leaves are used to weave mats and even curtains and other items. In Mexico the term frequently refers to a species of *Cyperus*, native to the lakes of the Central Plateau. It may also refer to *Seirpus californicus*, *S. lacustris*, *Typha angustifolia*, and *T. latifolia*. In the plural, "the tules" refers to an out-of-the-way or desolate place, or "the middle of nowhere." Hence the expressions "to be in deep tules," meaning to be in trouble with the law and "to pull freight for the tules," "to be on the lam." The term is also used in forming numerous compounds. Some examples include: tule elk, tule gnat, tule wren; tule lake, tule land, tule marsh or swamp. *Alternate forms:* toolie, tula, tulé, tuley.

Tulare:
(*tular* [tulár] < *tule* and suffix -*ar* 'place abounding in'). A place where bulrushes grow. Santamaría concurs. Common in place names, such as: Tulare County, Tulare Hill or Peak, and Arroyo del Tulare (now Oak Creek), in California. *Alternate form:* tulares (plural).

tule fog:
Ground fog that occurs inland and is not directly related to precipitation or high humidity. Blevins notes that, in California, it refers to fog on the Sacramento or San Joaquin Rivers.

tullies:
Pertaining to or native to the *tulares*, particularly with reference to human inhabitants or livestock.

tumbadore:
(tumbador [tumbaðór] < Spanish *tumbar*, from the imitative *¡tumb!* 'to knock down or throw down' and -*dor*, an agentive suffix). A cowboy whose job it is to rope and throw calves so that they can be branded. Simon and Schuster's International Dictionary references the related term *tumbadero* as a branding yard or pen in Venezuela. *Tumbador*, however, is not referenced in Spanish sources.

vaca:

(Sp. model spelled same [báka] < Latin *vaccam* 'cow'). Carlisle: 1846–47. The General Spanish term for *cow*. This term is commonly used in place names throughout the Southwest, especially in California. For example, Vacaville, Vaca Canyon or Valley (in both California and New Mexico), and Mount Vaca or the Vaca Mountains.

vacada:

(Sp. model spelled same [bakáða] < *vaca* [see above] and -*ada*, a collective suffix). A herd of cows. The *DRAE* glosses it as a herd of cattle in general, and Santamaría references it as a group of cows that are separated from the bulls in a herd in order to fatten them or for some other purpose.

vacher: *See* **vaquero.**

vamoose:

(*vamos* [bámos], first person plural conjugation of the verb *ir* 'to go' < Latin *īre*). *OED:* 1827. To leave, or clear out. This term originated in the Southwest, but has since become common slang throughout the United States. It is generally used as an intransitive verb, but as Blevins and the *OED* note, it also has a transitive usage, as in "they vamoosed the ranch." *Alternate forms:* bamoose, vamonos, vamoos, vamos, vamose, vampoose.

vaquero:

(Sp. model spelled same [bakéro] < *vaca* [see above] and agentive suffix -*ero*, 'profession or trade'). Hendrickson: 1800s. Usually a Mexican or California cowboy, but it may also refer to a cowboy in

general. It is most likely the model for cowboy and buckaroo. The
DRAE glosses it as a herder of cattle. Santamaría indicates that the
term refers to a person who works in the various operations of a
ranch, including the handling of cattle. *Alternate forms:* baquero,
buckaroo *(see* various forms of buckaroo), vacher.

varruga:

(*verruga* [beɾúɣa] < Latin *verrūcam* 'wart'). A cattle brand in the
form of a cut made in the wattle that caused a strip of flesh to hang
down from the neck of the animal. This term derives from *verruga*,
which Spanish sources gloss primarily as a wart, but Cobos indicates
that in New Mexico and southern Colorado, it can also refer to "a
scar or scarred tissue."

velada:

(Sp. model spelled same [belá ða], perfective participle of *velar* 'to
watch; to keep vigil' < Latin *vigilāre*). Referenced by Hoy as "a line
camp." He defines it as a structure with a **corral** and a source of water
nearby. It is located on a ranch at a point fairly far from the ranch's
headquarters. It is not occupied year round, but whenever it is needed
for working cattle or maintenance work. Sobarzo defines a *velada* as
a periodical gathering of cowboys for the purpose of rounding up the
cattle that are freely grazing in the pasturelands. The cattle are herded
toward a *manga*, or fenced-in watering place, where they may enter
but cannot escape.

vent:

(*venta* [béṇta] 'sale' < Latin *vēnditam*). California: 1888. (1) As a
verb, to vent a brand meant to invalidate one brand and apply a new
one to an animal's hide. A vented animal was one that had been
legally sold. (2) As a noun, a vent was a special brand that showed an
animal had been legally sold. *Also called* counter-brand, cross-brand,
sale-brand, vent-brand, venta. In Spanish, a *venta* is a business trans-
action or legal sale. Sobarzo, however, indicates that in the state of
Sonora, Mexico, it also refers to a brand placed on the left shoulder of
an animal as an indication that the animal had been sold. Cobos references *venta* as a branding iron or a quitclaim brand (a brand that can-
celed out the brand of a previous owner at the time of a sale).

vereda:

(Sp. model spelled same [beréδa] < Latin *verēdam* 'path' or 'cattle trail'). A trail. The *DRAE* glosses it as a narrow path, often one formed by the frequent passage of pedestrians and livestock. It can refer to the trail used to drive cattle from winter pastures to summer pastures or vice versa.

vigilantes:

(Sp. model spelled same [vixiláηtes], plural of *vigilante* < *vigilar* < Latin *vigilāre* 'to watch over or guard' plus the nominalizing suffix, *-nte*). *OED:* 1856. Men who organized themselves to fight crime in areas where effective law enforcement was lacking. They frequently took the law into their own hands in their efforts to suppress criminal activity and punish the alleged offender. *Also known as* committees of vigilance, vigilance committees, regulators.

vuelta:

(Sp. model spelled same [bwéɭta] past participle of < *volver* 'to return' < Latin *volvere* 'to roll; wind; turn around'). General Spanish term for 'turn,' also referenced by Carisle. In the Southwest, this term was generally used to refer to a turn of the rope around a saddlehorn or other object in the process of roping an animal. *See also* **dally**.

wagh!:
    (*¡gua!* [gwá] or *¡hua!* [wá], of uncertain origin). Blevins suggests that this expression of assent or admiration comes from the Spanish *¡gua!*, meaning "gracious!". He indicates that *¡gua!* was first borrowed by drivers on the Santa Fe Trail, where it meant "get along." The *DRAE* references *¡gua!* as an interjection used in Bolivia, Columbia, Peru, and Venezuela to express fear or admiration. *See also* hua!

wrangler:
    (*caballerango* [kaβaǰeráŋgo] < *caballo* 'horse' < Latin *caballum* 'pack horse, nag' plus *-ero*, an agentive suffix, plus *-ango*, a despective suffix). *OED:* 1888. The hand on a ranch or trail drive who cares for the herd of horses. This position was usually held by a young or inexperienced cowboy. This term appears in English as early as the sixteenth century, but with the very different meaning of 'disputant,' such as for the throne. The *OED* suggests that the term used in the West is a combination of the English term *wrangler* and the Spanish *caballerango*. It is also quite likely that the western term evolved without the influence of the original English term, which cowboys were probably not familiar with. Rather, it is possible that early cowboys heard *caballerango* and recognized the *caballo* element. Early variants, *caballo rango* or even *horse rango*, would have eventually been shortened to *wrango* and then *wrangler*. It is likely that the eventual spelling was influenced by the existing English word. The Royal Academy glosses *caballerango* as a Mexicanism for a servant on horseback. Santamaría gives a definition more similar to the western meaning. He defines it as the servant who, on a ranch or personal

estate, keeps and saddles the horses. *Alternate forms:* caverango, horse-wrangler, wangler, wrangatang, wrango. *Also called* horse pestler, horse rustler, **remudero**.

day wrangler:
The hand that cares for the **remuda**, or herd of horses, by day.

dew wrangler:
The wrangler who works the early morning shift.

dude wrangler:
A cowboy who cares for horses, leads rides for guests, and perform other chores on a dude ranch.

hen wrangler:
A boy employed for chores on a ranch.

law wrangler:
According to Adams, a common term for a lawyer.

wrangle:
OED: 1899. To care for or herd horses.

wrangle horse:
The horse that a wrangler keeps saddled in order to bring in the other horses.

Wrangler jeans:
Hendrickson calls these "the jeans brand of choice for a cowboy."

wrango:
A small pen for keeping horses. Watts indicates that it is uncertain whether this term derives directly from the Spanish *caballerango* or from the English wrangler.

xerga: *See* **gerga.**

yarner: *See* **llano.**

yegua:

(Sp. model spelled same [ǰéɣwa] < Latin *equam*, feminine form of *equum* 'horse'). General Spanish term for a mare. Islas references it as a female horse, three years old or older. According to Slatta, vaqueros as well as other Hispanic horsemen felt it an insult to their machismo to ride a mare. In the border **corrido** "The Ballad of Gregorio Cortez" (also a movie by the same name which is based on Américo Paredes's book *With a Pistol in His Hand*), the protagonist and the sheriff suffer a tragic fate when the deputy misunderstands Gregorio's claim that he didn't sell a horse (**caballo**) but rather a mare (*yegua*).

zacate:

(Sp. model spelled same [sakáte] < Nahuatl *zacatl* 'hay; fodder'). *OED:* 1848. A general term in the Southwest for forage grass. Santamaría references it as a generic name for various creeping grasses that cover the fields of Mexico and serve as forage for animals. It also refers to some cyperaceous plants that are similar to the grasses. Islas also defines it as a corn plant that is dried once the ears have been cut off.

zaino:

(*zaíno* [saíno], of uncertain origin, perhaps from Arabic *ṣâ'in* 'keeper of secrets,' then 'traitor.' Corominas indicates that dark-colored horses are said to be treacherous). Referenced by Smith as "a chestnut-colored horse." He does not indicate whether this term was common among English-speakers. Islas references it as a horse, cow, or steer of a solid color. In Spanish, the term often follows the color of the animal, such as a *prieto zaíno*, which is completely black, or a *colorado zaíno*, which is a horse that is completely red.

zalea:

(Sp. model spelled same [saléa] < Vulgar Arabic *salîha* 'undressed sheepskin' < *sálah* 'to skin'). Watts: 1890. An undressed sheepskin used as a blanket, protective garment, or as a layer on a pack that fits between an animal's back and a saddle blanket or between the animal's back and the pack saddle. The *DRAE* references it as a sheepskin with the hair left on. It is used as a protection against cold or damp weather. Santamaría and Islas concur. Cobos notes that it may also refer to a goatskin.

zerga: *See* **gerga.**

zopilote:

(Sp. model spelled same [sopilóte] < Nahuatl *tzopílotl* 'hanging trash' < *tzotl* 'filth' and *pílotl* 'hanging' < *piloa* 'to hang something'). Carlisle: 1927. A buzzard native to the Southwest (*Cathartes aura*), *also known as* a turkey vulture. It is commonly depicted in western literature and films. Santamaría references it as a Mexicanism for the black vulture (*Cathartes atratus*), which has a bald head and a curved beak. The bird is known by a number of other names throughout the American continents, including *gallinazo* and *zamuro*. *Also called* (in Mexico): zope, chombo, shope, nopo. *Alternate form:* sopilote.

zorrillas:

(zorrillo [soříǰo], of uncertain origin; probably from Spanish *zorro* 'fox' and *-illo*, a diminutive suffix). According to Santamaría, a *zorrillo* is a skunk. In the Southwest the term was applied to longhorn cattle whose hides have dorsal stripes. Watts indicates they often had white spots on their flanks and bellies, which made them similar in appearance to the above-mentioned animal.

Sources

Selected English Sources

Adams, Ramón F. *Western Words: A Dictionary of the Old West*. New York: Hippocrene Press, 1998.

Bentley, Harold W. *A Dictionary of Spanish Terms in English, with Special Reference to the American Southwest*. New York: Columbia University Press, 1932.

Blevins, Winfred. *Dictionary of the American West*. New York: Facts on File, Inc., 1993.

Carlisle, Rose Jean. "A Southwestern Dictionary." University of New Mexico: Unpublished Thesis, 1939.

Cassidy, Frederic G. *Dictionary of American Regional English*. Volume I: *Introduction and A–C*. Cambridge, Mass.: Belknap Press of Harvard University Press, 1985.

Cassidy, Frederic G., and Joan Houston Hall. *Dictionary of American Regional English*. Volume II: *D–H*. Cambridge, Mass.: Belknap Press of Harvard University Press, 1991.

———. *Dictionary of American Regional English*. Volume III: *I–O*. Cambridge, Mass.: Belknap Press of Harvard University Press, 1996.

Clark, Thomas L. *Western Lore and Language: A Dictionary for Enthusiasts of the American West*. Salt Lake City: University of Utah Press, 1996.

Hendrickson, Robert. *Happy Trails: A Dictionary of Western Expressions*. Volume II: *Facts On File Dictionary of American Regionalisms*. New York: Facts on File, 1994.

Hill, A. A. "*Buckaroo*, Once More." *American Speech* 54 (1979): 151– 153.

Hoy, Bill. *Spanish Terms of the Sonoran Desert Borderlands: A Basic Glossary,* 4th ed., rev. and enl. Calexico, Calif.: Institute for Border Studies, San Diego State University, Imperial Valley Campus, 1993.

Oxford English Dictionary, 2d ed., on compact disc: Windows Network Version 1.11. New York: Oxford University Press, 1995.

Rodríguez González, Felix. *Spanish Loanwords in the English Language: A Tendency Towards Hegemony Reversal. Topics in English Linguistics,* vol. 18. Herman Wekker, series ed. New York: Mouton de Gruyter, 1996.

Slatta, Richard W. *Cowboys of the Americas.* New Haven, Conn.: Yale University Press, 1990.

Smith, Cornelius C., Jr. *A Southwestern Vocabulary: The Words They Used.* Glendale, Calif.: The Arthur H. Clark Co., 1984.

Watts, Peter. *A Dictionary of the Old West.* Avenel, N.J.: Wings Books/Random House, 1977.

Selected Spanish Sources

Alvar Ezquerra, Manuel. "Pero ¿quiénes son tantos gringos?" *Homenaje a Humberto López Morales*, eds. María Vaquero y Amparo Morales, 75–89. Madrid: Editorial Arco, 1992.

Cabrera, Luis. *Diccionario de aztequismos, cuarta edición.* Mexico City: Ediciones Oasis, S. A., 1982.

Cobos, Rubén. *A Dictionary of New Mexico and Southern Colorado Spanish.* Santa Fe: Museum of New Mexico Press, 1983.

Corominas, Joan. *Breve diccionario etimológico de la lengua castellana, segunda edición.* Madrid: Editorial Gredos, S. A., 1967.

Corominas, Joan, and José A. Pascual. *Diccionario crítico etimológico castellano e hispánico:* vols. I–V. Madrid: Editorial Gredos, S. A., c. 1980–.

Real Academia Española. *Diccionario de la lengua española, vigésima primera edición (CD-ROM).* Madrid: Espasa Calpe, 1995.

Galván, Roberto A. *The Dictionary of Chicano Spanish/El diccionario del español chicano,* 2d ed. Chicago: National Textbook Co., 1995.

Garulo, Teresa. *Los arabismos en el léxico andaluz.* Madrid: Instituto Hispano-Árabe de Cultura, 1983.

Islas Escárcega, Leovigildo. *Vocabulario campesino nacional: objecciones y ampliaciones al vocabulario agrícola nacional publicado por el Instituto Mexicano de Investigaciones Lingüísticas en 1935.* Mexico: B. de Silva, 1945.

Santamaría, Francisco J. *Diccionario de mejicanismos, quinta edición.* Mexico City: Editorial Porrúa, S. A., 1992.

Sobarzo, Horacio. *Vocabulario sonorense.* Mexico City: Editorial Porrúa, S. A., 1966.